Public Communication: Behavioral Perspectives

Jerry W. Koehler
University of South Florida

Karl W. E. Anatol
California State University, Long Beach

Ronald L. Applbaum
California State University, Long Beach

Macmillan Publishing Co., Inc.
New York

Collier Macmillan Publishers
London

Copyright © 1978, Macmillan Publishing Co., Inc.

PRINTED IN THE UNITED STATES OF AMERICA

Macmillan Publishing Co., Inc.
866 Third Avenue, New York, New York 10022
Collier Macmillan Canada, Ltd.

Library of Congress Cataloging in Publication Data
Koehler, Jerry W
  Public communication.

  Bibliography: p.
  Includes index.
  1. Public speaking. I. Anatol, Karl W. E., joint author. II. Applbaum, Ronald L., joint author. III. Title.
PN4121.K923   808.5′1   77–23879
ISBN 0–02–365610–7

Printing: 1 2 3 4 5 6 7 8   Year: 8 9 0 1 2 3 4

Preface

The title of this textbook, *Public Communication: Behavioral Perspectives*, contains a number of important terms that require our immediate attention if we, as students of communication, are to understand the primary objective of this text. First, what is meant by "public communication"? Conventional definitions of public communication include concepts such as "an uninterrupted discourse," "a formal presentation given to a group of people," a "prepared presentation before an audience," or a "talk in public." Definitions such as these serve to give us direction, but do not adequately explain the public communication activity we are to study. Descriptions of public communication appear in a number of college textbooks. However, after describing or, in some cases, hinting at the complex process of developing and delivering successful public communication, most of these books emphasize only two basic topic areas: speech preparation and delivery.

These definitions and instructions on public communication may be adequate for telling us what a speech is, and telling us how to go about organizing and presenting it in the most effective manner, but they fall short of the more thorough behavioral approach developed in this text. First, they focus on specific elements in public communication, such as delivery or organization, treating each as a distinct element. Second, they often confine themselves to only two links, preparation and delivery, in the long chain of interacting events that actually make up the public communication process.

We view communication as a process involving numerous elements that build upon each other. These elements reach back into the predelivery period, and project into its aftermath. Rather than concentrating on specific functions as instructional entities, such as delivery, organization, or style, our focus is on the interactive relationships among the behavioral elements that affect public communication. We define public communication as the product of behavioral inputs, actions, and outputs that are measured by audience behavior in relationship to communicator objectives.

The text uses a systems approach that entails the study of interaction and related elements that directly affect communication outcomes. We perceive public communication as a process whose components are interrelated; it structures inputs that can produce previously defined outcomes in a given audience.

We do not attempt to dictate the "correct" method or format for public communication. We seek to provide you with the informational tools needed for understanding and developing the proper modes of public communication. Correctness is a situational phenomenon in public communication. It is possible for a speaker to organize, structure, and deliver a great speech in the typical textbook sense and fail to fulfill the desired public communication goals. A speech may stand out in the speaker's mind as a jewel with little thought for the setting into which it must fit. What is proper in one situation may, in fact, be incorrect in another. Thus, the successful public communicator must be able to assess what communication behaviors are needed to produce the desired results in a specific public situation.

An effective public communicator is a successful problem solver. He or she begins by recognizing the particular problem in a public communication situation, analyzes all the inputs that may operate in the public communication process, and selects the solution or mode of communication that accomplishes the intended goal. Therefore, we have organized this text with a problem-solving model in mind. We begin in Chapters 1 and 2 with an orientation to public communication by asking: What is a public communicator? What are the general misconceptions speakers have about public communication? How should the public communicator view the public communication situation? In Chapters 3, 4, and 5 we are concerned with problem recognition. We examine three primary goals of the public communicator: modifying cognitive systems, inducing resistance, and resolving conflict. Communication strategies are provided for accomplishing these goals. Chapters 6, 7, 8, and 9 are concerned with problem analysis. We investigate a number of input factors that can help or hinder public communicators in achieving their goals. In addition, suggestions are provided for utilizing the inputs for specific purposes or goals. The last four chapters of the text explore ways to resolve specific problems by actually constructing the public message. We provide potential public communicators with ways of preparing, organizing, delivering, and evaluating their public communication.

We cannot stress enough the concept that all the goals, strategies, and inputs we will discuss interact, and are by no means independent components of the public communication process. Basic elements are presented in separate chapters of this text merely to assist you in organizing the information we provide on public communication. However, we should never treat these elements as being mutually exclusive.

J. W. K.
K. W. E. A.
R. L. A.

Acknowledgments

This textbook would not have been possible without the time and efforts of those scholars who have spent many centuries studying the form of communication that we call public communication. We have endeavored to borrow, beg, and steal many of the strategies and ideas developed by these men and women in order to provide the type of public communication experience we endorse. We would like to thank Lloyd Chilton of Macmillan for his patient assistance and overall coordination during the developmental stages of the text. We also wish to thank Susan Stone Applbaum for her preparation of outlines in Chapter 11, and James Sauceda for his assistance with Chapter 12. In addition, our reviewers provided many insightful comments that were incorporated into the final manuscript. Last, but most important, we wish to offer thanks to our wives and children for their cooperation and love during the entire writing and production of the text.

J. W. K.
K. W. E. A.
R. L. A.

Contents

Part I
Orientation to Public Communication

Part II
Problem Recognition

Part I
Orientation to Public Communication

Chapter 1
Approaching Public Communication

P R E V I E W

¶ *What are some common misconceptions about public communciation?*
Communication apprehension is a sign of a poor communicator
Public communication is merely a performing art
People are born with an innate speaking ability
Successful speakers must use gimmicks
Inspiration is all you need to become a successful speaker
A good writer will be a good speaker

¶ *What are three perspectives of public communication?*
Informational
Rhetorical
Behavioral

¶ *When used in the technical sense, what is meant by the term process?*
A mechanism involving an input, an action, and an output

¶ *What are the limiting judgments and definitions involved in the public communication process?*
Establishment of goals, boundaries, and priorities

¶ *What is a system?*
A plan for selecting and organizing available elements in such a way that their interaction will achieve a desired objective

¶ *What is a system boundary?*
An arbitrary line separating those processes that will be included in the system from those that will not be included

¶ *What is an efficient system?*
It includes all the processes essential to the achievement of the objective

¶ *What are the three steps in the problem-solving process in public communication?*
Problem recognition

Problem analysis
Problem resolution

¶ What is communication noise?
The system of elements that interfere with the understanding and acceptance of the intended message

O B J E C T I V E S

After reading this chapter, you should be able to

1. discuss common misconceptions concerning the nature of public communication.
2. explain the informational approach to public communication.
3. identify three perspectives of public communication.
4. explain the rhetorical approach to public communication.
5. explain the behavioral approach to public communication.
6. explain the concept of communication process and its elements.
7. explain the concepts of input, action, and output.
8. discuss the interrelationship between the system and its subsystems.
9. explain the process of establishing goals, boundaries, and priorities.
10. explain the nature of the relationship between the output of one system and the input of the next within the system.
11. identify the variables that should be considered in the preparation of a speech.
12. describe the three-step process involved in planning a public communication.
13. describe the concept of noise in communication.
14. describe the components of communication noise.

To a far greater extent than we generally recognize, the complex form of behavior we label "communication" pervades and molds our lives. Whereas our senses give us the shape, color, sound, taste, and texture of the world around us, it is communication that invests these sensations with meaning and offers us the means for coping with our environment.

We will begin our approach to public communication by first examining the variety of communication behaviors manifested by a typical college student. Bob Smith, a college freshman, arrives on campus with a variety of academic and social goals. He wants to select a specialized course of study, join a particular fraternity, find congenial associates, engage in certain sports and entertainments, and maintain a rewarding interaction with the social and academic environment of the college community. He knows, of course, that he will be required to "communicate" with others as part of this interaction, but, if he is like most of us, he probably has only a vague idea of the important role communication will play in achieving these goals.

His ambition to join a fraternity, for example, will involve him in a subtle and highly sophisticated communication encounter. He must find ways of communicating his availability (but not his eagerness), and of introducing himself gracefully into the pledging procedure with a proper blend of humility and self-assurance. His resourcefulness will be tested in his efforts to demonstrate that he is sociable (but not dutiful), aggressive (but not pushy), independent (but not rebellious), and a competent student (but not a drudge).

His task would be easier if he could simply verbalize all these things, but communication rarely operates in such a straightforward manner. His verbal behavior may function more to conceal than to reveal. Other students will attach importance to the form and quality of his speech, as well as its actual content, by noting whether he talks too much or too little, his tone and voice quality, grammar, vocabulary, responsiveness, wit, speech mannerisms, and so on. His dress, grooming, appearance, carriage, demeanor, and social skills will also communicate information about him. He will communicate, in short, by the words he chooses and his general behavior. The response he evokes from others will depend upon the degree to which his overall behavior strikes a responsive chord in his auditors.

Bob's verbal communication will be particularly significant in his college classes because academic success requires a high degree of proficiency with written and spoken forms of communication. Even in the classroom, much of his success in evoking the behavior he desires from teachers, for example, good grades, will depend upon the quality of his nonverbal behavior—his class attendance, participation, deportment, promptness with which he completes assignments, and even his penmanship and typing skills.

If Bob should decide, at some point, that the college is not responding to his needs, that the quality of instruction and content of courses is not preparing him for the "real world," he may wish to produce a change in the instructional practices. As he starts planning ways to achieve this goal, he will begin to recognize the many types of communication behavior that will be needed to accomplish this task. As a first step, he may articulate his complaints in a letter to the campus newspaper. But if his goal is to effect a significant change in his educational environment, he will learn quickly that written communication is only one form of communication that can be utilized.

He may recognize that for change to occur he will need to elicit the support of his institution's administrative officers. Thus, he may seek out the dean of students. But as on most campuses, Bob has limited access to institutional administrators. Bob must make an appointment and justify his mission in order to avoid being shunted off to a subordinate. Should he be fortunate enough to have his message heard, he may undoubtedly discover that his complaint contains nothing new. He may learn that most of what he expresses has been said repeatedly in student course evaluations, which he is assured are taken seriously. He may discover that many deans and vice-presidents agree wholeheartedly with his criticisms. He also may discover that they have no intention of taking any action to correct the shortcomings.

At this point, Bob must make a crucial decision. He has engaged in two basic types of conventional communication: interpersonal exchanges and letters to the campus newspaper. Although his previous communicative behavior has produced certain results, it is obvious that he has not achieved his goal. He must select a form of communication that will actually permit achievement of his goal. The information he has received from others may convince him that sentiment for change exists, but in an unproductive form. What he needs is a communication mode and a forum that will dramatize the need for change and motivate those who hold it to translate their feelings into behaviors that will command response at the decision-making level of the college. Bob must recognize that his goal may only be achieved by utilizing public communication in the form of an oral presentation to listeners who are also involved with his problem.

This form of public communication has traditionally been called "public speaking." The campus upheavals of the late 1960s demonstrated the power of public speaking as a tool for reaching and motivating large numbers of students in a compact institutional environment. However, most speakers learn quickly that effective public speaking involves more than a proper environment. It involves an understanding of the special kinds of behavior by which speakers and audiences exchange information and feelings.

Some very fortunate speakers appear to have intuitive knowledge of these behaviors. Most people, like Bob Smith, must arrive at this understanding through experience. And, some students, like yourselves, are fortunate enough to receive training in public communication, instruction that provides knowledge of oral communication in a public forum. It is the purpose of this text to provide you with a basic understanding of oral public communication. We don't guarantee you will become a great speaker, but we do hope that the information provided will make you a more effective speaker and listener in public communication situations. One factor that hinders the development of many public communicators is the misconceptions they hold about oral public communication. Let's examine some of the more common misconceptions before developing our basic approach to public communication.

Misconceptions About Public Communication

Some people believe that *communication apprehension is a sign of a poor communicator*. The first time that one of the authors of this text was called on to speak publicly, he was in a beginning speech class like yours. Having the reputation as a "talker" in informal social situations, it had never occurred to him that he could not speak indefinitely on any subject in any setting. It therefore came as a surprise to him when he became panicked about standing up before an audience of classmates and talking for five minutes on a single subject.

He approached class the morning of his first speech like a man going to his execution. At the classroom door he nearly turned and bolted. His shirt was soaked with sweat, his stomach churned audibly, and a chill surged through his veins when his name was called by the instructor. He strode to the podium and turned upon his classmates a fixed, sick smile. Then, after the first half dozen halting words, a strange thing began to happen to him—he could feel the discomfort his audience was sharing with him. He could see it in their faces: some turned to him with determined attention, others just as determinedly averted. He could read it in their postures, half rigid for fear of distracting him even further. They were feeding back to him their reaction to his communication behaviors.

Suddenly making them relax became the most important thing in the world to him; that short term objective became the organizing focus and communication goal of his remarks. He began to talk naturally and relatively easily about his birthplace, parents, and childhood. There were still some rough spots in the talk, but he quickly discovered that these occurred only when he allowed his contact with the audience to be broken and returned his attention to himself.

Gratified, he discovered that when he relaxed, his audience relaxed. The sick apprehension was replaced by an exhilirating sense of power and control. He confesses that he still feels nervous at the beginning of a talk, but that he would rather talk than listen. He rates his discovery of the audience as the single most important lesson in his life as a public speaker.

The lesson was given a new dimension several years later when he was interviewed for the first time before television cameras. Surprisingly, he felt himself beginning to freeze up as the interview started. His host, however, was an old pro to whom unfreezing communication channels was part of the daily routine. In this case, interestingly enough, the host did it not by asking a simple, easy-to-field question, but by asking a very personal question that required a good deal of thought.

It had the same calming effect as the discovery of audience feedback had in his first experience in public speaking. The two lessons seemed contradictory but, although the question seemed to turn attention back to the speaker in this second case, it was actually turning it to him as the topic of the discussion, not as a self-conscious speaker. As long as he could focus attention on the reactions of the audience or on the message, even though he himself was the subject of the message, he was freed from the panic that comes with thinking of oneself as the performer afflicted with stage fright. While the speaker's nervousness and self-consciousness are parts of all public communication situations, they can be reduced to the extent that the attention can be focused on the audience or the message.

The reasons for the extraordinary dread with which most people face the task of addressing an audience for the first time are no doubt complex and deeply intertwined with the human ego. However, most apprehension about communication is similar to any other form of anxiety. We experience it when we face a task for which we feel inadequate or unprepared.

Apprehension about public speaking may persist even among people who are highly articulate and perfectly at ease in interpersonal conversations. They recognize that speaking in public involves special skills and special vulnerabilities. Knowledge of oral public communication techniques provides tools with which to focus on the audience and message.

Much of our apprehension about speaking arises from other common misconceptions we have about the nature of public communication. Some people believe that *public communication is merely a performing act.* People often fear public speaking, and fail at it, because they think of their appearance as a theatrical performance and, as a result, may engage in stilted and distracting behaviors. In reality, audiences almost invariably respond best to a speaker who acts perfectly natural.

Some people continue to believe that speakers are born with an inate speaking ability. The "Born Speaker Theory" suggests that certain people inherit the ability to be good speakers, and if you are not one of the chosen few, then you can't learn to become an effective communicator. Although some speakers do have fewer problems learning to be effective public communicators, there are relatively few who cannot become accomplished speakers with proper training and practice.

Some people believe *a successful speaker must use "gimmicks."* There is a popular assumption that one can become an effective speaker by developing a bag of tricks for manipulating and influencing the audience in the form of attention-getting devices. A speaker might believe that, by showing a great deal of enthusiasm, or smiling a lot while speaking, he or she will automatically be a successful speaker. Gimmicks may help a poor speaker for a short period of time, but a speaker who depends on gimmicks will likely fail in the long run.

Some people believe *a good writer makes a good speaker.* The assumption that written and oral communication are identical is the cause of many unsuccessful public presentations. What reads well silently rarely reads as well aloud. When difficult words and convoluted sentences are employed in written material, the reader can always go back over the material if something was overlooked or misunderstood. The public communication listener has no such opportunity and may simply lose some of the ideas presented by the speaker. Oral communication invariably uses simpler, shorter words and less complex sentence structure than written communication.

Some people believe *inspiration is all you need* to become a successful speaker. Many individuals, faced with the awesome task of preparing a speech, persuade themselves that they can depend on the inspiration of the moment to carry them through. It seldom works. There are speakers, of course, who are quite effective in extemporaneous performance, but they are usually experienced lecturers who are thoroughly grounded in their subject matter.

A part of this misconception is the belief it takes more time to prepare a long talk than a short one. This is not necessarily true. It often takes far longer to condense material so that it is complete and structured, and still achieves the communication goal within a few minutes. In a longer talk you have a chance to ramble more before arriving at the desired goal. Herbert Hoover, when asked how long he would need to prepare a talk, was said to reply that if he was required to talk ten minutes, he would need three weeks, an hour, one week; but if they would give him three hours for his speech, "I'm ready to start now."

The misconceptions we have discussed are not uncommon among beginning speakers. As one beginning to learn about public communication, you should cast aside any previously held misconceptions and begin to build a new framework for examining public communication. In the next section, we will examine three ways of looking at public communication and indicate the approach we will utilize throughout the remainder of the text.

Three Perspectives on Public Communication

It is possible to classify most public communication (as distinguished from entertainment or purely social conversation) into three perspectives: (1) informational (scholarly, scientific); (2) rhetorical (persuasive, argumentative); and (3) behavioral (combination and extension of the informational and rhetorical perspectives).

THE INFORMATIONAL PERSPECTIVE

A famous newspaper slogan reads: "Give the People light and they will find their own way." This could be the theme of those who subscribe to the objective or informational approach to communication, which is based on the assumption that the speaker should present the audience the facts without any attempt to influence their judgment, leaving it to each individual to evaluate the information presented.

This is the typical model used for scientific or scholarly presentations and reports. The model assumes that an audience can be led to the "right" conclusions if all the facts are presented clearly and objectively.

In developing informational communication, you are engaged in a task similar to that of the librarian who carefully assembles a well-balanced collection of books, arranges them in an orderly fashion on the shelves, and provides a comprehensive catalog of their contents and location, without any attempt to tell the reader which books should be read and which should be ignored. The librarian's job is to make the books readily available, not to judge them.

Scientists are expected to communicate in this way, as are reporters and, in a somewhat modified manner, teachers who, because of the inexperience or immaturity of their audiences are sometimes expected to give greater guidance in helping the student to develop a basis for judgment and discrimination. This poses a particularly delicate ethical problem for teachers, as they are sternly enjoined from imposing their private political, social, and religious views on their students.

The informational presentation is considerably easier to describe than to emulate. Some observers even go so far as to deny the possibility of a truly "objective" presentation of even the most neutral subject. The serious defender of informational presentation can only reply that the speaker is obligated to do the best he or she can.

Despite its critics, objectivity is universally regarded as a virtue, so much so that even the most blatantly biased speaker can usually be counted on to assert that he or she is "merely presenting the facts." It is probably true that even the most scrupulously honest report is not totally free of unconscious bias at some point, but the hearer or reader must be especially wary of the amount of deliberate distortion that can be built into a seemingly objective presentation by the clever selection, manipulation, and omission of facts, stress, and order of presentation.

An extreme example of distorted "objectivity" appeared on the front page of a small-town California newspaper a number of years ago in a report of an altercation involving a local businessman with whom the paper's editor was feuding. The front page was dominated by a three-column picture of a man with blood running down his face, his hair disheveled and his shirt bloody and torn, captioned "Victim of Attack by ———" and subheaded "Struck from Behind with Metal Object, Customer Says." The headline and lead paragraph repeated the photograph caption, with the details buried in a long carryover on a back page. After a lengthy description of the victim's treatment for superficial wounds at a local hospital, his family's reaction, and his recent financial difficulties, the report recounted the actual conflict in brief detail.

The reader learned deep in the second column of close type that the customer had come into the businessman's office in response to a demand for payment of an overdue bill. Finding no one in but the owner's elderly mother, he engaged in a violent argument with her. The owner entered from the street just as the customer lunged across the counter and grasped his mother by the throat. He struck the man on the head with the nearest weapon, a floor lamp (the "metal object"), and called the police.

When criticized for his treatment of the story, the editor maintained piously that he had "merely reported the facts" and challenged his critics to point out a single important fact that had been omitted from his account.

Such crude perversion dishonors the objective approach, of course, and seldom misleads the more careful and thorough readers. But not all audiences are careful and thorough, and not all pseudo-objectivity is this crude. Some of it, particularly when major social or political issues are being debated, is quite sophisticated and difficult to detect.

Nevertheless, the informational approach in the hands of an informed and honest communicator is the most powerful tool of knowledge our society possesses.

THE RHETORICAL PERSPECTIVE

Twenty-five hundred years ago, Aristotle defined rhetoric as "the art of discovering the available means of persuasion." This definition has stood the test of time. There is strong support for the belief that all public communication is, and should be, persuasive in nature and that, if we are honest about it, we communicate only to influence others. Even when the speaker presents a set of facts objectively, some will argue, he or she is actually making a subtle case for the acceptance of that set of facts. When a professor scrupulously avoids injecting his own biases and beliefs into his lecture, he is nevertheless influencing the student simply by his selection of the material that he considers, however honestly, to be relevant to the subject.

The rhetorical or "adversary" approach to communication has peculiar appeal to Americans. We love debates, arguments, political confrontations, and dramatic courtroom clashes in which each side makes the strongest possible case for its point of view. Advertising has taught us to expect that if toothpaste is composed of two ingredients—soap and flavoring—one firm will urge us to buy its product because it has "more flavor" whereas its competitor will make the same case for "more cleansing power."

If we examine a debate that will probably go on in America for many years—our attempt to hammer out a satisfactory approach to handling our energy needs, we can see that the roots of the rhetorical approach are buried in the very structure of our society. One faction composed of environmentalists, public advocates, and representatives of alternate energy sources marshal all possible arguments to show that the development of nuclear energy will be dangerous for the populace, destructive to the environment, and a further monopolization of energy control and profits in the hands of the power companies. The opposite faction includes the major power companies and corporate power consumers, who will argue that nuclear energy development is actually safer and less destructive to the environment, cheaper in the long run, and in any event absolutely necessary to meet our future requirements. Both sides believe they are acting in the best interests of the country and, given equal distribution of their conflicting cases, make it highly unlikely that a single important fact that bears on the issue will remain hidden from exposure by one side or the other. Each side will attempt to influence the general populace to accept its particular view rather than merely providing the information upon which the audience can arrive at a particular position.

THE BEHAVIORAL PERSPECTIVE

When we attempt to inform or persuade an audience in order to achieve our goal, we are dealing with a "black box"—the human mind—if we endeavor to explain all of the influences operating on any audience in any public communication situation. We have a pretty good picture of the behavioral inputs or factors affecting our listeners and of the changes in behavior that result. What we do not always know is what goes on inside the "box," the mind of the individual.

The behavioral approach simplifies our problem by making it unnecessary to ask the unanswerable question "What goes on inside the box?" and asks instead, "What kind of behavioral inputs can be counted on to produce our desired behavioral output?"

It should be noted that most of our daily communication takes place on a behavioral basis without our giving the subject much thought. If you walk into a store and a clerk who is a stranger to you smiles and says "Hi. How are you?" the chances are that you will respond with the same cheerful informality. You are involved in a situation in which the maintenance of a pleasant surface relationship is more important than what may actually be going on inside either of you.

You may, in fact, be thinking "Idiot!" while you are smiling and saying "Fine, thank you," but unless you betray the thought in some gross behavior aberration, there is no reason for it to intrude upon what is essentially a ritualistic encounter.

If Bob Smith from our earlier example were to discover that he established better rapport with his audience, and evoked a more positive behavior response, with a rambling, disjointed speech accompanied by erratic gestures than by one that was carefully organized and smoothly delivered, he would be foolish not to adopt the style that most effectively advanced his goals, no matter what a speech handbook might indicate as proper in a public communication situation.

This is the essence of the behavioral approach: it seeks a behavioral description of the oral communication inputs that will produce the output behavior that indicates we have achieved our communication goal. The behavioral perspective encompasses both the informational and rhetorical perspectives. It is concerned with achieving the communication goal regardless of whether it be to transmit information, influence the audience's views on a particular subject, or motivate the listeners to take a specific action.

Systems Approach to Communication

In order to clarify our approach to public communication we will start with a definition of public communication that emerges from the behavioral perspective in the previous section. *Public communication is the product of behavioral inputs, actions, and outputs that are measured by audience behavior in relationship to a communication goal.*

This text uses a systems approach that entails the study of interacting and related elements directly affecting communication outcomes. We are not concerned with whether public communication conforms to a model of rhetoric or information. We are concerned with public communication as a process that interrelates and structures inputs that produce desired outcomes in a given audience.

DEFINITIONS

We have employed a number of terms—*process, system, input, action, output*—that must be defined to facilitate our focus on the specific elements of public communication.

The term *process* involves an input, an action, and an output. In a process an action transforms the input into something that becomes the output. A boy converting a straight pin into a fishhook is a simple example. He takes the pin (input) and subjects it to pressure (action), which converts it into a "J"-shaped hook (output).

Inputs and outputs need not be objects. They may be ideas or attitudes. Nor does the process action have to be a physical one. The action could be thinking. In a chain of related events, the output of one process may become the input of the next. The boy who formed a hook in the example above may now use the output, the hook, as the input of the succeeding process—stringing the hook, and so on.

Inputs and outputs may be simple (a pin) or complex (a

speech). A large process may be made up of many subprocesses. It is not the nature of the elements involved, nor their complexity, that identifies a process: a process is identified by the conversion of an input to an output.

SYSTEMS AND SUBSYSTEMS

A system is a special type of process. It is composed of a number of interacting, interrelated processes with an ultimate output— the objective or goal. It is the existence of the objective that gives a system its character and definition. The "objective" of a natural group of processes such as the Mississippi River "system" can be said to be the waters reaching the Gulf of Mexico. Most of the systems we will refer to can be described as telic, or purposeful, and are deliberately structured to achieve specific outcomes, e.g., a student who wants to improve existing classroom practices through the use of an oral public communication.

Effective system design involves the establishment of objectives or goals, boundaries, and priorities. A simple example will define and illustrate the relationship between these three system elements.

My family needs a home that offers shelter from the elements, a place for belongings, and space for both privacy and togetherness. This is our general objective, but we define it more precisely in order to make our system for providing a house more efficient. A multitude of factors will influence the objective's definition— our present and future requirements as a family, our resources of money, time, and skills, building codes, the physical environment, the style of the neighborhood, aesthetics, and so on. Out of the interplay of all these factors comes a decision that we want to design and, as far as possible, construct for ourselves, a house in the traditional Spanish, southwest ranch style, with a tiled roof and exterior walls of adobe brick.

Further analysis convinces us that it is impractical to attempt such specialized projects as foundations, interiors, or roof, but that it is quite feasible for us to build our own exterior walls. The boundaries of our system can now begin to take shape. We will contract out those parts of the structure we do not feel competent to do for ourselves, relying on the usual procedure for selecting competent contractors and maintaining general surveillance over work in progress. Our principal system will be concerned with supplying adobe bricks and constructing the walls.

It is clear at this point that coordination of the various parts of the job will be a critical problem. Because we will be responsible for an important part of the work, we must schedule the construction stages so that there are no unnecessary delays or conflicts. We cannot begin erecting the walls, for example, until the foundation is laid; the walls and roof must be completed before the interior work, and so on.

We must wait for the foundation work before beginning to put up the walls, but we can begin supplying brick as soon as we have the site. We read up on how to manufacture adobe brick and learn that the skills and equipment required are well within our means. It is a job in which all members of the family can participate and, if necessary, we can hire unskilled help to make sure we meet our schedule.

As a test, we secure a small quantity of materials and experiment until we have perfected the procedure for making a single brick to our satisfaction. Our brickmaking system can now be reduced to creation of a format for repeating this process until a sufficient quantity of bricks has been produced. Note that the inputs to this process have been both tangible and intangible. Besides clay, fiber binder, water, forms, and drying equipment, we also supply ideas, energy, plan, skills, and the accumulated brickmaking experience of our society acquired in our research.

Note also how the procedure has a natural tendency to narrow and focus on the immediate job at hand as we develop our system. Beginning with a generalized objective, we have now reached a process for the first task to be undertaken. The procedure can be represented schematically this way:

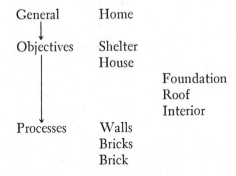

When we survey the overall system, we see immediately that it is made up of groups of related processes—subsystems—that have to be coordinated if the system is to work properly. Not only must the foundation be in the right place for the walls to be erected, it must be ready at the right time, just as the bricks must be. Now all of the elements that were inputs to the brick-making process— the clay, fiber, water, energy, skills, ideas, planning, and so on— have been synthesized in its output (bricks), which now become a part of the input to the next process, wall-building. The wall-building subsystem, in turn, must be coordinated with the system flow that will bring together the right combination of materials, energy, and skills to produce a roof and interior elements.

As can be seen, all of the small and large processes and subsystems are ultimately inputs to the larger objective-concept, *house*, which, in its turn, is an input to the concept *shelter*. And shelter is an input to the still-larger concept *home*; and home to the concept *family*, and so on. Thus, a system can be ordered in such a way that it includes all the processes from the digging of a shovelful of clay to the most abstract concepts of human relationships. It can likewise be restricted to the operations necessary to produce a brick.

In either case, the scope of the system depends upon the definition of its boundaries. In its simplest terms, a system boundary is no more than an arbitrary line separating those processes that will be included in the system from those that will be excluded. As our house-building example shows, the boundaries can be expanded to include additional processes and subsystems, such as wall-erection and brick-making, or contracted to exclude others, such as all the foundation, roof, and interior construction processes.

The selection of boundaries is obviously one of the critical tasks of systems design. An efficient system includes all the processes essential to the achievement of its objective, and excludes all that are unnecessary or counterproductive. Identifying the boundaries of such a system requires the clearest possible statement of the objective, and a thorough analysis of the inputs available to it. In our example, it might not be practical from a purely economic point of view for the family to undertake the tasks of making bricks and erecting walls. The savings in labor cost might very well be offset by the loss of time that family members might spend more productively in other activities. But from the point of view that family participation in the actual construction of their own home is an important objective, extending the system boundaries to include these processes is both practical and desirable.

A system, therefore, is simply a plan for selecting and organizing available elements in such a way that their interaction will achieve a desired objective. The general definition holds true whether we are talking about a system for making bricks or for public communication. In each case, there is a technology for achieving the specific objective based, in the first place, on our observation of how such objectives have been attained in the past and, in the second, on the skill and imagination with which we select and combine our system elements.

The principal difference between the two cases is one of complexity. Compared with the communication process, brick-making is a simple and static operation as we still make adobe bricks pretty much the way they have been made for generations. Weather conditions or material shortages may require some process modification, but in general the system is highly stable and repeatable.

Far greater process flexibility is required to meet the constantly changing conditions of the public communication process. The brickmaker is not likely to receive new inputs that require radical process changes while the process is going on. The public speaker, by contrast, is continuously adjusting to new inputs. Even while the speaker is selecting a particular symbol or illustration to fit into a particular sentence or train of thought, new inputs may be received that make it necessary to reconsider the appropriateness of the elected material. Every seasoned speaker can recall at least one instance when last-second feedback from an audience caused the elimination of a potentially disastrous figure of speech or reference.

To a lesser degree, every sentence uttered by a speaker who is sensitive to the audience is affected by perceived audience feedback, whether or not the issue is critical. One of the authors recently spoke before an exceptionally receptive audience that responded very well to a series of jokes and humorous references he had included in his text. The last of these, and the one he liked best, had always received the best audience response. However, he decided to eliminate it at the last moment, because the ultimate purpose of his talk was serious, and the unusual receptiveness of the audience had created a situation in which he felt any further attempt at humor might not only seem excessive, but actually distracting. Thus, a new input—evidence of the favorable predisposition of the audience—dictated a change in a speech process that was under way.

In a particular public speaking event, there is always at least one system and one or more subsystems. To a very large extent, their effectiveness depends upon the conscious effort that has gone into their design and coordination. The system is the overall design into which the individual speech fits. Its objective is to achieve a goal, for example, to elect a candidate or administration, to reform the prison system, to build school spirit, to generate public support for space exploration, and so on, all of which may require many inputs. This system may include many forms of public communication, including public speeches.

The subsystems have as their principal objective the assembly of the public communication for presentation to an audience. The public communicator must understand the objective of the system or the output of the subsystem may be ineffective or counterproductive as an input to the system.

In structuring the subsystem, the speaker attempts to take into account as many as possible of the input elements that will have a bearing on the outcome. As with any other system, the first and most critical of these is the definition of the subsystem objective and its place in the larger system. At a certain level of a political campaign, for example, the total objective of a speech might be to merely emphasize the shortcomings of an incumbent's performance, without mentioning the name or program of the opposing candidate; or to spotlight an incumbent's accomplishments without specifically advocating his or her re-election. Members of presidential cabinets have become quite adept, in election years, at defending administration programs and attacking the proposals of opposition candidates without appearing to be electioneering.

Once the objective has been defined, the single most important element of the system becomes the audience—its anticipated size, age range, partisanship, grasp of the issues, ethnic composition, and educational level. The speaker's credibility, prior contacts, and rapport with the audience, or the absence of such factors, are important considerations, of course, as are the information and platform skills the speaker brings to the task.

For the experienced public speaker, most of the speech inputs are applied (or omitted) more or less automatically, depending on individual proficiency and professional skill. Most of these will be dealt with in the appropriate sections to follow. They include

1. Message introduction.
2. Message organization.
3. Visual materials.
4. Order of arguments.
5. Audience analysis.
6. Emotional appeals.
7. Type of arguments.
8. Message presentation.
9. Supporting materials.
10. Organizational patterns.
11. Message style.

These, and many more, elements are among those that affect speech behavior and effectiveness. They emerge from literature, research, personal experience, observation, and practical understanding of the subject. Later in the text they will be discussed in greater detail in relation to their place in system development.

AREAS OF PLANNING

Our system approach to public communication from a behavioral perspective involves three areas of planning:

1. Problem recognition.
2. Problem analysis.
3. Problem resolution.

If we look at the prior list of inputs, we note that each is actually a statement of a problem with which the speaker must deal, or an obstacle to be overcome. Thus, an early stage of the development of an effective speech for a particular audience and situation consists of defining the problem reflected in each input. Audience size, for example, presents one kind of problem for a speaker, audience age range another. An audience of retired people requires a certain specialized approach; an audience of high school students a different one; a mixed audience ranging from high school students to retired people still a third.

Analyzing the problem is a natural sequel to defining it. In practice, it means simply that the speaker tries to visualize the practical implications of the problem as defined, in terms of the specific communication situation and objectives involved. Given a certain goal and an audience basically hostile to that goal, what approach offers the best chance of obtaining the type of behavior desired? An appeal to evidence? To emotion? Seeking another issue to which there is less resistance that might produce the desired behavior? Other inputs will undoubtedly provide clues to the correct solution.

Problem resolution is the process of selecting the better of the available responses to each of the problems defined by the inputs to the speech process.

Once the interactive nature of the systems approach is grasped, it becomes a powerful organizing tool for the speaker. A common problem of speakers who do not use the systems approach—trying to accomplish too much in a single speech—is greatly simplified by a clear definition of the subsystem (speech) objective, as dictated by its position as an input to the larger system. Analyzing the speech in the light of its system function usually makes the task of drawing its boundaries much simpler. Whereas the overall objective of a political campaign may be to elect a candidate, the objective of a particular public speech may be merely to get certain ideas or facts before a certain audience, or to enlist a certain number of volunteers. It is far easier to organize an effective talk within these boundaries than it is to begin with the vague generalization that the goal of the speech is to help elect candidate X.

The interacting nature of system elements is helpful in developing effective public speaking because it accurately reflects the interaction of real forces in the public communication process. Not only in the speaker's analysis, but in real life, the age and educational level of the audience are important factors in determining its positive response to one approach and negative response to another. The speaker's success in establishing credibility with an audience does play an important role in determining whether or not the desired behavior will be evoked. The ability to obtain, interpret, and respond effectively to audience feedback *can* make the difference between success and failure as a public speaker.

The systems approach saves time and energy and increases effectiveness in a variety of other ways as well.

Having defined in advance what the speech objective is—what the larger system requires it to accomplish—the speaker will find the task of researching, structuring, and preparing the speech materials greatly simplified. Research can be confined to the specific points that fall within the speech boundaries; material that does not contribute directly to producing the specific audience behavior desired can be eliminated. However relevant or fascinating, material that is not meaningful to this particular audience at this particular time can be ignored. The effectiveness of the speech is not determined by its conformity to a textbook model, but by its success in producing the audience behavior required by its objective.

A second subsystem may be employed to evaluate the success of the speech. This may involve a very simple or a very complex analysis. If the objective of a particular speech is to raise a specific amount of money or to prevent a lynching, it is not difficult to determine whether or not it has succeeded. But if the objective is less concrete—to create a favorable image of an individual or program, for example—special processes may be required to evaluate the effect indirectly.

In the speech to which we referred a few paragraphs earlier, the speaker's objective was to challenge the thinking of the audience with what he felt were valid new ideas and insights, and to do it with sufficient force that he would be valued as a speaker by the sponsoring organization for future occasions.

He had prepared by obtaining advance information about the audience and making notes on material that had been successful with similar groups in the past, adding new material that seemed likely to be effective with these particular listeners. Much of the information was supplied by the sponsoring organization in response to a questionnaire asking for details about the composition of the anticipated audience.

When he arrived, he had this information in mind, as well as the elements of his talk, and was able to check his advance information against his on-the-spot observation of the audience. In this case, he had an opportunity to watch and listen to a fairly good sample of the group that he would be addressing as they entered the hall.

He continued to watch the audience for clues during the preliminaries and the introduction by trying to catch any indication of either positive or negative response to his name, the mention of his book's title, the introductory speaker's humor, reference to issues, and so on. By the time he began to talk, he had a pretty good understanding of the audience; hence, the process of selecting and deleting among the elements he had collected for the speech went on almost automatically as he spoke.

He had a variety of means of estimating the effect of his talk—applause, laughter, eye contact, restlessness, inattention, coughing, general behavior, and body language. Also he had post-address evidence in the form of comments, book sales, and ultimately an invitation to speak again.

Viewed from a systems-behavioral approach, this particular public address offered a variety of aspects for analysis. Its goal, for example, was a fairly general one. It was intended to influence primarily the thinking, rather than the physical behavior of its audience through the promotion of certain ideas and concepts. To the extent that it was intended to influence behavior directly, it was aimed not only at the audience, but also at the program's sponsors who, it was hoped, would conclude that the message was desirable and the audience response positive, and would therefore seek a return engagement.

Although the speech was not meant to be geared into a sharply purposeful larger system, such as a political campaign, its effectiveness nevertheless depended on its meshing in some way with the general educational purposes of the meeting and its sponsors. The likelihood that it would succeed was increased by the processes of the larger system that had gone into effect before the speaker began to shape his talk—the selection of a conference theme and agenda, title for talks, the shaping of the audience through the type and distribution of publicity used and the invitations extended, and selection of speakers based on reputation and prior performance.

The boundaries of his system for developing and delivering his remarks did not have to include any of these areas—it was only necessary that he understand them and develop his subsystem accordingly. His problem-recognition process began with the question: what does this organization want me to accomplish, and under what circumstances? This question was reasonably simple to answer (problem analysis) from experience with similar situations in the past and the information supplied by the sponsor describing this particular event and its audience.

The solution then became a relatively routine process of putting together the elements that his judgment and experience told him would best produce the desired effect under the indicated circumstances—a process that, as he has already noted, continued right through the delivery of the talk.

The Concept of Noise. Few systems are perfectly efficient, and no system produces only those outputs that are desired, no matter how narrowly its boundaries are defined. Some effects of system interaction always run counter to the desired objective. Friction in a mechanical system is a good example, or noise in an electronic system. In fact, "noise" has become generally accepted in the communication field as a term describing the system elements that interfere with understanding and acceptance of the intended message. Just as static reduces the intelligibility of radio messages, noise reduces the effectiveness of messages in public communication.

Naturally, the amount of noise in any system can be increased by careless selection of inputs or by faulty or improper processes, or decreased by elimination of all noise sources that are not inherent in the system itself. The speaker, for example, who writes his speech purely as an academic exercise, without regard to the nature of the occasion for which it is to be delivered, the size and composition of the audience, or the ultimate purpose it is to serve, runs a high risk of excessive noise in his communication system. On the other hand, each element that he correctly plans in advance, each input that he properly evaluates, each contingency he makes adequate provisions for, decreases the system's noise, and consequently increases the chance for effective communication and acceptance of the message.

Overview

Public Communication: Behavioral Perspectives is divided into four parts. The first, an introductory/theoretical section, is composed of two chapters. The three remaining parts are organized around a simple problem-solving model. We believe that a successful public communicator must be a successful problem solver. Thus, the second part, which includes Chapters 3 through 5, is concerned with recognition of the particular task or problem that must be addressed by the public communicator. The third part, which includes Chapters 6 through 9, is concerned with an analysis of the public communication problem, that is, examining the inputs affecting the public communication system. The final part of the book (Chapters 10 through 13) describes the tools and procedures needed to resolve our public communication problem, by offering guidelines for preparing the public communication, from recognition of the problem through its actual presentation.

In Chapter 1 we describe misconceptions that most people have about public communication. Then we describe the three perspectives one can take in examining public communication. Finally, we examine the systems approach to public communication.

Chapter 2 focuses on the theoretical role of the audience in public communication. One of the most important elements in improving public communication effectiveness is the ability of the speaker to interpret and adapt to audience behaviors. A distinction is made between dyadic, small group, mass, and public communication.

Chapter 3 discusses how the cognitive system influences audience responsiveness, and what a communicator must do to ensure that the audience processes information according to plan. First, we identify and define four components of the cognitive system— values, attitudes, beliefs, and needs. Second, we explain how the audience's cognitive system serves as an information-processing mechanism, and how existing needs, beliefs, values, and attitudes facilitate or frustrate the cognitive realignments desired by the communicator. Third, we discuss the general terms of a design for audience motivation, and then go on to describe the steps of a strategy that may aid you in modifying cognitive systems.

Chapter 4 deals with ways to influence an individual so that he or she does not yield to future persuasive attempts. First, we describe some of the tactics that are used in a behavioral commitment approach. Second, we investigate anchoring techniques that attempt to strengthen new beliefs or cognitions by anchoring them to cognitive elements that are highly cherished in the listener's experiences. Third, we present strategies that are derived largely from the "instincts" of the listener. Fourth, we present a brief description of a systematic process for creating greater immunity, which involves a sensitizing, training program called inoculation. Finally, we consider the tremendous, resistance-inducing impact of groups to which people belong.

Chapter 5 shows how we may resolve conflict more effectively. First, we discuss the nature of conflict. Second, we attempt to discover what causes conflict. Third, we attempt to detect the manifestations of conflict. Fourth, we examine the various audiences that prevail in a "conflict" arena. Fifth, we set up various processes for "managing" the conflict. Sixth, we develop a particular conflict strategy, and we discuss how we should launch the strategy.

Chapter 6 is concerned with the examination of environmental and social inputs in the public communication process. We begin with an examination of the historical inputs. We review only certain high points and significant currents of the history of public communication. The second part of the chapter is concerned with contemporary social and environmental inputs. We examine media, education, consumers, business organizations, world concerns, government, political, and legal environments.

Chapter 7 examines the main elements of the source that influence the public communication. We concentrate on the individual or speaker as source. First, we examine the perceptual inputs describing the components and effects of the perceptual inputs. Second, we describe how source-receiver identification effects public communication. Third, we provide suggestions for improving your source input effects.

Chapter 8 investigates the main elements of the message in the public communication system. Three message areas are separated for analysis: the organizational characteristics, or the form of the message; the ideas and arguments presented, or the content of the message; and methods for expressing the content. As we examine each message area we identify the input variables affecting the public communication system.

Chapter 9 deals with audience analysis, that is, the collecting and analyzing of vital information about the audience. We discuss this subject by studying six crucial conditions:

1. The relationship between audience and message.
2. The relationship between speaker and audience.
3. The bias of the audience.

4. The ego-involvement of the audience.
5. The demographic characteristics of the audience.
6. The unique "personality" of certain audiences.

Chapter 10 examines the foundations of speech development. We begin with a definition of communication goals and expected outcomes. This is followed by a discussion of how the public communicator collects and records the data needed for construction of the message. Finally, we examine how one develops the topic.

Chapter 11 examines the major elements of speech structure. Organizational patterns are described, enabling us to fit the most appropriate pattern to the selected topic. Included are specific outlines illustrating the organizational patterns. Finally we discuss the use of supporting materials, the information that transforms the "skeleton" outline into a speech.

Chapter 12 will be concerned with the final stage in message development—the selection of a message style and the presentation of that message to a group of individuals—an audience. We explore the concept of style and how it affects our messages. We examine how visual aids may be utilized to assist the speaker in effectively reaching their intended goal. Special attention is given to input factors that affect the speakers vocal delivery. Finally, we investigate audience participation in message presentations.

Chapter 13 illustrates the complexity of outcomes that can be influenced by public communication. It also presents a general framework upon which evaluation of public communication can be implemented.

K E Y C O N C E P T S

Can you define and give examples of the following terms?

Informational perspective	Output
Rhetorical perspective	Communication boundaries
Behavioral perspective	Communication priorities
Verbal communication	Problem recognition
Nonverbal communication	Problem analysis
Public communication	Problem resolution
Process	Noise
Input	

1. Apprehension can also be reduced by shifting the focus of attention from the speaker to the message or to audience feedback.
2. Getting the audience to agree to the need for change does not necessarily lead them to acceptance of your plan for reform.
3. Public speaking is not a function of acting.
4. Very few people are "born speakers" with innate speaking ability. Most speaking skills are learned.
5. The use of gimmicks does not necessarily insure effective or successful communication.
6. Most speakers need more than the "inspiration of the moment" to communicate effectively.
7. The oral style differs from the written style in language choice and structure.
8. Informational discourse presupposes a certain objectivity on the part of the speaker in reporting facts for the consideration of the audience.
9. Informational discourse does not seek to provide direction to the audience, rather, it should provide the necessary facts to allow the audience to find its own direction.
10. Rhetorical discourse imposes an adversary relationship on the situation, in that the aim of the speaker is persuasion or argumentation.
11. The behavioral approach seeks to examine the behavioral inputs that produce the desired behavioral outputs in communication situations.
12. In order for a public speech to be effective, it must conform to both the communication goal and the long-range goal.
13. The term *process* is defined as a mechanism involving an input, an action upon that input, and an output that is the product of the action upon the input.
14. A system is usually a very complex process involving a number of interrelated processes tending toward the objective of the system.
15. Certain judgments and definitions work to limit the scope of the system, among them the establishment of goals, boundaries, and priorities.
16. Generally speaking, the public speaking situation involves at least one subsystem as well as a primary system.
17. The first critical step in the preparation for a public speaking occasion is defining the objective of the subsystem and its place in the larger system.

18. The systems approach to public communication involves three areas of planning; problem recognition, problem analysis, and problem resolution.
    a. Problem recognition involves the definition of the problem as reflected in each input, e.g., audience size, sex, age, and so on.
    b. Problem analysis is the visualization of the practical implications of the problem as defined in terms of the specific communication situation and the desired objective.
    c. Problem resolution is the process of selecting the best of the available responses to each of the problems defined by the inputs to the speech process.
19. Having defined the speech objective, the speaker will find the task of researching, structuring, and preparing the speech materials greatly simplified.
20. The effectiveness of the speech is not defined by its conformity to a textbook model, but rather by its success in producing the audience behavior required by the objective.
21. Speakers should be able to interpret audience feedback and adjust the speech content to accommodate such feedback.
22. "Noise" refers to the elements of the system that interfere with understanding and acceptance of the intended message.

Chapter 2
Adapting to Audience Processes

P R E V I E W

¶ *What are the two types of information modification that are utilized by the mind in processing inconsistent information?*
Censorship and selective attention

¶ *What is a coactive system?*
Each participant in the dyad is involved in a direct exchange of influence with the other

¶ *What is synergy?*
The components of a system work together to produce a whole that is greater than the sum of its parts

¶ *What is an opinion leader?*
An individual in an audience who is capable of influencing the behavior of others in the audience

¶ *What is the bandwagon effect?*
That phenomenon that encourages individuals to go along with the crowd

O B J E C T I V E S

After reading this chapter, you should be able to
1. discuss the concepts of censorship and selective attention.
2. explain how the listener determines what is communicated.
3. explain co-active and interactive systems.
4. explain the concept of synergy and its implications on group processes.
5. identify the elements of interaction in the mass media.
6. explain the use of shills and claques in public communication.
7. discuss the importance of isolating opinion leaders.
8. discuss audience interaction effects and processes.

FRANK WILLIAMS is a county employee in charge of developing a long-range land-use plan. He is responsible for developing and gaining acceptance of the overall program for effective use of the county's lands and resources. In developing the plan, he must take into account present and future needs of the population for goods and services, transportation, utilities, recreation, housing, jobs, education, and health facilities.

As difficult as his job is, the challenge of persuading people to accept his plans may prove to be even more difficult. Every new issue developed is a potential source of conflict for groups with vital interests in land-use. He may have to negotiate with and persuade scores of people in many different settings, ranging from small committees to mass meetings.

Many people in Frank Williams' situation believe that a public presentation providing the "facts" is all that is necessary to achieve the desired goal. People holding this misconception do not understand that the human mind has a remarkable facility for maintaining order and consistency among data. The mind simply refuses at times to accept information that does not conform to its intellectual and emotional preconceptions. At other times the mind may subtly alter the information to make it conform to preconceptions. Simply stated, we often seek and take note of information that reinforces our preconceptions and tend to avoid or ignore data that challenges them. Merely outlining the facts usually does not suffice even when it may appear that all one has to do is "give the facts" to the audience and let its members draw their own conclusion. The real-life difficulties created by this apparently sensible approach are familiar to almost every experienced speaker. Particularly with a subject of Frank Williams' complexity, there can be scores of equally valid "facts," depending on the relative stress and detail devoted to one fact or another.

Seldom will any two listeners or audiences concur completely on which facts are significant enough to be included in a public presentation. The expansion of an airport facility, for example, would certainly be regarded as a significant event by business people, environmentalists, and local residents, but in considerably different factual contexts. A presentation before an audience of business and industrial representatives might emphasize the plan's contribution to the speed and convenience of transportation while ignoring such details as proposed flight patterns and anticipated noise levels, or mentioning them only in passing. The same presentation, however, might be considered incomplete and evasive if presented to an audience of homeowners living near the airport.

If there were enough time and interest, and if the speaker possessed the stamina, it might be theoretically possible to "give the facts" unselectively to every listener. Unfortunately, this is seldom the case. Moreover, the speaker usually has a personal point of view and objective. Frank Williams, for example, no doubt wants his plan to be accepted. In addition to its professional importance to him, it represents many hours of labor and thought. It is a product of his judgment. Its acceptance represents a major personal and professional triumph. Naturally, he hopes that the plan is widely accepted and adopted.

Synergy

Frank Williams' first major test comes with the unveiling of his completed plan at a County Board of Supervisors meeting. This situation will offer him a significant challenge. Besides the supervisors, his audience will undoubtedly include representatives of various segments of the community. His goal is to persuade not only his supervisors, but also developers, business people, consumer and environmental groups, utility companies, unions, and generally all taxpayers to accept his plans.

At first glance, it might appear to be a hopeless task to seek common ground in such an assembly, that is, finding a single issue or position upon which all listeners or even a majority of listeners can agree upon. However, experienced speakers learn to disregard their initial reactions to speaking situations and to concentrate on isolating or identifying areas of common interest that exist in every audience. He or she often begins by analyzing the shared interest that brought the audience together. For example, Frank Williams may conclude that what has motivated the people in his audience to come together is their common interest in the future of the county. Each of them lives, works, or does business in the county, and so each has a vital stake in the direction in which it will be developed. Also, from his analysis, he will come to realize that the outcome of his presentation will be determined by *what* he says, his message, and *how* he says it, as well as how specific members of the audience evaluate his presentation. Reactions to his presentation will vary, and individual reactions often depend or hinge upon the reaction or evaluation given by the leader of specific interest groups, that is, opinion leaders. Their nod of approval or disapproval can often signal the success of a project. In today's environment, an effective speaker understands the powerful impact of individuals located within the audience and spends considerable time adapting and adjusting his or her behavior to the interaction that occurs between and among audience members.

One result of the interaction described above is that the components of this system work together to produce an effect that is greater than the sum of their efforts taken separately. In other words, the whole is greater than the sum of its parts. This effect is called synergy. People in a system produce a different output from the same people working in isolation, for example, a choir singing an anthem may be spiritually transported to a degree that would be impossible for the same people singing separately.

The synergistic effect is not always positive. Blockage and inhibition can be multiplied no less than positive reinforcement; undesirable products can be magnified as well as desirable ones. For example, the destructive world of a mob often surpasses the viciousness of its individual members. One distinguishing characteristic of a public communication system is that it provides equal, or at least substantial, opportunity for audience members to mutually influence each other as well as the behavior of the speaker.

In public communication, the audience usually presents a complex communication environment, as in Frank Williams' case. The audience is, in effect, a many-segmented organism, with a potential for a high degree of direct interaction as well as feedback interaction with the speaker.

DEVELOPING SYNERGY

The ultimate objective of a speaker is to create a system of public communication where the components of the system work together to produce an effect greater than each of the components working independently. Frank Williams, for example, wants to develop positive synergy. He wants each member of the audience to respect his proposal, wants each member to influence other members to accept the proposal, and ultimately wants members in the audience who are also members of specific interests groups to influence their group to accept the proposal. If this were to occur, Frank Williams might develop this thematic outline for his presentation:

1. We all share a common goal: creating the best possible future for everybody in our county.
2. This goal can not be achieved unless everyone's interests and needs are taken into account—that's why planning is necessary.
3. The plan's criteria are designed to make sure that the proposed land use represents an optimum balance of interest.

4. This balance has been preserved in each section of the proposed plan.

Frank may believe that if he dwells on these four areas he is likely to achieve a positive synergy effect. In the introduction of his speech, Frank may suggest:

In many ways, a county is like a living organism. It can not enjoy health and growth without a great number of healthy activities, all going on at the same time, all interacting with and contributing to each other. Sometimes the well-being or even the life of the whole organism is threatened because some seemingly insignificant function is cut off from oxygen or nutrition. The organism can prosper and grow only so long as the needs of all its functions are met. This is the philosophy that has guided the development of each detail in the proposed plan for the future health and growth of the organism we all "Progress County."

This introduction does several things for Frank. It makes a bid for a sympathetic hearing based on mutual interest. It offers assurance in advance that a responsible philosophy and concern for the general health of the community have gone into the plan. It reminds the listeners graphically of their interdependence and the penalty for sacrificing the general good to satisfy selfish interests. At the same time, it calls attention to the fact that the plan is an integrated whole that should not be picked apart piecemeal without considering the effect of one part on all of the others.

As soon as the opening is concluded, Frank may move directly into the second point of his outline, with concrete reminders and illustrations of the interest they all share in the county's future, and of the interdependence that makes the welfare of each a function of the climate of health and progress. Industry can not prosper if pollution drives employees and customers out of the area; environmentalists will lose in the long run if they make it impossible for industry to function profitably; merchants need adequate transportation and parking facilities, but they will be wasted if green space, recreational areas, and schools are neglected; and all plans will become pointless if the cost becomes so great that the taxpayers rebel.

Frank can then proceed to describe all of the studies, research, comparison, and consultation that has gone into the master plan to guarantee that all interests have been recognized and integrated into a balanced program for economic health, good living, and sound land-use development. This same theme can carry over into his description of the plan details. In explaining the proposed increase in airport size, traffic, freight, and passenger service he says:

Now, we could have proposed a much larger expansion, which would have pleased the people who rely heavily on airport facilities—at least, it would have pleased them on paper. But right along with it, we would have increased the noise, hazards, service traffic, and parking problems to an unacceptable level. That's what they did in another county and the public opposition was so great that not only were they prevented from completing the plan, they were not even able to complete the parts of it that were reasonable and acceptable. This plan will give us an expanded facility to meet our needs, and still allow us to stay well within the limits the studies have shown to be safe and acceptable.

This is only one of the number of possible approaches to developing a presentation based on the general theme Frank chose. He might, for example, open with a description of one facet of the plan that illustrates all of the care and concern for a sound, balanced program that have gone into the preparation of the proposal. Or he might have begun with a projection of the county's needs in ten to twenty years, and then demonstrated how the plan was developed to meet those needs.

Whatever the details, however, he will find it an advantage to keep the approach as flexible and as adaptable as possible. This simplifies adjustments that may be required to meet the individual interests of different audiences. It is equally important in making on the spot modifications indicated by the speaker's interpretation of audience reactions to his presentation. To achieve a positive synergy, the speaker, in most cases, must rapidly adjust his message to maximize audience receptivity and mutual influence among members of the audience.

Interpreting Audience Behavior

One of the more important tools for evaluating and improving public communication effectiveness is the ability of the speaker to recognize and interpret audience feedback. Feedback is represented not only by the overt expressions of approval or disapproval such as applause or booing, but also by the dozens of unconscious signals such as cough level, facial expression, restless movement, posture, cross-talk, gestures, and similar reactions.

It is not enough for the public communicator merely to be aware of audience feedback. He or she needs to perfect the ability to make instant evaluations of audience behavior, by relating it to communication goals and expected outcomes, and by adapting to the communication process accordingly. The ability to interpret audience behavior effectively is usually the product of experience combined with sharp observation, a certain amount of intuition, and above all a clear understanding of both the audience composition and the group processes that influence the reactions of its members.

In Chapter 9 we will focus directly on audience analysis. Here, we are concerned with the effect of a special set of influences that are generated by the presence of other members of the audience. These group interaction effects include both structural factors such as setting, group size, and personality factors such as individual self-image and public image concepts. These factors play significant roles in individual and group reactions to a specific message, subject, or speaker.

Traditionally, speakers tend to predict the listener's response to a particular message based upon such details as income, age, political and religious affiliation, education, family, ethnic and geographical background, life style and social activities, and so on. Then, the speaker accumulates this data and begins to visualize a single composite of people. Based upon the composite of audience details, the speaker then develops an audience profile and, with some accuracy, predicts the overall audience response to his or her message.

This is a practical and usually very effective approach to public communication. It is important, however, for an effective speaker to keep two other key factors in mind: (1) that the "typical member" of an audience is a fictional entity that seldom bears any resemblance to any real member of the group and, (2) that the reactions of individuals in groups are often quite different from their reactions when they are alone. The mere presence of others has a significant influence on individuals' behavior. For example, most people have at least one model image of the kind of person they believe they are, or would like to be, or would like others to think they are. The tendency to behave as one thinks one's model would behave in a given situation is sometimes compelling, and is usually heightened by the presence of other people, particularly if their admiration or good opinion is desired.

Thus, a public communicator such as Frank Williams, faced with the task of making a persuasive presentation on a complex subject to a diverse, partisan audience, needs to know as much as possible in advance about the responses that he can expect through audience analysis. He also needs to understand the ways that variables such as organizational loyalty, interest group identification, the reaction of opinion leaders, seating location, and similar factors will affect interactions among members of the audience. Frank Williams will have to accurately evaluate this behavior, perhaps by making some adjustments on his own, and capitalizing on the interacting influences that occur as he speaks.

Effects of Dyad and Small Group Behavior

A listener's persuasibility can differ drastically according to whether the persuasion takes place in a one-to-one communication situation, in a small group, or in a large audience. It also can vary with different media (a private letter, newspaper, radio, television, or public address), and with the format (a form letter as opposed to a personal one, an advertisement or a commercial, a news item, a report, a conventional speech, a panel discussion, or a debate). A dyadic communication system exists when two people communicate directly with each other. This is the most common communication system in our everyday lives, and it takes a multitude of forms. A brief exchange with a door-to-door salesperson is obviously of a different order than one that takes place between husband and wife, even when the content is similar. In general, the briefer the contact the more the exchange is characterized by impersonal, stereotyped responses. Consider, for example, the following exchange

"Would you be interested in . . . ?"
"No."

taking place between a householder and a door-to-door salesperson on the one hand, and between husband and wife on the other. In the first instance, it probably expresses the second speaker's resentment of intrusion and resistance to the idea of being sold anything, no matter what it is. It probably has no antecedents, and is virtually automatic and impersonal.

Between husband and wife, however, the same exchange is almost certainly anything but impersonal, and speaks volumes about what has gone on before it. The opening question, rather than being merely the prelude to a presentation, may signify, "I want to make up," or "I'd like to resume our prior discussion," or "I have an idea." The response may mean "I'm too busy for anything right now," or "I know exactly what you're talking about and there is no point in discussing it any further," or "I'm still pouting."

Each participant in dyadic communication is involved in a direct exchange of influence with the other; this is sometimes called a "coactive" communication system. For example, an individual's response to a presentation often is affected by who they sit next to, the way the rest of the audience responds, or even by who they talk to after hearing the speech. This behavior has a significant impact on communication outcomes.

A listener affiliated with a specific interest group attending a public communication event will probably not only experience coactive influence, but will also be influenced by the specific affiliated group. The smallest "interactive" system is a group of three—a "triadic" system. With the addition of only one person a small quantitative change indeed, its qualitative effect on the communication process is significant.

There is a familiar comedy routine involving a jeweler, a well-to-do elderly man, and an attractive young woman, discussing the price of a pair of earrings.

"They're $200.," says the jeweler, and pauses to check the man's expression for a negative reaction. Seeing none, he adds, ". . . each," pauses again, and then adds rapidly, "plus, of course, fitting them to the lady's ears."

Here, feedback and the unspoken influence of the young woman on both the jeweler's boldness and the reluctance of her escort to protest are obviously crucial to the exchange.

The effects of coactive and interactive systems on a public communication are indeed potent. The public communicator must be aware of the powerful impact of these influences. For years, strategists have advocated that a public speaker should seek out an affirmatively responding audience member, and focus on him or her. The idea is that the speaker not only would feel good about his or her speaking, but it is hoped that the members in the audience would observe the supporting behavior and begin reacting in the same manner.

Effects of Mass Communication

One evening one of the authors attended a speech where the speaker presented his views on the subject of pornography. It was a rather informal affair and from time to time the speaker was interrupted by questions from the audience. He pleasantly responded and upon completing his answer went on with his talk. The audience tended to be favorably impressed with the speaker and his message and seemed to become more interested as he spoke.

Suddenly a door opened and within a few minutes a TV camera was focusing on the speaker. The presence of this camera, a camera man, and a reporter had a profound effect on audience behavior as well as speaker behavior. The communication climate moved from informal to formal, from relaxed to rigid and tense. At first everyone observed what was happening and then seemed to decide to return to normalcy. However, both audience and speaker were unsuccessful. The speaker began reading more from his manuscript, looking directly at the camera, and ignoring his audience. The audience changed their behavior accordingly. They began watching the speaker "interact with the camera." Rather than being an audience, they were now observers of a media communication event. They did not interrupt the speaker with questions, nor give the impression that they were highly motivated or actively involved in the communication situation. However, when the speaker concluded and asked if there were any questions, the audience was quick to respond and a number of hands went up. When asking the question, the person would stand up and very formally address the speaker while paying careful attention to the camera.

In today's environment, it is not uncommon to have mass communication systems present at public communication events. In many cases, the presence of equipment and mass communication personnel have a profound effect on speaker and audience behavior.

Public Communication: An Interactive System

From the simplest midway concession to national political conventions, those who are professionally concerned with influencing the thinking and decision-making processes of large groups of people attempt to manipulate mood, setting, and interpersonal influence to produce the effects they desire. Shills and claques, hired to feign interest and enthusiasm, are familiar allies of speilers and pitchmen of all stripes. Politicians routinely plant supporters in their own audiences, and hecklers in the audiences of their opponents. Evangelists welcome the presence in their congregation of "Amen-shouters" and perennial penitents who regularly "answer the call" to public salvation. Noisy demonstrations in the aisles, designed to stampede political conventions for one hopeful candidate or another, are familiar enough to draw chuckles from Walter Cronkite, and pained protests from time-conscious chairpersons.

The reason is simple. Audience-wise professionals know that reactions are contagious in groups—that the response of some members of the audience can influence the response of others. An important part of this phenomenon is the concept of the opinion leader, the individual in a group who exercises extraordinary influence. Lawyers routinely try to spot such individuals among jurors, and when they believe they have located one, they are inclined to direct their message to him or her, and give special weight to the feedback signals they receive from such individuals.

Wyatt Earp, the famous upholder (or corrupter, depending on which source you choose to read) of frontier law, once gave a graphic example of the value of communicating directly with opinion leaders. Determined to protect a prisoner from a lynch mob, he watched the gathering crowd until he located the three or four men who were most actively urging it on. When he was given the traditional challenge that "You can't stop us all!" he responded that he *could* stop three or four, adding, "And they'll be you, and you, and you, and you," pointing out the leaders. According to Earp, the effect was little short of miraculous as the determination of the entire mob melted before his eyes.

Upon occasion, every speaker is brushed by the uneasy suspicion that he is facing a potential lynch mob. Unfortunately, the situation is usually less deadly than it may appear and although the audience processes at work may be subtler, they are nevertheless discernible to the alert speaker.

At their simplest level, audience processes are dyadic. If two people attend a speech together, the chances are very high that the response of each will be affected to some degree by the presence of the other. If one is a more forceful personality, or more knowledgeable than the other, he or she may exercise a disproportionate amount of influence. A similar but more complicated interaction process is apt to influence the responses of a group that attends together, or recognizes each other in the audience.

An important role is also played by the individual member's perception of the character of the audience. Crowds have a tendency to have an intimidating effect upon those who are, or believe themselves to be, in the minority. At the same time, there is a "bandwagon" effect that encourages individuals to go along with the crowd. This is well understood and thoroughly exploited by the employers of shills, the organizers of convention demonstrations, and the producers of television shows, who shrewdly provide laugh tracks and canned applause to guide the responses of home audiences.

All of the factors affecting communication that we have learned to look for in the individual continue to operate in the audience situation. Self-interest, self-image, ego considerations, censorship, and selective attention all take their toll on clear message reception, just as they do in one-to-one and small-group systems. But the effect is sometimes significantly different, both for the audience as a collective entity and for its individual members—at least so far as immediate response is concerned. There is reason to believe that individuals tend to revert partially or wholly to their original views when the persuasive influence is withdrawn.

The public nature of audience response makes some individuals more cautious in exposing their true feelings. The employee who knows that his or her boss is in the audience may refrain from applauding sentiments the boss may disapprove of, or hypocritically applaud those the boss approves, and thus distort the influence exercised on other members of the audience by falsifying the apparent division of opinion.

In a similar way, a powerful form of censorship is exercised by individual group identification. If you think of yourself as, say, a conservative in an audience in which you recognize many other conservatives, you may well feel a certain sense of group solidarity that you are reluctant to violate. You may be inclined to defer to what you believe your fellow conservatives expect of you, even though it may not always reflect your precise view. This appears to be a fairly universal human tendency, to some degree affecting just about everybody who feels loyalty to an identifiable point of view, be it political, fraternal, social, or religious.

From the foregoing, it is perhaps apparent that the task of the speaker who wishes to utilize understanding of audiences and interpretation of feedback effectively is a formidable one. At the most fundamental level, it involves a grasp of formal logic and analogy to provide the presentation a sound basic structure. But this is only the beginning of a public communication.

To this basic foundation, the effective speaker must add an understanding of the human factors that work against ready reception and acceptance of new or different ideas, however logically or colorfully they may be presented. The speaker also needs to understand the limits an audience places upon its willingness to be led, and how these limits are communicated through feedback to the speaker.

It is important to know the forms of interaction that operate among the participants in a communication system, and the special conditions imposed by the size and nature of the system, as well as by the medium and format employed. A dyadic system operates on different principles than a small group, a small group on different principles than a public speaking audience. In the public speaking audience, a group of people are brought together in close proximity with each other and a speaker, creating an arena for new kinds of interaction. In general, the effect of the audience setting is to suppress highly individual responses, to invest expressed responses with a certain uniformity, and to heighten the authority of perceived groups and majority opinions. There is a greater tendency for individuals in an audience to conceal views they perceive as unpopular, and to respond to the bandwagon effect of crowd psychology.

It can be argued with a good deal of reason that the effective speaker's skill is an art as much as a science—that it relies at least as much on intuition as on sober analysis. This is no doubt true, however, the public communication can improve with patient practice and persistent application.

KEY CONCEPTS

Can you define and give examples of the following terms?

Selective attention	Opinion leader
Dyadic communication	Group identification
Coactive system	Bandwagon effect
Synergy	Interactive systems
Synergy effect	

PROPOSITIONS

1. The mind may refuse to accept information that does not conform to its intellectual and emotional preconceptions or alter the incoming data to make it conform to our preconceptions.
2. It is the listener, not the speaker, who determines what is communicated.
3. A listener's persuasibility can vary according to the communication context, message, and other audience members.
4. Any small group that provides the opportunity for each member to interact with each other member is an interactive system.
5. In the mass media, there is usually no interaction between the audience members and the sender.
6. If two people attend a speech together, the chances are very good that the responses of each are affected by the presence of the other.
7. Crowds have an intimidating effect on those who perceive themselves to be in the minority.
8. The bandwagon effect encourages individuals to conform to the wishes of the crowd.

9. Self-interest, self-image, ego considerations, censorship, and selective attention each take their toll on message reception.
10. The public nature of audience responses makes some individuals more cautious about expressing their true feelings.
11. A powerful form of censorship is exercised by individual group identification.

Part II
Problem Recognition

Chapter 3
Modifying Cognitive Systems

P R E V I E W

¶ *What are the components of the cognitive system?*
Values, attitudes, beliefs, and needs

¶ *What is the nature of values?*
A frame of reference within which new orientations are assessed

¶ *What is an attitude?*
Our predispositions toward or against objects, persons, and issues

¶ *What are the components of an attitude?*
Cognitive, affective, and behavioral

¶ *What is a belief?*
Our conviction that something is true or false on the basis of evidence, authority-suggestion, experience, or intuition

¶ *What is the role of needs in the cognitive system?*
They are the drives that motivate our search for and choices of information

¶ *How does the cognitive system operate as an information-processing mechanism?*
It helps us to anticipate and cope with recurring events, and provides a quick, economic method for assessing, processing, and sorting data

¶ *What are the three ways in which the cognitive system works as a frustrator of message acceptance?*
It causes an unwillingness to ask questions, or to understand
It leads to an avoidance of relevant information
It causes a tendency to overlook crucial differences

¶ *What are the four ways in which the cognitive system works as a facilitator of message acceptance?*
It operates as a vector, compass, or pointer
It helps to organize the effects of needs, attitudes, values, and beliefs

It helps to supply a context

It arouses expectations that lead to subsequent changes in the existing cognitive system

¶ *What are the essential steps in the information-processing strategy?*

Presentation, attention, acceptance, and retention

O B J E C T I V E S

After reading this chapter, you should be able to

1. identify the components of the cognitive system.
2. explain the nature of values, attitudes, belief, and needs.
3. identify some of the significant values of American culture.
4. explain how the cognitive system influences audience responsiveness.
5. explain how the cognitive system operates as a frustrator of message acceptance.
6. explain how the cognitive system operates as a facilitator of message acceptance.
7. explain the "safest" assumptions that a speaker should formulate about the prospective audience.
8. identify the steps in the information-processing strategy.
9. explain the nature of the saliency approach.
10. explain the nature of the functional approach.
11. explain the factors that influence an effective presentation.
12. explain the factors that influence audience attention.
13. explain the factors or circumstances that are conducive to message acceptance.
14. explain the factors that frustrate or facilitate message retention.

A MEMBER of the citizen's policy advisory board stood before an overflowing audience in the city council chambers surveying the anxious faces. "Gentlemen," she said, turning toward the council chair, "the advisory board believes that we need to establish a more highly educated police force." As she proceeded with her discourse, she presented the audience with a basic argument to support her position. "We recognize that effective policing depends upon a police officer's ability to make decisions of high quality. Better decisions are a result of a proper education. Therefore, our police need to be better educated. It is your responsibility to provide the funds necessary for an educational program for our police."

The speaker's goal was to persuade the council members to fund a program for educating police. The communication goal was to modify the cognitive systems of the receivers who would make the ultimate decision on the speaker's recommendation. Modifying cognitive systems is the primary goal of public communication. In most public communication situations, the speaker confronts an audience in order to change the audience's orientation toward a particular situation, idea, object or issue to thereby change the receivers' existing cognitive system.

In this chapter, we'll discuss how the cognitive system influences audience responsiveness, and what a communicator must do to ensure that the audience processes information according to plan. *First*, we'll identify and define the four components of the cognitive system—values, attitudes, beliefs, and needs. *Second*, we'll explain how the audience's cognitive system serves as an information-processing mechanism, and how existing needs, beliefs, values, and attitudes facilitate or frustrate the cognitive realignments desired by the communicator. *Third*, we'll discuss the general terms of a design for audience motivation, and then go on to describe the steps of a strategy that may aid a communicator in his or her attempt to modify cognitive systems.

Components of the Cognitive System

Values, attitudes, beliefs, and needs are the key components in a receiver's cognitive system. They serve to influence the quality of audience responsiveness. Consequently, a speaker must understand the characteristics of these components in order to maximize their effectiveness in a public communication system. Before proceeding, we must define each cognitive component.

Values constitute a yardstick or frame of reference against which audiences measure and evaluate new ideas, suggestions, or viewpoints proposed by the speaker. According to Jones and Gerard, "values animate a person; they move him or her around the environment because they define its attractive and repelling sectors."[1] People use values to assess the goodness, soundness, or acceptability of situations or behaviors. Americans, for example, extol the values of *puritan and pioneer morality, human or civil rights, achievement and success, change and progress, a sense of*

1. Jones, E., and H. Gerard, *Foundations of Social Psychology* (New York: Wiley and Sons, Inc., 1967), p. 158.

ethical responsibility, efficiency, practicality, and pragmatism.[2] Minnick has suggested that a communicator should develop communication inputs to fit one or more of six general value categories: *theoretic, economic, aesthetic, social, political,* and *religious.*[3] By establishing a linkage between the speaker's values and those of the audience, the communicator may provide a basis for modifying the existing cognitive system.

Attitudes are our predispositions for or against objects and issues, and are affected by our ideas, feelings, and customary behaviors. Stated more technically, we may say that our attitudes consist of three components: cognitive (pertaining to information), affective (pertaining to feelings), and behavioral (pertaining to actions). When our feelings and cognitions about a particular issue change as a result of persuasion, our behavior usually changes. When a politician argues convincingly, we may gain some new insights from him; we may begin to have good feelings about him and his message, and we may eventually go to the polls to vote for him. In other instances, we may change our behavior and find that our cognitions and feelings change as if to catch up with our new behavior. In reaction to a physician's arguments for more bulk in our diet, we may begin eating cereals we once despised, acquiring a more positive feeling for the cereal and accepting the importance of the product in our diet.

Attitudes are rather complex states or orientations that tend to be stable and enduring, and can change only through proper motivation. Sensing a certain attitude, the communicator's task is to skillfully convince the audience that existing attitudes no longer serve a useful purpose.

Beliefs are our convictions that something is "true" or "false" on the basis of evidence, authority-suggestion, experience, or intuition. For example, we may be led to believe that water fluoridation is good for our community because a speaker has presented us with evidence derived from dental studies. Or, we may believe that Lee Harvey Oswald was not the sole participant in the assassination of President John F. Kennedy, not because of convincing evidence, but on the basis of sheer intuition.

Research has found that some beliefs, particularly those formulated through superstition, stereotypes, delusions, and prejudice,

2. Steele, E., and W. C. Redding, "The American Value System," *Western Speech*, 26 (Spring 1962), pp. 83–91.
3. Minnick, W. C., *The Art of Persuasion* (Boston: Houghton Mifflin Company, 1957), pp. 211–214.

are rather resistant to change. The amount of resistance is related to the intensity of the belief, the confidence with which it is held, the amount of social support given by other significant persons, and the length of time over which the belief has prevailed.

Needs are the substance of our daily existence. Although each individual brings specific, and potentially different needs into a public communication situation, almost all of these needs may be conveniently subsumed under seven general categories: (1) need for freedom, (2) need to help others, (3) need for new experiences (particularly among young people), (4) need for power and influence, (5) need for recognition, (6) need for response and affection, and (7) need for security.

Our needs create drives that motivate our searches and choices. Public communication that extends a promise of satisfying or fulfilling a need may be effective in motivating a receiver to change his or her cognitive systems.

These four components—values, attitudes, beliefs, and needs—constitute a communicator's targets in a public communication situation. They are the elements of the receiver's cognitive system. They act like gatekeepers by maintaining constant vigil and monitoring every bit of new information that comes by.

INFORMATION PROCESSING AND AUDIENCE RESPONSIVENESS

An audience's cognitive system is formed through experience, and, despite relative stability, can be changed by public communication. Speeches are made by government personnel to enlist our support for a legislative proposal or executive action; political candidates appeal to our sense of logic and often to our prejudices and passions in order to influence our vote, and ministers and evangelists exhort us to forego our self-centered urges in favor of a more "righteous" existence. Every day our values, attitudes, beliefs, and needs are the targets of numerous messages that create pressures toward changing our attitudes and inducing behaviors that we would not otherwise manifest. Most communicators assume that every belief, attitude, or value-orientation has a vulnerable spot that can be penetrated with a sound strategy. However, we should realize that although change is being solicited there are also counterforces operating to bolster and maintain the existing cognitive structure and its habitual responses. The task of inducing change in cognitive systems is not an easy one; some members of your audience may manifest no change in attitude, and most of those who do change, do so reluctantly.

In the title of this section, we characterized the audience's cognitive system as an *information-processing* mechanism. What's involved in this information-processing capability? Beliefs, attitudes, values, and needs help the individual to anticipate and cope with recurring events. Because these cognitive components evolve from our victories and defeats, or from what has pleased or displeased us, they are not usually discarded easily. We utilize them to provide quick, economical methods for assessing, processing, or sorting out new data and information. In fact, we are inclined to impose as much order on our environment as we can.

Our information-processing system is crucial to our survival. Without attitudes, beliefs, values, and needs, we could not make quick decisions when choosing between alternative courses of behavior. Instead, we would have to perform a sophisticated, time-consuming calculus of anticipated gains and losses in each new situation. Imagine the effort involved in shopping if a homemaker, with grocery list in hand, had no predictions toward brand names; or the dilemma confronting a voter in choosing a candidate for elected office without having some type of system from which to base judgments. We rely upon prior patterns developed in our cognitive system to assist us in making these choices. The homemaker buys the can of beans that carries the *Del Monte* label because she has been satisfied with other *Del Monte* products. The potential voter chooses candidate X because X is a Republican, because he or she is a Republican, and because Republicans generally vote for Republican candidates. In both instances, we can see how people process information, responding to new events and ideas in ways appropriate to old response patterns. Despite the benefits we derive from such a system, there is also a potential cost. If we aren't careful, we may become too rigid and unchanging when change is to our advantage.

Although audiences manifest a tendency toward conservatism or "unchangingness," there are also internal drives that contribute to openness and flexibility. Cognitive systems—attitudes, beliefs, values, and needs—do change (though slowly and reluctantly) when a communicator causes audience members to see that their attitudes or beliefs are inconsistent with their individual goals and objectives. We need to know how the cognitive system operates if we are to become better public communicators. We should understand how our cognitive system functions as a frustrator by blocking and slowing message-acceptance, and how it can serve as a facilitator to hasten and enhance message-acceptance.

FRUSTRATORS OF MESSAGE-ACCEPTANCE

There seem to be three basic ways in which a listener's cognitive system could work to frustrate the attainment of the communicator's goal.

First, existing needs, attitudes, beliefs, and values may cause potential listeners to be unwilling to ask certain questions, or may diminish their desire to understand for fear that the response may furnish information disturbing to their comfort, complacency, and ways of viewing life. A mother might not request information on her child's classroom behavior because she would not want to be confronted with evidence that her child was creating problems.

Second, existing needs, attitudes, beliefs, and values may also lead listeners to avoid considering relevant evidence, or from seeing the relevance of presented information. For example, residents of southern California may not listen to the Governor who implores that they conserve water because they have sufficient water to meet their current needs.

Third, existing needs, attitudes, beliefs, and values may cause potential listeners to overlook differences, or to fail to make distinctions. For example, a debate on the merits and drawbacks of a guaranteed annual income was held before an audience that was bitterly opposed to such interventions by the federal government. The audience did not seem to appreciate the fact that it was indeed a debate, and insistently heckled both speakers for advocating "more meddling by the bureaucrats in Washington." They seemed unable to see the important difference between the two positions presented. Common experience suggests many such occurrences in the realm of social, political, and religious attitudes. To a conservative person, every idea left of center may seem to be radical, while the more radical person may view every idea right of center as reactionary. The range over which fine distinctions can be made appears to be shortened.

FACILITATORS OF MESSAGE-ACCEPTANCE

There are four basic ways in which the cognitive system could assist the communicator in achieving the desired goal.

First, existing needs, attitudes, beliefs, and values may operate as a compass, pointing the audience in the direction of a solution. Frequently a listener, because of "pointing" attitudes or needs, will latch on to a relatively obscured idea or suggestion that would otherwise have gone unnoticed. Under the influence of particular attitudes or needs, people become attuned to events to which they would not otherwise be sensitive. However, effective communicators normally will not leave things to chance. They realize they must furnish the audience with something to point toward. Consequently, the appeals and need-satisfying elements of the message must be clearly presented.

Second, closely related to pointing are the organizing effects of needs, attitudes, values, and beliefs. When a strong need is aroused, facts, information, and ideas organize themselves around it. For example, when you are working on a term paper, everything you read appears, at first glance, to be relevant to the topic with which you are concerned. First, there's the need, and then every bit of information seems intent on rushing in to fill that need. It seems that under the influence of the aroused need, we perceive similarities not otherwise noticeable. If a speaker is adept at getting the audience to perceive an urgent need, it makes it easier for all of his or her ideas to be accepted.

Third, existing needs, attitudes, beliefs, and values may supply context. Since the context may influence the manner in which an argument is perceived, it follows that a given argument may be viewed differently in accordance with a particular need or attitude. For example, a speaker confronting an audience known for its stolid opposition toward any program of socialized medicine may be skillful enough to convince the audience of the need for better care for the elderly, and motivate them to vote for a national health insurance program. The need, in this case, care for the elderly, supplies the context, available medical care, and moves the audience to opt for the speaker's proposal, a national health program.

Fourth, existing needs, attitudes, beliefs, and values may arouse expectations that, in turn, may lead to a change in an audience's cognitive system. Needs that are aroused could influence a "softening" of existing negative attitudes and beliefs. According to Henle, "the stimulus for which we are predisposed requires less time than a like stimulus for which are are unprepared, to produce its full conscious effect."[4] Recall our example about the national health program. In that instance an audience was "softened" by being convinced of the misery and suffering of the elderly. Given the conviction of need-arousal, the audience may be "self-persuaded" to desire or *expect* some type of nationwide solution. The speaker puts the frosting on the cake; he or she reveals the "best possible solution"—a national health program.

Let's summarize. Existing needs, attitudes, beliefs, and values—

4. Henle, M., "Some Effects of Motivational Processes on Cognition," *Psychological Review*, 62 (1955), pp. 423–452.

the cognitive system that each individual brings to the audience —may be so constituted as to cause some members to be unwilling to understand, to avoid considering relevant information, and to fail to make major distinctions. All of these behaviors are indicative of closed-mindedness. The communicator's effectiveness will be generally minimal or nonexistent unless some way is found to lure the audience into openness.

On the other side of the coin, the existing cognitive system may greatly facilitate the communicator's goal. When attitudes, needs, beliefs, and values facilitate audience responsiveness to a communicator's intent, they are characterized as contributing to open-mindedness. In such instances, the existing cognitive system operates as a vector, pointing the way to anticipated solutions. It serves as a focus or point around which arguments may be organized, supplies a ready-made context into which a communicator imbeds persuasive arguments and arouses expectations.

Whether cognitive systems are potentially frustrating or facilitating will not be known by the communicator unless he or she has explored or analyzed the audience before the actual encounter. Whatever the prospect, we should anticipate the worst of conditions. There's safety in assuming that (1) the audience will be closed-minded and unyielding in its commitment to its opinions, and (2) they will not budge until they are motivated by arousing or establishing needs, and offering need-satisfiers. How we go about the task of need-arousal will be influenced by the type of motivational design we utilize. In the next section we'll discuss the general nature of such a design, which may constitute a foundation for an *information-processing* strategy that is effective in dealing with most audiences.

A General Design for Motivating the Audience: An Information-Processing Strategy

Our major concern in drafting a design for motivating the audience is to point up the necessity for making information relevant to the needs and drives of the potential listener. Public communication achieves its greatest success when it "enables people to bring about more satisfying relationships between themselves and the world around them."[5] Consequently, the design should derive from the audience's point of view. It should ask the crucial question: "What audience input variables are

5. Davison, W. P., "On the Effects of Communication," *Public Opinion Quarterly*, 13 (Fall 1959), p. 344.

likely to be prominent in the communicator-audience transaction, and how may they affect the quality of responsiveness?" With the answer as our guide, we can proceed to develop a foundation for a step-by-step *information-processing* strategy.

We must begin by recognizing that an audience is *not* a passive gathering of people who merely wait to fulfill the whim of every speaker. An audience is composed of people who are alive, dynamic, resisting, and rarely yielding unless motivated or rewarded. Audiences seem to operate with a type of "cost accounting" orientation. They seek bargains by demanding much from the speaker, and yielding little by little in exchange. A design for motivating an audience should be predicated on the idea that neither attention nor acceptance will occur in the absence of unfulfilled needs or desires. Once the audience members become aware of a particular need, they will scout and forage among the presented ideas for the necessary satisfiers. However, as Lerbinger points out, "we must go further by showing the audience the best path to the goal."[6] In the field of marketing research, motivation experts suggest that attempts should always be made to discover consumer motives that might be related to a product, and if necessary to reshape a product so that its ability to satisfy the discovered needs are more obvious. In public communication, the speaker should (1) discover the audience's motives or needs that relate to a proposed issue or viewpoint; and (2) highlight the potential value of our ideas for satisfying these audience's needs.

How do we discover the motives or needs that relate to an issue? The discovery process involves analyzing the audience before the actual encounter (we'll discuss in depth the question of audience analysis and audience inputs in Chapter 8). For the moment, it is sufficient to say that we should not only try to discover *what* are the prevailing needs, attitudes, beliefs, and values, but also try to discover *why* they exist. Once we have learned the *what* and *why* about the various dispositions or biases, the major task—laying out the information-processing strategy—can be undertaken.

The major assumption underlying an *information-processing* approach to inducing change in cognitive systems is that a listener presented with new information will try to absorb and deal with informational inputs as efficiently and economically as possible and alter his or her behavior accordingly.

6. Lerbinger, O., *Designs for Persuasive Communication* (Englewood Cliffs, N. J.: Prentice-Hall, Inc., 1972), p. 80.

William McGuire[7] has described a series of behavioral steps through which a communicator should guide an audience. These steps are: *presentation, attention, comprehension, yielding, retention,* and *action.* McGuire devised his model for the fields of marketing and advertising. Because the advertiser and public speaker are both involved in the business of public communication, we feel that McGuire's model, with minor modifications, can be used to outline a strategy for inducing change in cognitive systems. Our version of his information-processing model is presented in Figure 3–1. Each step in the model is linked to the pre-

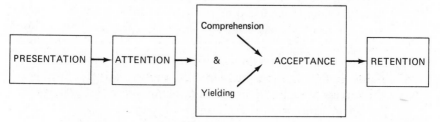

FIGURE 3.1. An information-processing model for indicing changes in cognitive systems.

ceding one, and the listener must be brought through each of the steps before he or she can be effectively persuaded.

As indicated in Figure 3–1, a message designed to affect an audience's cognitive system in a certain manner may or may not be *presented* effectively. There is a probability, and only a probability, that the audience will pay attention to the speaker's arguments or issues. Of those who attend, some will *accept* the speaker's induction, others will not. Will the audience *yield* to what has been *comprehended?* Will they consider your arguments to be convincing or sound? If they do, will they *retain* the information long enough to act upon it when the situation arises?

Several factors may be responsible for impeding the listener's journey through each of the four steps. For example, *presentation* may be hindered because a speaker fails to convince the audience that the ideas would be beneficial to them. *Attention* may be reduced because of the audience's existing beliefs or because of their disinterest or low involvement in the issue. *Acceptance* may be frustrated by personality factors such as low intelligence, closed-

7. McGuire, Wm., "An Information-Processing Model of Advertising Effectiveness." Paper presented at the symposium on Behavioral and Management Science in Marketing, Center for Continuing Education, The University of Chicago, July 1969.

mindedness, or because of group pressure. *Retention* may be reduced because of the speaker's inability to structure the message so that ideas flow smoothly, clearly, and logically.

The various influences that are exerted on an audience during any given public communication event may be attributed to factors that are identified as communication input variables. *The success of the communication in gaining attention, acceptance, and a manifested response is the result of the interaction between the source, message, and audience input variables.* The dynamics of this interaction is the essence of a fundamental framework for analyzing the effectiveness of the public communication process. In later chapters, we will discuss the input variables of the source, message, and audience in greater detail. For the moment, we are merely interested in discussing the general impact of these three factors on the *information-processing* behaviors inherent in the public communication situation. We want to see what influences the success of each step in our information-processing strategy for inducing change in audience's cognitive systems.

MESSAGE PRESENTATION

In Chapters 10, 11, and 12, you will read how a message should be packaged in terms of content, structure, and style. In this chapter, we'll talk about the "philosophy" of message presentation. We are now at the drawing-board phase, and we must ask questions such as: What are the concerns that govern an effective presentation? How can I make the speech engaging? How can I make my ideas salient and valuable to my audience? The answers may rest in one of two approaches, or rather, a combination of the two. The first is a saliency approach; the second is a functional approach.

The Saliency Approach. As a speaker, you probably will be confronted with one of three tasks: (1) you may try to create a "new" audience attitude or orientation toward a particular point of view; (2) you may try to change the direction of an existing attitude; or (3) you may try to increase the intensity of the existing attitude, for example, moving an audience from low commitment to high commitment.

When the task involves an attempt to entice the audience into *forming a new attitude* or favorable bias toward an issue, for example, a national health insurance plan, we should make use of a value premise that the audience already holds, and we should point out why and how our point of view enhances that particular value premise. For instance, if we are dealing with an audience that knows little or nothing about a national health plan, we might associate or identify our proposal with the value our audience places on the need to maintain a healthy citizenry—rich and poor alike.

Changing the direction of an existing attitude can be a difficult task. In this situation, we should try to show the audience that their existing attitude and behavior do not really reflect the basic values they cherish. We must convince them that the conclusions under which they operate, and the responses they have been manifesting are not truly representative of the "kinds of things they deeply believe in." We may attempt to convince them that what they believe is really not so. For example, if an audience believes that having a federally subsidized health program is undesirable because it eventually leads to a "communistic state of affairs," we should try to change that belief by citing relevant evidence drawn from facts and data pertaining to successful, humane, and noncommunist health programs in other countries. In addition to this evidence, we also should emphasize the benefits that are to be gained. In essence, we attempt to heighten the saliency or value of the issue.

If we are fortunate in finding an audience that's already favorable to our position, we may try to *increase the intensity of their existing attitude.* Our major task should be to make the audience more aware of the importance of both the issue and their attitudinal orientation toward it. We also should be prepared to demonstrate the number of important values that will be served by their activity. Suppose that we were planning to speak to an audience already in favor of fluoridation, and our task were to motivate them to canvas the neighborhoods to enlist community support for an impending referendum. What should we do? We should emphasize the great hygienic advantages of having good, sound teeth. But we also should link our arguments and appeals to other values such as dedication to community service, saving on dental costs, being a progressive-minded individual, having attractive children, having faith in American scientific know-how, and so on.

Whatever the task, the conduct of the saliency approach is clear. We must begin by tapping values that are already existent and potentially salient. Unless the values exist, or can be made to exist, a speaker will not be successful in bringing about positive responses toward his or her ideas.

The Functional Approach. The leading advocate of the functional approach to the modification of cognitive systems is Daniel

Katz.[8] Katz suggests that in order to change someone's attitudes we should first assess the functions the attitudes perform, and adjust our presentation accordingly. Attitudes perform *four* basic kinds of functions: (1) *utilitarian* or *instrumental*; (2) *ego-defensive*; (3) *value-expressive*; and (4) *knowledge*. We'll begin by discussing each function, and then indicate how we may entice our audience to process information through these functions.

The *utilitarian* function implies that people form or maintain certain attitudes largely as a means of achieving goals, maximizing rewards, and minimizing losses. Attitudes are used as a means to calculated ends. For example, a student who is intent on getting a good grade from an instructor may manifest a friendly, earnest attitude. This might be affected by lingering after each lecture to express appreciation for "a very fascinating idea" that the instructor touched upon and being extremely complimentary, even if the student hates the class and considers the instructor to be "a real turkey." If a person has a vested interest in off-shore petroleum drilling, he or she may manifest a positive attitude by making contributions to or voting for certain politicians supportive of that view. In both examples, the attitudes are manifested in order to bring about certain goals that establish their utility or instrumentality.

The *ego-defensive* function is manifested when some of our attitudes help us to form a shield or barrier against certain harsh "truths" about ourselves, people around us, or our environment. A negative attitude toward college education, for example, may protect a person from facing the reality that he or she "just can't hack it" as far as studies are concerned. The person projects the failure outward—"Nothing's wrong with me! It's the system that's loused up!" Racial prejudice, for example, may be a manifestation of an ego-defensive attitude through which a person projects his or her feelings of inferiority or inadequacy on to some person or group in the immediate sphere of reference.

The *value-expressive* function enables us to give positive expression to our central values, and aids us in portraying ourselves as we would ideally like to be. Value-expressive attitudes help us to reflect and confirm the notion of what we like to think we are. People who work in certain agencies or industries may come to value toughness, masculinity, and hard work. Consequently, they may manifest attitudes that express that toughness or obsession with "hard work," and may demonstrate negative attitudes toward

8. Katz, D., "The Functional Approach to the Study of Attitudes," *Public Opinion Quarterly*, 24 (Summer 1960), pp. 163–204.

those who work at less physically-demanding jobs or toward those who, for whatever reasons, do not work at all.

The *knowledge* function is served by those attitudes that help us to understand and give meaning to situations and phenomena that may not be instantly meaningful to us. Robertson puts it this way: "Individuals acquire knowledge to provide meaning and order for what would otherwise be a conglomeration of sensations in a chaotic environment."[9] For example, someone who has no clear-cut understanding of the objectives of the Women's Liberation movement may rush to the judgment, conclusion, or "knowledge" that it is intent on emasculating American men so that women can take over jobs and stop being good mothers and wives. Likewise, we may not know much about certain ethnic or racial groups, but we may rush into our own scripts or data about what we'd like to believe anyway. Some of our "knowledge-forming" attitudes cause us to behave unfavorably toward people, issues, and objects; some may cause us to behave favorably.

We have the *four* attitudinal functions: instrumental, ego-defensive, value-expressive, and knowledge. Each is a sieve or filter through which new information passes. An understanding of these functions is vital to planning our presentation for modifying the audience's cognitive systems. Let's see what's involved in developing presentation strategies.

You will encounter many audiences characterized by attitudes that are instrumental or utilitarian in scope. Such attitudes can be changed if you convince your audience that their orientation does not maximize the fulfillment of their goals, and that their acceptance of other beliefs, opinions, or inclinations can be more instrumental in satisfying needs. For example, when viewed as an isolated political issue, a national health insurance program may smack of socialism to an ultraconservative audience; consequently, they would have a negative attitude toward the idea. However, by showing them *how* such a health program could be vital to their survival, or convincing them that a national health plan removes the pressures of having to respond to constantly escalating medical fees, you would enhance your chances of changing their orientation to the issue.

Two basic approaches are recommended for working with ego-defensive attitudes or behaviors. First, you must make sure that your message does not imply threat or coercion to the listener. Because the audience's attitudes may have been intially brought

9. Robertson, T. S., *Consumer Behavior* (Glenview, Ill.: Scott, Foresman and Company, 1970), p. 61.

into focus because of a threatening circumstance, any additional threat on your part may further alienate the audience. Second, you should try to create as supportive a climate as is possible. An objective, matter-of-fact approach can serve to remove threat, especially in situations where people have been customarily bombarded by highly charged emotional appeals. Humor also can be used to establish a nonthreatening atmosphere, but it should not be directed against the audience or even against the problem. For public communicators, the importance of ego-defensive attitudes derives not so much from what we must do to change them, but rather from what we must do in order to avoid provoking or intensifying them.

Value-expressive attitudes can be changed through a presentation that skillfully induces an audience to become dissatisfied with the images they project. Katz suggests a basic mode of presentation for affecting attitude change.[10] Somehow, you must try to influence the audience to feel a measure of dissatisfaction with their self-image. This is your opening wedge, because people who are smugly and complacently pleased with all aspects of self will be immune to attempts to change their value-expressions. Here's an example of such a presentation strategy used by former Israeli foreign minister Abba Eban when he spoke to the General Assembly of the United Nations on June 16, 1967:

> Together with the supply of offensive weapons the Soviet Union has encouraged the military preparation of the Arab States.
>
> Since 1961 the Soviet armaments have assisted Egypt in its desire to conquer Israel. The great amount of offensive equipment supplied to the Arab States strengthens this assessment. *Thus, a Great Power which professes its devotion to peaceful settlement and the rights of states has for fourteen years afflicted the Middle East with a headlong armaments race: with the paralysis of the United Nations as an instrument of security: and with an attitude of blind identification with those who threaten peace against those who defend it.* (Authors' italics)

Notice how the italicized portion of Eban's comments attempts to chide the Soviet Union for the discrepancy that it allows to exist between its professed value orientation and its actual behavior.

Change may also be induced by providing your audience with information that makes it evident that their current beliefs or opinions are inaccurate or incomplete. Your major concern would be to find ways to overcome the audience's tendency to

10. Katz, D., op. cit., pp. 163–204.

avoid information that conflicts with their notions. Solid evidence derived from sources respected by your audience would be an essential aspect of your presentation.

As we complete this discussion about the mode of presentation as a factor in inducing change in cognitive systems, we will suggest a method that will guide you effectively through your choice of either the *saliency* or *functional* approach.

Whichever presentational mode you choose in attempting to induce change in cognitive systems, the impact on the audience would be mediated largely by the audience's tendency to either *assimilate* or *contrast*[11] new information. An understanding of what's involved when an audience assimilates or contrasts should help you to plan your approach more effectively.

Let's begin by examining an audience's contrast tendencies. Your audience will *contrast* your ideas if those ideas advocate a position very different from their own. The term *contrast* means that the audience will very likely distort your message and see it as being extremely radical in tone and intent. They'll be "turned off" or "ticked off" by it.

Assimilation tendencies operate in an opposite manner. Your audience will assimilate your ideas or statements if your position is not too different from theirs. The audience will still distort the information you provide, but this time, the distortion works in your favor. The audience will perceive your message as advocating a less extreme position and bring it into harmony with their own thinking. Assimilation is the goal we generally strive for as public communicators.

A primary factor affecting the influence of public communication upon inducing change in cognitive systems is the audience's judgment of the amount of discrepancy between the speaker's position and their own. It is for that reason that we recommend that you do your homework on the audience in planning your presentation. You must be able to put your ideas across so that they are not perceived as being extreme. You must be equipped with some knowledge of how your audience stands on the issue.

Attention. You cannot effectively change a person's attitudes, opinions, or beliefs without first gaining that person's attention to your message. Consequently, an awareness of *how* attention operates, and how it may be gained, diverted, and attracted is

11. Hovland, C. I., and M. Sherif, *Social Judgment: Assimilation and Contrast Effects in Communication and Attitude Change* (New Haven, Conn.: Yale University Press, 1961).

very important to your strategy. Our cognitive system influences the quality of attention that we pay to objects, arguments, ideas, and events. If we are hungry, we may be inclined to attend to a *Burger King* commercial; if we are not hungry, we may ignore it. If one has a positive attitude toward environmentalism, one may be motivated to attend to a speech given by an environmentalist. Just think of the number of speakers you have already ignored and will ignore during your stay in college. Frequently, it's not that we don't care about some of the crucial issues, but rather that we are so bombarded and overwhelmed by information that we can't really be bothered.

Readiness or willingness to attend, or the intensity and longevity of that attention may be influenced by (1) prior information-satisfaction, overkill or overload; and (2) whether the new information is tantalizing, controversial, interesting, exciting, pleasing, or surprising. The question is: How do we increase the probability that our audience will attend to our public communication? People are generally willing to listen to messages that increase their understanding and help them to organize the complex data that they receive from their environments, do not attack their self-esteem, do not reveal unpleasant truths about themselves, help them to adjust in a complex world by making it more likely they will obtain rewards and avoid punishments and give them an opportunity to express their values more convincingly to others.

The key to gaining audience attention is indicating to the audience that your ideas are *worthwhile*. Accomplish this goal by showing them how your ideas are relevant to their satisfaction, and you will win attention. That which is salient is normally interesting! Once audience interest is aroused, you must sustain it. If your message-appeals are strong and consequential, you may be successful in sustaining the audience's attention.

Thus far, we have examined strategies for effective presentation and gaining audience attention. We will now examine how the speaking gains acceptance.

Acceptance. We view acceptance as consisting of two very crucial behaviors: audience comprehension, and audience yielding. The audience must understand what you're trying to say, and on the basis of that understanding yield to your inductions.

Comprehension resides mainly in the audience even though there is much that you, as a speaker, can do to facilitate it. People bring different mental abilities to the public communication situation. The quality of comprehension is dependent on the kind of interaction developing among the source, the message, and the audience. If the source is competent, intelligent, and has useful knowledge about the audience, the message will be planned to meet whatever contingencies that audience presents. That message should be clear in the listener's mind. Also, as we pointed out earlier, the message must fit into the audience's frame of reference—their values, beliefs, needs, and so on—and should not make them feel defensive.

Yielding is the other part of the twofold process. According to Kelman,[12] yielding behavior may consist of three different qualities: compliance, identification, and internalization. A significant consideration of our information-processing strategy would be to determine what kind of yielding (and acceptance) we want from the audience.

You will probably get *compliance* when your audience accepts your ideas or suggestion solely to get a favorable reaction from you or the agency you represent. Here, acceptance is indicated not because they believe fully, but because they are interested in being rewarded instead of being punished. *Identification* may occur when the audience yields because of their need to establish a satisfying relationship with the speaker. If the audience likes you, that is, if they perceive you as an attractive source, they will tend to go along with your point of view. *Internalization* is perhaps the most solid and enduring kind of yielding. It occurs when the audience accepts the speaker's influence because the message is congruent or compatible with their existing values, attitudes, or beliefs.

We suggest that your perceived power of authority as a source, particularly the manner in which you wield that authority, would most likely lead to compliance. Your attractiveness as a source would lead to identification. And, your credibility, (if it's high) could be conducive to identification. As for the impact of the message, we suggest that if the message makes it clear that there will be rewards for adopting a given position punishment for not adopting that position, compliance may occur, especially if the reward or punishment is plausible. If your message clearly shows that your ideas are consistent with the audience's values, you may get the audience to internalize your ideas.

Once we have created a strategy that induces an audience to accept our arguments, we must concentrate on an item that is most frequently overlooked in the planning process: How does a

12. Kelman, H. C., "Processes of Opinion Change," *Public Opinion Quarterly*, 25 (Spring 1961), pp. 57–78.

speaker get the audience to remember or retain what has been said? What happens, for example, if we have been arguing on behalf of a proposition, but the vote on the proposition does not occur for another three or four weeks? We've successfully changed some cognitions, but, will they be retained? We'll now attempt to answer that question.

Retention. If you've been assured of a "second crack" at the audience, you may increase the audience's retention of your message. As Triandis writes "Powerful or attractive sources that are constantly present to re-assert their messages are most likely to increase the retention of the message.[13] Or, if each member of your audience continues to exist in an environment that reinforces your ideas, retention may be heightened. However, if we cannot guarantee such circumstances, it becomes a matter of creating a message that works on the audience after we've gone.

Under normal circumstances, an audience may be expected to retain information that supports their attitudes, and may have difficulty remembering information that is not supportive. However, there are conditions under which people do retain messages that are uncongenial or threatening to existing attitudes. Individuals may remember a message simply because it does not fit their scheme or ways of looking at things. It could be that when a cognitive system is ripe for change (and it's up to the speaker to provide the stimulus), such disturbing or contradictory material is favored. Points with which we disagree may stand out in contrast to repeated evidence for something we already believe. The key to producing retention is getting the audience to accept your value premise.

Also, the more frequently an argument is presented, the longer it's likely to be retained. You should devise a method for repeating your arguments during the actual presentation. Some skill and thoughtfulness is required; you must be adept at rephrasing arguments using other words.

Conclusion

In this chapter, we have explained how an audience's cognitive system serves an information-processing filter, and how it, in turn, influences audience responsiveness. In order to induce changes in the cognitive system, we must focus our appeals on existing needs,

13. Triandis, H. C., *Attitude and Attitude Change* (New York: John Wiley and Sons, Inc., 1971), p. 62.

beliefs, attitudes, and values. We also have discussed a design for audience motivation, from which we outlined the conduct of a basic, step-by-step, information-processing strategy. In that strategy, we advised that effective public communication is contingent on (1) a sound, motivating plan of presentation; (2) techniques for stampeding the audience into attending the message on the basis of need-arousal, and sharing of value-orientations; (3) an awareness of the various kinds of message-acceptance and the factors influencing each kind; and (4) whatever mechanisms you may utilize for helping the audience to retain the thrust of message for an appreciable length of time following the actual public communication event.

The process of inducing changes in cognitive systems is akin to a teaching and learning process. To be effective, the speaker must be able to educate the audience. Moreover, that education must take place under conditions that are conducive to learning. Such conditions require that we construct messages and package information in such a way as would lead our audiences to "habituate" or to rehearse the ideas we propose. We must be able to stimulate our audiences to respond through a careful attention to appeals that contribute to the arousal of basic drives and urges. In every message, "payoffs" must be clearly indicated because people will not willingly opt for change unless they can see incentives. Finally, we should be able to anticipate and account for the factors or features that, when ignored, tend to create inhibitions and frustrations that impede desirable speaker-audience interactions.

K E Y   C O N C E P T S

Can you define and give examples of the following terms?

Cognitive system
Components of the cognitive
    system:
Values
Attitudes
Beliefs
Needs
Information-processing
    mechanism
Information-processing
    approach
Saliency approach

Functional approach
Functions of attitudes:
    Utilitarian or instru-
        mental
Ego-defensive
Value-expressive
Knowledge
Assimilation
Contrast
Selective perception
Selective exposure

Message-acceptance: Compliance
    Comprehension   Identification
    Yielding   Internalization

P R O P O S I T I O N S

1. Modifying cognitive systems is the primary objective of public communication.
2. The key components in an individual's cognitive system are values, attitudes, beliefs, and needs.
   a. Values constitute a sort of yardstick against which audiences measure or evaluate new information or suggestions.
   b. Attitudes are characterized by our predispositions for or against objects and issues.
   c. Attitudes consist of three components: cognitive, affective, and behavioral.
   d. Beliefs are our convictions that something is true or false on the basis of evidence, authority-suggestion, experience, or intuition.
   e. Needs are the drives that motivate our search for and choice of alternatives.
3. Values, attitudes, beliefs, and needs constitute the communicator's real targets in public communication.
4. An audience's cognitive system is formed through experience.
5. An audience's cognitive system functions as an information-processing mechanism.
6. Although audiences manifest tendencies toward inflexibility, there are internal drives that contribute toward flexibility and and openness.
7. The cognitive system can be changed when a communicator leads the audience to see how their orientation is out of focus with their goals and objectives.
8. The existing cognitive system sometimes operates as a frustrator of message-acceptance when it:
   a. causes listeners to avoid information.
   b. leads listeners to be unwilling to understand.
   c. causes listeners to overlook significant differences.
9. The existing cognitive system sometimes operates as a facilitator of message-acceptance when it:
   a. functions as a vector or compass pointing in the direction of a solution.

b. functions as an organizer when strong needs are aroused.

c. supplies a context for incoming solutions.

d. arouses expectations.

10. The success of a public communication message in gaining attention, acceptance, and a desired response is the result of the interaction between the source, the message, and the audience.

11. A primary factor affecting the influence of public communication to induce changes in cognitive systems is the audience's judgment of the amount of discrepancy between the speaker's position and their own.

a. An audience tends to contrast arguments which advocate positions very discrepant from their own.

b. An audience tends to assimilate arguments that advocate positions not too discrepant from their own.

12. Message-acceptance consists of two crucial behaviors: audience comprehension, and audience yielding.

13. Yielding behaviors are characterized by three separate qualities: compliance, identification, and internalization.

14. Material with which we agree is better remembered than material with which we disagree.

15. The more frequently an argument is presented, the longer it is likely to be retained.

Chapter 4
Inducing Resistance

P R E V I E W

¶ *What are the basic approaches that may be utilized in making people more resistant to counter-attitudinal communication?*
Behavioral commitment approach
Anchoring or linking techniques
Cognitive balancing
Inoculation programs

¶ *What is involved in the behavioral commitment approach?*
The behavioral commitment approach involves the use of certain suggested behaviors or activities that should be performed following a shift toward a communicator's advocated position

¶ *What are the techniques underlying the behavioral commitment approach?*
Private decision
Public decision
Active participation
External commitment

¶ *What are the qualitatively different types of commitment behaviors that may be induced through behavioral commitment techniques?*
Compliance, identification, and internalization

¶ *What is anchoring?*
Anchoring is the process whereby a communicator attempts to demonstrate the acceptability of his or her ideas by showing how compatible the ideas are with those already held by the audience

¶ *What types of anchoring or linking may be utilized in inducing resistance?*
Anchoring to beliefs, values, and goals
Anchoring to other individuals or groups

¶ What is cognitive balancing?
Cognitive balancing is a human information process wherein we alter our perception of incoming information so as to reduce the need to change already accepted viewpoints

¶ What are the various types of defensive behaviors involved in cognitive balancing?
Source derogation, denial, bolstering, differentiation

¶ What are inoculation programs?
They are techniques that utilize weakened forms of counter-attitudinal arguments to immunize persuadees against attack from other persuaders

¶ What role does a group to which a person belongs play in inducing resistance to counter-attitudinal communication?
It provides an environment in which our beliefs may be validated
It provides a blockade against reneging on one's commitments because of the persistence of group pressure

O B J E C T I V E S

After reading this chapter, you should be able to
1. identify four *general* plans for inducing resistance to persuasive communication.
2. explain the nature and requirements of the behavioral commitment approach.
3. explain the comparative strengths of each of the four behavioral commitment techniques.
4. explain the impact of private decision on resistance.
5. explain the impact of public decisions on resistance.
6. explain the impact of active participation on resistance.
7. explain the impact of external commitment of resistance.
8. identify and discuss the nature and effects of compliance, identification, and internatlization.
9. explain what is meant by anchoring or linking techniques.
10. explain the nature and effects of anchoring to accepted values, beliefs and goals.
11. explain the nature and effects of anchoring to other individuals, and groups.
12. explain the general process of cognitive balancing.
13. discuss what is meant by source derogation, denial, bolstering, and differentiation.

14. explain the nature of inoculation programs for inducing resistance to persuasion.
15. compare the effectiveness of supportive defenses versus inoculating defenses.
16. explain how membership groups and reference groups function as agents for resistance to change.

A GROUP of irate New Yorkers residing in areas adjacent to the Kennedy International Airport petitioned the New York Port Authority to forbid the supersonic aircraft known as the Concorde to enter the airport because of hazards posed by take-offs and landings. When the petition failed, they mounted a campaign to recruit participants for a "massive protest rally that would snarl traffic during the rush hours" on a particular day. Immediately following the campaign, thousands of people signified their intentions to participate in the protest. However, on the day of the protest, only 500 showed up. By several accounts, the rally was a failure.

In our example, the organizer's objective was twofold: (1) to get the people to sign up to participate, and (2) to ensure participation on the appointed day. The first objective was accomplished; the second was not. Winning commitment to an idea is very crucial to the effectiveness of public communication. Many endeavors fail because we do not understand the processes involved in inducing commitment and fortifying resistance against change of commitment.

Some authorities have expressed grave doubts that individuals can retain their identity of independence when constantly barraged by public communication on issues from every side. Although it is probably true that modern men and women are subjected to many more influence attempts than their predecessors they have many resources at their command for resisting influence. It is important that we who are engaged in the process of packaging and delivering public communication understand what those resources are, not only because we are in the general business of persuading people, but because we desire to keep people committed to our ideas once they have been persuaded.

This chapter deals with ways to influence a persuadee's processing of intended persuasive messages so that he or she does not yield to future persuasive attempts. We will discuss the various means by which the individual maintains the integrity of his or her attitudes in the face of strong pressures to change. We have divided the chapter into five major sections. The first section has been devoted to a description of some of the tactics that we may utilize in what is generally called the *behavioral commitment approach*. Through this approach, the communicator guides the listener into certain activities that eventually contribute to resistance. The second section describes *anchoring* or *linking techniques*. In this method, we attempt to strengthen new beliefs or cognitions by anchoring them to cognitive elements that are highly cherished in the listener's experiences. The third section presents strategies that are derived largely from the instincts of the listener. We refer to these strategies or tendencies as *cognitive balancing*. The fourth section presents a brief description of a systematic process for creating greater immunity. It involves a sensitizing, training program that is called *inoculation*. Finally, in the fifth and final section, we consider the tremendous, resistance-inducing impact of groups to which people belong.

We need to understand these processes because the effectiveness of public communication depends not only on our ability to change cognitive systems, but also to maintain those cognitive systems.

Behavioral Commitment Techniques

The basic assumption underlying a behavioral commitment approach toward inducing resistance against opinion, or attitude shift, is that *a person's belief should become more resistant to change if he or she becomes more committed to the belief.* An understanding of the general role of *commitment* is vitally important to anyone who is involved in the process of public communication. You will be successful in influencing people over the long haul only if you succeed in preventing them from committing themselves to any position other than yours. Moreover, you may even find it necessary to reduce or minimize the effects of any other previous commitment that they might have had. Once you have succeeded in changing the audience's orientation, attitudes, or beliefs, you must go one step further—you must get them to commit themselves to the new position.

Cronkhite has suggested two reasons for getting an audience to commit themselves to a new position. First, *commitment makes behavior less changeable.* An act or behavior to which we have become committed will be likely to occur, because opinions will be brought into line with the act, making it easier to perform next time. Second, *the greater the degree of commitment, the greater its effect in perpetuating consistent attitudes and changing inconsistent ones.*[1]

COMMITMENT ACTIVITIES

William McGuire,[2] a leading researcher on methods for inducing resistance, has provided us with a list of four basic types of commitment-clinching activities.

First, we can at least coax our listeners into *making a personal, private decision.* The strategy is to get the person to *think about* his or her stand on an issue, so as to believe more intensely in that stand. This *private decision* activity merely attempts to set up a "good faith" contract between the communicator and the listener. In our example at the beginning of the chapter, the organizers of the protest rally appear to have relied mainly on their listeners' private decisions.

Second, we may move beyond the private decision strategy, and entice the listener (if we have swayed his or her attitudes) to make a public decision. The strategy, in this case, is to force the person into becoming publicly identified with the position. For example, the organizers could have suggested to the people who signed the petition that they should tell their neighbors and friends about their intent to participate in the rally.

Third, we can urge the listener into *acting out or behaving overtly* in such a way as to give a clear indication of his or her stand. For example, an individual who has decided that the protest rally against the Concorde is worthy of public support could be driven toward greater commitment if he or she were influenced to go out and actually work in behalf of getting other supporters for the rally. In this case, actual participation strengthens the private opinion and the commitment.

And, fourth, we can make the decision to participate in the rally even more binding by *convincing the person that other people* (of some significance to the person, of course!) know the decision that's been made, or of the stand that's been taken. For example, the organizers could have reported back to the "signer," at a later opportunity, that his or her intention had been brought to the attention of certain civic leaders and that they have expressed considerable delight and appreciation.

1. Cronkhite, G., *Communication and Awareness* (Menlo Park, Calif.: Cummings Publishing Company, 1976), p. 179.

2. McGuire, W. J., "The Nature of Attitudes and Attitude Change," in G. Lindzey and E. Aronson (eds.), *The Handbook of Social Psychology,* Vol. 3 (Reading, Mass.: Addison-Wesley Publishing Co., Inc., 1969), pp. 136–314.

It is reasonable to assume that publicized decisions and those that have incurred some effort or investment on the part of the listener will be more difficult to change. This is exactly what we're aiming for in our attempts to secure audience commitment. A decision made in private is committing—but how strong or enduring will that commitment be? It would be more practical to have the person make a public announcement to people who are considered important or significant. With this ploy, we have moved the person from deciding to pledging. Even though pledges are often broken, they are substantially more revealing and binding than mere private decisions. However, in order to be doubly sure that the pledge will be maintained, we need to go further—get the person to invest in the idea. Time, money, and effort expended publicly generally make pledges stick.

The effectiveness of a method wherein we conduct or lead the audience through the four behavioral commitment strategies has been borne out by many studies. Festinger, Rieken, and Schacter have given us an excellent example of the strengthening effect of behavioral commitment in their analysis of the actions of members of a religious group whose leader predicted the end of the world. The leader predicted the time of the end, and announced that only those in a specific place would be saved. Some people not only accepted or believed the leader's opinion, but they *committed* themselves by publicizing their beliefs and selling all of their worldly possessions in order to be saved from the holocaust.[3] Well, the prophecy failed. However, most of the followers were so committed to the idea that they decided to stand by their leader anyway. The results were not so surprising if we consider just how much it *cost* the followers to share in their belief. To the extent that they could not overlook the cost, even after failure or disappointment, they were forced or committed to stay with or stand by their beliefs.

According to Miller and Burgoon, "the dynamics of inducing resistance to persuasion by involving people in public acts that reinforce their private beliefs are probably similar to the more persuasive impact of . . . role playing."[4] The strategy, then, is to let the audience role-play and "really play out" their commitments. However, *the conditions under which active participation occurs, will determine the magnitude of subsequent commitment.*

3. Festinger, L., Rieken, H., and S. Schacter, "When Prophecy Fails," in E. Macoby, T. Newcomb, and E. Hartley (eds.), *Readings in Social Psychology* (New York: Henry Holt, 1958), pp. 156–163.

4. Miller, G., and M. Burgoon, *New Techniques of Persuasion* (New York: Harper and Row Publishers, 1973), p. 29.

If the person is enticed into acting, behaving, participating, and publicizing without too much pressure, reward, or justification, he or she will show more resistance to subsequent attacks than if he or she were extremely pressured or liberally rewarded. The important point here is that if an individual believes that he or she was coerced into a statement, expression, or action by being offered a high reward or by being strongly threatened, the individual may feel obligated to act without feeling any constraint to force their attitudes or beliefs into consistency with their action. The natural response would seem to be "Heck, I just did it for the money!" or "I did it because it would have been hell to pay if I didn't!" Later on, the person can more easily recant.

Table 4.1 presents a summary of the kinds or levels of commitment-inducing activities that we have discussed. Let's consider

TABLE 4.1 THE LEVELS OF COMMITMENT-INDUCING ACTIVITIES

1. Private decision:	Person is coaxed into making a private "commitment." This activity constitutes the minimum requirement for inducing resistance to subsequent counter-attitudinal messages.
2. Public decision:	Person is forced into endorsing his or her belief publicly.
3. Active participation:	Person is urged to "act out" or behave, or do something overtly so as to give a clear-cut indication of his or her position on an issue.
4. External commitment:	Person is informed that other people are fully aware of what his or her position is.

the total picture by referring to a hypothetical example. Let's reexamine the example of our attempt to get an audience to adopt our idea of a national health insurance program. We'll assume, at this point, that the audience has accepted the idea, and we want to make them committed. If they are to resist and reject messages opposed to national health insurance, we must lead them into the basic activity of "reminding" themselves that they do, indeed, believe in the insurance plan, and that the belief is grounded on positive values and logical, ethical premises. To make the commitment even firmer, we could increase their resistance to future messages by motivating them to talk publicly about their position, letting others hear of the value of their idea. On the third level, we could encourage them to become committee-workers, canvassers, or even spokesmen to drum up support and win new converts. Here, our hope is that the investment of effort will increase the strength of commitment. Finally, we could remind our audience during the ensuing days that many other people are aware of their dedication to the idea of national health insurance. We might, for example, call them on the telephone, call on them at home or write them a letter. Obviously, this entails quite an amount of follow-up on our part. (As a matter of strategy for any type of public communication, we believe that a "one-shot" type of public communication is rarely effective. You must find opportunities to remind your audience several times beyond your first encounter with them. The first shot should be followed by booster shots!) Similarly, *the degree of commitment is increased by increasing the number of committing acts*; by the audience members and that *the acts ought to be important, explicit, public, and irrevocable.*[5] Most important, even though you are the one who actually entices or motivates the audience into some type of commitment, they must be led to perceive that whatever they do will have been accomplished through their own *deliberate choice*.

At this point in our discussion on inducing resistance, we should talk about the impact that you as a public communicator can exert on the audience to "commit" to your position. Once again we'll examine the three audience behaviors, compliance, identification, and internalization. However, rather than examining their relationship to changing cognitive systems, we'll examine how each of these three behavioral responses to a speaker influences the nature and endurance of the listener's commitment.

Qualities of Committing-Behavior

The extent to which a value, attitude, or behavior is permanent or can be induced into permanence depends upon the dynamics of the influence process. Remember that Kelman suggested there are three distinct processes and qualities of social influence: *compliance, identification,* and *internalization.*[6] These behaviors are in response to the communicators public expressions. They also provide different levels of commitment by the audience.

5. Kiesler, C., and J. Sakumura, "A Test of a Model for Commitment," *Journal of Personality and Social Psychology*, 3 (1966), pp. 349–353.
6. Kelman, H., "Processes of Opinion Change." *Public Opinion Quarterly* 25 (1961), pp. 57–78.

AUDIENCE COMPLIANCE

Audience compliance occurs when individuals accept your influence and go along with your suggestion because they hope to achieve a favorable reaction from you. The risk is that people may really disagree with you *privately* even though their outward behavior indicates agreement. Why the duplicity? It could be due to the fact that they are pretending merely to gain some type of reward or avoid punishment. People who go along with an idea on the basis of compliance will usually go along only as long as you (the rewarder, or punisher) are around to keep rewarding or punishing. For example, if you urge someone to adopt a positive attitude toward a national health insurance program, and you further instruct him to go out and campaign for it by threatening to expose his drinking problem to his fellow executives, it's safe to bet that he will comply. But is he committed? What would happen if you died? Would he continue to work on behalf of the idea? Slim chance! The idea, then, is not to browbeat, cajole, strong-arm, muscle, or even overpay people into endorsing things. In light of the dubious endurance or longevity of this kind of committing behavior, we should avoid this strategy unless the situation will allow or afford no other.

AUDIENCE IDENTIFICATION

Identification will occur when people adopt behavior suggested by you because the behavior is associated with a satisfying, self-defining relationship.[7] One form that identification takes is shown in attempts to be like another, or to actually be the other person. We see this quite frequently in children who copy the behaviors and attitudes of their parents, peers, or other models. In another form of identification, a person does not attempt to be like another person, but forms a relationship to him that demands behaviors quite different from his. The individual behaves in terms of the expectations that the other person has with respect to his behavior. For example, a client behaves in accordance with the expectations of his lawyer and adopts his advice and suggestions. The same type of identification is inherent in relationships between patient-doctor, student-teacher, and so on.

Identification, like compliance, does not occur because the position to be adopted is intrinsically satisfying in itself. Rather, it occurs because of the desire to maintain a satisfying relationship with another person, and because the particular act or behavior defines, strengthens, or consummates that important relationship. Unlike the compliance situation, however, the individual actually

7. Ibid., p. 63.

believes in the attitudes and actions that he adopts as a result of identification.

How do we get an audience to behave at this second level? For one thing, the behavior (identification) may result from the kind of *power* that you appear to have or to exercise over your audience. Attraction power, legitimate power, and a high level of credibility may be just what the situation calls for. The audience must like you, be attracted to you, see you as having some right to do what you're doing; and they must perceive you as being trustworthy, competent, and dynamic. If you're lucky to get this much commitment, how do you keep it so strong? According to Kelman, individuals who perform activities largely because they "identify" with someone, will continue to perform those activities only as long as the relationship remains important. In other words, if the person continues to like you and to want to be like you, identification will persist and commitment will hold.

AUDIENCE INTERNALIZATION

Internalization will occur when your audience accepts your influence, and does what you ask because the content of the behavior; the ideas,' and suggested behaviors, are consistent with their value system. People will internalize if what you propose appears to be useful for the solution of problems, and congenial to their needs. Thus a person with a liberal political attitude is likely to support a government program for medical care for the aged because one of the values to which he subscribes is that government should promote the public's well-being. As long as the issue remains relevant, important, and crucial, the audience will remain motivated and committed whether you're around or not.

Remember that the quality of the "committing behavior" will depend upon your source of power as an influencing agent. If you have strong controls over rewards and punishments that your audience is likely to receive, you may achieve *audience compliance*. If, on the other hand, your audience enjoys or desires to enjoy or maintain a satisfying relationship with you, you may get *audience identification*. And, if you're perceived as being highly credible, and as having the best possible solutions to crucial problems, you'll get *audience internalization*.

Remember also that each of the three types of behavior carries different implications for the permanence of attitude change. *Audience compliance* is likely to be abandoned if you are no longer perceived as having control over your audience. Compliant behaviors are generally isolated or unrelated to attitudes and values. *Audience identification* is likely to be maintained only so long as you maintain a satisfying, exciting relationship between you and your audience. *Audience internalization* is likely to persist as long as the values relevant to the adoption are maintained. Often two or more of these behaviors occur simultaneously, or all three may operate together. In this section, we have discussed the characteristics of various techniques for influencing behavioral commitment, and we have examined some of the "committing behaviors" that are likely to develop. Essentially, we have argued that changing one's mind is difficult to do in public especially after one has taken a publicized position on an issue. We also have suggested that swaying, reneging, "waffling," or "copping out" will be discouraged even more when a person has "chosen" to perform several acts that are consistent with the adopted opinion. Commitment, through the methods suggested, places limitations or restrictions on opinion change; people become more rigid, less free, and less capable of evaluating new ideas or orientations with their usual amount of objectivity. We've made them resistant.

Of course, obtaining commitment through induced behaviors is not the only available method. In fact, there are three other methods that can be utilized with considerable success. Let's examine a second method that is based on a fundamental assumption of what is generally referred to as consistency theory. The assumption is that people have a need, or feel pressure to maintain consistency among their beliefs, attitudes, behavior, and so on. In order to take advantage of that pressure, many public communicators resort to a technique called *anchoring* or *linking*. We present the general idea behind the anchoring or linking technique in the following section.

Anchoring or Linking Techniques

The commitment technique that we described in the previous section was predicated on the idea of getting our audience to feel committed or hooked because of having invested their behaviors in support of a given position that they had adopted. *Anchoring or linking techniques attempt to induce commitment and subsequent resistance to persuasion by linking one belief to other beliefs that an audience already holds or professes.* The assumption is that when a belief (such as, the one expressed by a communicator) is anchored or linked to beliefs held by an audience, resistance to counterattitudinal messages (at a later date) will result. When two beliefs become anchored or linked, a person must change both beliefs in order to renege his or her commitment, otherwise cognitive inconsistency or "dissonance" will occur. Generally speaking, people do not relish the idea of having to make changes through a wide range of their beliefs—it's disconcerting enough to change one's belief. Thus, if the anchoring or linking is done properly, commitment to your idea or belief could be strengthened.

McGuire suggests methods for inducing resistance by linking or anchoring beliefs to: (1) accepted beliefs, values or goals; and (2) liked (valenced) individuals or groups.[8] Let's deal with each method separately.

ANCHORING TO ACCEPTED BELIEFS, VALUES, OR GOALS

People tend to hold beliefs that enable them to achieve certain goals. That being so, we can make our audience resistant to subsequent counterattitudinal messages in two ways. *First,* we can emphasize the saliency or importance of particular goals; *second,* we can emphasize the extent to which the beliefs or ideas we have suggested would be extremely instrumental in achieving those goals. We must constantly remind our audience (during our presentation, and later on) about the goals that they have frequently enunciated. We must constantly remind them of the importance of those goals to their happiness and survival.

If the issue is "the need to maintain a national enforcement of the 55 mph speed limit," we could remind the audience of their enduring belief in fuel conservation and traffic safety. Furthermore, we could remind them (remember those booster shots!) that their steadfastness to *their* belief in the "55 mph law" is very essential to the goal-achievement of conservation and safety. What we're really doing is anchoring a new position to their old, trusted beliefs or positions.

ANCHORING TO OTHER INDIVIDUALS AND GROUPS

Linking a person's beliefs to his relationship with other individuals or groups can also induce resistance to later persuasive appeals. We believe that the impact of groups as an agent in inducing resistance is so powerful that we have devoted a large section of this chapter to a more expanded discussion of the processes involved. However, our discussion, here has to do with your strategy in anchoring or linking beliefs to significant individuals or groups. There are several techniques for conferring resistance utilizing this method. Here's how Miller and Burgoon[9] describe one method: "Suppose a persuader demonstrates the linkage of a

8. McGuire, op. cit., pp. 136–314.
9. Miller, and Burgoon, op. cit., p. 33.

particular belief to a person by saying to an intended persuadee, 'Since you believe in X, person Y likes you.' If the person values the opinion of person Y (or group Y), he will think that believing *not-X* will result in psychological discomfort. His apparent alternatives are to end his relationship with Y or to change Y's beliefs." Suppose, for example, that you have persuaded someone that drinking alcoholic beverages is bad. Further, suppose that you have informed him that Dulcima Goodbody—the woman he daydreams about constantly—really likes him because he decided not to drink anymore. If he really likes Dulcima (i.e., if she is a liked or valenced Y as in Miller and Burgoon's description), and if he is really concerned about what she thinks of him, it stands to reason that he is going to try desperately to stand by his decision on X: "that drinking alcoholic beverages is bad." But he has a few choices—he could stop being goofy about Dulcima; *or*, he could try to get her to change her thinking on the subject of booze. Both alternatives would appear to be too costly, so he chooses to resist any message that would try to sway him from the position that he's adopted.

Bennett[10] argues that a linkage even with anonymous individuals or groups can induce persistance to persuasion. The persuadee does not even have to know the individual or groups referred to to appreciate his shared beliefs with them. Students in their many campaigns for "better conditions or policies on campus" often refer to a nebulous group called "students on other campuses"; and they try to get us to link our belief to that group. Quite frequently, we become quite reluctant to give in or to change our beliefs or attitudes that are linked to these anonymous individuals.

Resistance can also be created by reinforcing and strengthening established links. You don't always have to go out of your way to fabricate a valenced individual or group. We can raise the positive feelings a person already has toward some individual or group and thereby make him or her more resistant to persuasive attacks.

So, we can either anchor or link a new idea or belief to the individual's accepted beliefs, values, and goals; or, we can anchor or link a new idea or belief to other significant individuals, or a group. Either way makes it more difficult for people to change their position because such a change would require simultaneous changes throughout their chain of beliefs.

Thus far in this chapter, we have discussed two major approaches—the behavioral commitment technique, and the anchor-

10. Bennett, E., "Discussion, Decision, Commitment, and Consensus in Group Decisions," *Human Relations* 8 (1955), pp. 251–274.

ing or linking technique. The first attempts to bring behaviors into "sync" or line with adopted positions. The second attempts to demonstrate vital connections between newly adopted positions and established goals, values, beliefs, and so on. Let's look at a third general strategy—*cognitive balancing*—which involves methods for reducing the cognitive inconsistency that may develop whenever our persuadees or converts run into convincing countermessages.

Cognitive Balancing

Resistance to opinion or attitude change may be viewed in terms of the need that exists in all human beings to retain a state of consonance, cognitive balance, congruity, or consistency. Any public communication that is dissonant or inconsistent with existing attitudes will arouse defensive reactions. When such defensive reactions are aroused, people resort to various tactics to *avoid* having to make belief changes. Remember, we stated earlier that people generally do not spring too readily to change established orientation, particularly if those orientations have assisted them in attaining certain objectives.

In order to understand the nature of *cognitive balancing*, we should first understand the general nature of how cognitive elements are balanced or imbalanced.[11] Cognitive elements have either a positive or a negative value. In addition, the relation between elements may be either positive or negative. Thus, such concepts as mother, money, God, and America have positive value for most people, and death, corruption, communism, injury, shortages, and injustice have negative values. Positive relations between elements are illustrated by such terms as *likes, helps, supports, endorses, is consistent with*, whereas negative relations are depicted by such terms as *dislikes, fights, opposes, is inconsistent with*, and so on. A *balanced* state would exist under the following conditions.

1. Two positive elements have a positive relation: the United States (+) helps (+) her Latin American neighbors (+).
2. Two negative elements have a positive relation: the Soviet Union (−) and the Chinese communists (−) are working together (+).
3. A positive element is negatively related to a negative ele-

11. Rosenberg, M., and P. Abelson, "An Analysis of Cognitive Balancing," in C. I. Hovland & I. L. Janis (eds.), *Attitude Organization and Change* (New Haven, Conn.: Yale University Press, 1960), pp. 112–163.

ment: Yugoslavia (+) has resisted domination (−) by the Soviet Union (−).

An *unbalanced* state would exist under the following conditions:

1. One positive element is negatively related to another positive element: Latin America (+) is not supporting (−) the United States (+).
2. Two negative elements have a negative relation: the Soviet Union (−) and the Chinese communists (−) are highly critical (−) of each other.
3. A positive and a negative element have a positive relation: example: the United States (+) and the Soviet Union (−) have entered into a trade agreement. (+).

States that are imbalanced or unbalanced tend to be rather disturbing. Just imagine the impact of the headline: PRESIDENT CARTER AND UGANDA'S DICTATOR 'BIG DADDY' AMIN SIGN PACT FOR MILITARY AID. Such a headline is bound to create a belief dilemma for many people. They believe *in* President Carter, so they must find some way to secure that established belief. Some modes of resolving belief dilemmas are: (1) *source derogation*, (2) *denial*, (3) *bolstering*, and (4) *differentiation*.

SOURCE DEROGATION

An idea or position can be made more resistant to persuasive attacks by attempting to lower the credibility of the sources or persons responsible for the countermessages. If you anticipate such an assault, you could discredit the message-source long before it actually occurs. Politicians do it all the time. For example, "I am sure that next week Senator Bafflebag will come here and tell you that a national health insurance program is bad for this country . . . but remember, friends, that Bafflebag is the same fellow who proposed a tax cut for corporations and a tax increase for people in the lower-, and middle-income brackets!" This technique is also used quite often in the courtroom. A defense attorney takes every opportunity to discredit a prosecution witness before the witness has time to deliver too much damaging testimony. If the defense attorney successfully discredits the witness (source), the jury can be made resistant to the prosecution's persuasive countermessages.

DENIAL

This is the most often used and simplest method of resolving a belief dilemma. For example, the heavy cigarette smoker values smoking positively, but values cancer negatively. Suddenly, the smoker is bombarded with a series of appeals from the American Cancer Society. The smoker is upset (cognitive imbalance), and so is the tobacco industry. Both the smoker and the tobacco companies must find a way to resist the countermessages from the Cancer Society. Denial can be used to explain away the positive relation between lung cancer and smoking (i.e., smoking is related to cancer) by suggesting that the correlations do not really demonstrate or prove a cause and effect, or that the evidence is not really sufficient.

BOLSTERING

Through bolstering, the smoker who is becoming anxious about lung cancer may tell himself that smoking is extremely enjoyable, soothes his nerves, and adds to his social life. If the smoker does not get around to doing the bolstering for himself or herself, the tobacco company—through commercials and assorted ads—will be eager to do the chore. By bolstering, the imbalance between smoking (+) and lung cancer (−) is not eliminated, but the total balance in the entire system or related elements is improved.

DIFFERENTIATION

If denial and bolstering are defenses that preserve the identity of elements, *differentiation restores balance* by splitting an element into two parts that have a negative relation to each other. For example, the testing of nuclear bombs is positively valued (+) by many people because they reason that such testing is necessary for America's defense, but they also think that it is obscene to poison the atmosphere (−) through these tests. So, there is a dilemma stemming from an imbalance in the belief in bomb testing! How can we resolve the dilemma? We can differentiate! That is, we can split the attitude object into two parts: testing "dirty" bombs that pollute the atmosphere, and "clean" bombs that do not. Or, we could differentiate between Soviet bombs and American bombs. What the Soviets do pollutes; what the Americans do protects. The same process could be applied to our smoking–lung cancer dilemma. We can differentiate by talking about smoking ordinary cigarettes (−) and smoking filter cigarettes (+). If you believe that filter cigarettes protect against lung cancer, you can *restore balance* by smoking them.

We can see, then, that the individual who perceives that persuasive communication threatens cognitive balance or consistency may resort to a variety of resources for restoring balance without yielding to the pressure exerted by communication. Examples of mechanisms used to maintain balance are source derogation, denial, bolstering, and differentiation. In source derogation, an attempt is made to lower the credibility of the source of the countermessage. In denial, the value of the object that is creating the imbalance is denied or declared to be just the opposite of what is stated, or the relation that creates the imbalance is explained away. Bolstering does not completely restore balance, but it adds additional cognitive elements having values that increase overall balance. Differentiation, unlike the other mechanisms, restores balance by changing the identity of one of the elements, splitting it into two parts that have a negative relation to each other.

Let's recap the kinds of resistance-inducing strategies that we have examined thus far in this chapter. We have discussed the *behavioral commitment approach*, through which we try to make the persuadee express his or her position publicly; *anchoring* or *linking techniques*, whereby we tie or link the person's beliefs to other cognitions; and *cognitive balancing*, or ways of reducing the cognitive inconsistency that is around when people are confronted by powerful counterattitudinal messages. Some experts on public communication argue that although the methods discussed thus far will guarantee some measure of resistance, their effect could be strengthened further if we could find a systematic way or a "programmed" method for preparing an individual to resist persuasion in crucial circumstances. McGuire's *inoculation programs* appear to do just that.

Inoculation Programs

In 1961, William J. McGuire and a group of fellow social psychologists launched a series of research experiments under the assumption of a *Theory of Inoculation*.[12] McGuire's inoculation

12. See W. J. McGuire, "Inducing Resistance to Persuasion: Some Contemporary Approaches," L. Berkowitz (ed.), in *Advances in Experimental Social Psychology* (New York: Academic Press, Inc., 1964), p. 192; W. J. McGuire and D. Papageorgis, "The Relative Efficacy of Various Types of Prior Belief-defenses in Producing Immunity Against Persuasion," *Journal of Abnormal and Social Psychology* 62 (1961), pp. 237–337; D. Papageorgis and W. J. McGuire, "The Generality of Immunity to Persuasion Produced by Preexposure to Weakened Counter-arguments," *Journal of Abnormal and Social Psychology* 62 (1961), pp. 475–481; W. J. McGuire, "The Effectiveness of Supportive and Refutational Defenses in Immunizing and Restoring Beliefs Against Persuasion," *Sociometry* 24 (1961), pp. 184–197; W. J. McGuire and D. Papageorgis, "Effectiveness of Forewarning in Developing Resistance to Persuasion," *Public Opinion Quarterly* 24 (1962), pp. 24–34; W. J. McGuire, "Anticipatory Belief Lowering Following Forewarning of a Persuasive Attack," *Journal of Personality and Social Psychology* 2 (1964),

programs for conferring resistance to persuasion draw on a biological analogy. In medicine there are certain diseases for which the body can build a natural immunity. The body may need some assistance in order to accomplish this task, so a small amount of the disease-causing virus is inserted in the body. Not enough of the virus is inserted to cause the disease, but just enough to stimulate the natural body function of developing defenses against the virus in the system. Of course, a person could also acquire some sort of defense against a disease by undergoing supportive therapy such as adequate sleep, tonic, vitamins, and so on. So, there are two possible ways of setting up the defenses: inoculation and supportive treatments.

Let's carry the analogy over to the public communication environment. Just as people are immunized by preexposing themselves to weakened doses of a disease, so can a public communicator immunize audience members against future appeals. *Inoculation programs* require messages that will stimulate defenses but not destroy them, so that a person becomes resistant to later attacks. *Supportive programs* consist of the method whereby we attempt to build a defense in the listener by "supporting" or constantly providing him with arguments that support his established belief.

The consensus among researchers is that *the supportive program is not as effective as the inoculation program.* According to McGuire and Papageorgis, the supportive technique of strengthening attitudes is relatively ineffective in producing resistance to persuasion because it does not carry any *defense-alerting* energy. In other words, a supportive program, packed with positive reinforcements, merely informs an individual that his or her belief or position is good or acceptable. It really does not provide information as to how secure the position is, or how successfully someone else could argue against it. Presenting supportive arguments and evidence *does not motivate* the listener to seek out additional information, and consequently does not prepare the person for later attacks. Let's be honest about this: a supportive program is useful, if it's the only thing available, but its immunizing effect does not last very long. On the other hand, inoculation provides significantly better resistance.

Most people never fully realize that many of their beliefs could

---

pp. 471–479; W. J. McGuire, "Resistance to Persuasion Conferred by Active and Passive Prior Refutation of the Same and Alternative Counter-arguments," *Journal of Abnormal and Social Psychology* 63 (1961), pp. 326–332; W. J. McGuire, "Persistence of the Resistance to Persuasion Induced by Various Types of Prior Belief Defenses," *Journal of Abnormal and Social Psychology* 64 (1962), pp. 241–248.

be rationally and logically attacked. As a consequence, their na-ivete makes them rather defenseless. They are not alerted for trouble, and they are not prepared for defense. So, *the first step* in the inoculation program would be to unsettle that complacency by convincing the person that their belief could be successfully challenged and overcome. How do we do this? We use counter-arguments. The counterarguments, remember, should be mildly theatening (a weakened dose of virus), so that the person will feel that he or she has a sporting chance of arguing against the counterarguments, and will be motivated to generate the neces-sary rebuttals. So, we present arguments on the opposite side of the belief, and then we refute those arguments, or encourage the other person to refute them.

Here's another suggestion. It seems reasonable to assume that if we *combine* the strengthening effect of the supportive program with the immunizing effect of the inoculation program, we should be able to generate an even tighter defense against counter-messages.

We should consider still another feature of the inoculation pro-gram, which is derived from the well-known adage: "To be fore-warned is to be forearmed." Would a person be better prepared to resist an attack on his or her belief if there were some *forewarning* about the attack? McGuire and Papageorgis found that *warning* people of a persuasive attack, or *threatening* them with the possi-bility of a future attack, is more effective when utilized both in the case of supportive programs and inoculation programs. Again, motivation is the key. It seems that the mere knowledge of an impending threat motivates a person to make sure that defenses are being put to good use.

The inoculation program is perhaps the most effective of the methods that we have presented in this chapter. We suggest that whenever possible most of the other methods could be boosted by the inoculation technique. McCroskey and Wheeless sum up the value by suggesting that:

Once people have been inoculated, they tend to reject subsequent communication from other sources that includes the arguments to which they have been exposed and which have been shown to them to be faulty. But equally important, they also tend to reject new ar-guments to which they have not been previously exposed. Apparently, when we have been made suspicious of some of a source's arguments, we tend to become suspicious of her or his other arguments as well.[13]

13. McCroskey, J., and L. Wheeless. *Introduction to Human Communica-tion* (Boston: Allyn & Bacon, Inc., 1976), p. 419.

Up to this point we have talked about the things that we ought to do to secure people to the ideas that we cherish. But we have talked of individuals as though they ventured through life isolated and alone, and have given rather short shrift to the idea that most of the people that we meet are deeply and psychologically imbedded in some group, somewhere. People are group-oriented, for the most part; and much of what they believe, how they believe, and why they believe, is determined by standards that their groups impose upon them. Therefore, no discussion of the conditions that influence resistance can be considered complete without some commentary concerning the natural shelter that groups provide to help us withstand the crossfire of countermessage.

Groups as Agents for Resistance to Change

The various groups to which our listeners or receivers belong may reinforce or interfere with the effect of the messages that we direct toward them. For example, a group may (1) influence the extent to which a person would be willing to be exposed to new information, ideas, opinions, or arguments; and (2) provide social support for existing attitudes. Let's discuss these two operations separately.

EFFECTS OF GROUPS ON EXPOSURE TO COMMUNICATION

The structure or nature of a group may affect the way in which a message is filtered as it passes from one person to another. This filtering process determines the degree to which group members are exposed to various inputs of public communication. Most group members filter or tune out communications that are dissonant with or contrary to group opinion, and focus on those that are consonant or consistent with their orientation. Research on voting behavior points up the principle rather well. For example, studies have shown that people talk politics *primarily* with members of their family and friends. The implication is that because family and friends usually have similar political attitudes, the chances of encountering dissonant or other views through interpersonal channels are reduced. Consequently, exposure has been limited.

The degree to which family members have similar political attitudes is emphasized by a study of a panel of voters in one county where it was found that only four per cent of the voters had relatives voting differently from themselves.[14] Moreover, discussion with others who disagree with one's opinions is likely to be strictly avoided; as one Republican said forthrightly, "All of my neighbors are Democrats, so there's no use talking with them about politics."[15]

GROUPS AS SOURCES OF SOCIAL SUPPORT
FOR ATTITUDES

Regardless of the tightness or "knit" of the group, people are going to be confronted with some type of contrary or countercommunication anyway. The basic question, then, is, how does one hold firm to one's attitudes, values, beliefs, and so on. Or, better yet, how does a group serve our purpose in keeping people committed to our viewpoint?

The major source of resistance to continual bombardment of new information is found in the social support provided by the group. Basically, the support of the group may be described in the following terms. Individuals are attracted to others who have attitudes similar to their own. Festinger[16] suggests that this attraction comes from our constant need to validate our attitudes or to find support for them. In other words, a constant, unrelenting pressure toward uniformity binds us toward the group. This pressure is particularly effective in small, intimate groups, because individuals in such groups are normally highly dependent on each other for the satisfaction of their emotional needs such as affection, companionship, and encouragement. We may refer to such groups as *primary* groups. An excellent example of how membership in a primary group may produce strong resistance to persuasive communication is described in a study by Shils and Janowitz.[17] According to the study, the most important factor accounting for the strong resistance of German troops to allied propaganda in World War II, in spite of the hopelessness of their situation toward the end of the war, was *the loyalty of a soldier*

14. Lazarsfeld, P., B. Berelson, and H. Gaudet. *The People's Choice* (New York: Columbia University Press, 1948).

15. Berelson, B., P. Lazarsfeld, and W. McPhee. *Voting: Study of Opinion Formation in a Presidential Campaign* (Chicago: The University Press, 1954).

16. Festinger, L. "A Theory of Social Comparison Processes," *Human Relations* 7 (1954), pp. 117–140.

17. Shils, E., and M. Janowitz. "Cohesion and Disintegration in the Wehrmacht in World War II," *Public Opinion Quarterly* 12 (1948), pp. 280–315.

to his own unit. The unit met his physical needs, providing him with food, clothing, shelter, and protection, and also offered him affection, esteem, and support. Allied propaganda disseminated among German troops in the form of leaflets urging surrender had little effect upon soldiers belonging to such units. Asking the soldier to surrender had a small chance of success if it meant that the soldier must desert his buddies.

However, once the primary group was broken up, or its functions were disrupted by lack of food or ammunition, the need for survival often became so strong that persuasive communication urging surrender and guaranteeing safe conduct were often effective. So, either a total breakdown of the primary group or a group agreement on surrender was a necessary condition for the effectiveness of allied persuasive communications. Similar feelings of loyalty to the primary group existed among American soldiers, who, when asked what factors enabled them to keep going when things got tough, stressed that they couldn't let their outfit down, that their buddies depended on them, and so on.

Other examples of how the group helps people to resist influence comes from the study of prisons and of delinquent gangs. Although prisons are supposed to rehabilitate the criminal, influences in that direction are usually effectively blocked by the formation of strong informal groups or cliques among prisoners. These groups support and perpetuate attitudes that are favorable to continuation of criminal activity after release. Similarly, members of delinquent gangs are strongly resistant to reform efforts of police, social workers, and other community workers. A laboratory experiment conducted by Kelley and Volkhart[18] has shown that *placing a high value on one's group is associated with resistance to communications running counter to the group's values.*

It appears convincing, then, that groups do indeed support members in resisting communications that run counter to shared attitudes representing the central values of the group and strongly sanctioned by it. Another question is whether attitudes that are shared by the members but which are not *too* relevant to the goals of the group are also resistant to change because of group support. The answer is a resounding "yes." Several studies show that *even on issues of low relevance the group does exert some pressure on persons who deviate.*

In summary, we have seen that the various groups to which the

18. Kelley, H., and E. Volkhart. "The Resistance to Change of Group-Anchored Attitudes," *American Sociological Review* 17 (1952), pp. 453–465.

members of our audiences belong may frustrate the impact of our messages, but we have also seen that groups may help to secure some of the opinions or ideas that we have planted through public communication. If we understand how *group pressure* works, we would be able to get that pressure to work in our behalf. Remember that the communication structure that's existent in a given group sometimes serves to filter out dissonant communication. Remember, also, that groups frequently aid an individual in determining the kind or amount of credibility that will be attributed to a communicator. Sometimes, the group even sets the standard for judging how dissonant or consonant new ideas or arguments are. Finally, groups provide social support for the attitudes of their members by providing rewards for conformity and disapproval and punishment for deviation. The degree to which sanctions are exercised against deviators varies directly with the power of the group and the relevance of the attitude to the group's central values.

Groups are sometimes akin to impenetrable barriers, keeping ideas out, but they also function as prison walls by locking ideas in. Know your audience; learn of the various primary, referent, and interest groups in which they hold membership. Know who their opinion leaders are, and, having used them to gain entry into audience acceptance, use them later to lock up audience commitment.

Conclusion

In this chapter, we have discussed four basic strategies for inducing resistance to counterattitudinal communication, and we have also discussed the fortification that group membership provides for members of our audience. Some of the strategies are derived from the skillfulness of the communicator, whereas others spring spontaneously from the audience itself. Some strategies are better than others, and it is the communicator's task to analyze the situation before committing himself to any single one. Whatever the analysis, we trust that you will be mindful of the need to "follow through" with your audience. The first encounter in public communication may merely convince; it is the constant follow-up that commits.

KEY CONCEPTS

Can you define and give examples of the following terms?

Resistance
Commitment
Basic resistance-inducing formats:
  Behavioral commitment approaches
  Anchoring techniques
  Cognitive balancing techniques
  Inoculation programs
Qualities of commitment behavior:
  Compliance

Identification
Internalization
Behavioral commitment:
  Anchoring
Cognitive balancing:
  Source derogation
  Denial
  Bolstering
  Differentiation
Inoculation:
  Threatening defenses
  Supportive defenses

PROPOSITIONS

1. A person's belief should become more resistant to change if he or she is induced to be more committed to that belief.
   a. Commitment makes behavior less changeable.
   b. The greater the degree of commitment, the greater its effect in perpetuating consistent attitudes and changing inconsistent attitudes.
2. Publicized decisions and those that have incurred some effort or investment on the part of the listener will be more difficult to change.
3. The conditions under which active participation occurs will determine the magnitude of subsequent commitment.
   a. If a person is enticed into acting, behaving, participating, and publicizing without too much pressure, he or she will show *more* resistance to subsequent attacks than if he or she were extremely pressured or liberally rewarded.
4. The degree of commitment is increased by increasing the number of committing acts: such acts should be important, explicit, public, and irrevocable.
5. There are three distinct processes and qualities of social influence: compliance, identification, and internalization.
   a. Compliance occurs when individuals perform a behavior because they hope or desire to gain a favorable reaction from the person requesting the behavior.
   b. Identification occurs when individuals perform a behavior

because the behavior is associated with a satisfying, self-defining relationship.

    c. Internalization occurs when individuals perform a behavior because the behavior is consistent with their value system or orientation.

6. Compliance is likely to be abandoned if an influencing agent (speaker, source, message-sender) is perceived as no longer having control over the audience.

7. Identification is likely to be maintained only as long as the influencing agent is able to maintain a satisfying, exciting relationship between himself/herself and the audience.

8. Internalization is likely to be maintained as long as the values relevant to the proposed behavior are maintained.

9. When a belief or opinion (e.g. the one expressed by a communicator) is anchored or linked to beliefs or opinions held by an audience, resistance to counterattitudinal messages will result .

10. Resistance to subsequent counterattitudinal persuasions can be induced by linking a person's belief or opinions with other individuals or groups that may potentially serve as a referent for that person.

11. A public communication that is dissonant or inconsistent with the existing attitudes of an audience will arouse defensive reactions.

12. In inducing resistance, supportive programs generally are not as effective as inoculation programs.

13. The combination of a supportive program and an inoculation program is generally more effective in inducing resistance than would either of the programs used separately.

14. The major source of resistance to continual bombardment of new information is found in the social support provided by the groups to which people belong.

15. Placing a high value on one's group is associated with resistance to communications running counter to the group's values.

Chapter 5
Resolving Conflict

P R E V I E W

¶ *What are the three perspectives from which the nature of conflict may be understood?*
We may look at conflict as a type of clash; a kind of process; or a phenomenon deriving from certain irrational bases or behaviors

¶ *What are some of the inputs that create conflict?*
Roles, issues, perceptions, expectations, decisions, goals, and communication

¶ *What are a few of the behavioral manifestations of conflict?*
The variety of possible behaviors falls under one broad general category that we call the exercise of power. Some of the behaviors that represent the exercise of power in conflict relationships are threats, coalitions, and symbolic activity

¶ *Who comprise the various audiences in conflict relationships?*
Supporters; committed, active membership; the general public; influential agencies; the leadership of the opposition

¶ *What are three basic processes through which conflict may be negotiated?*
Bargaining, mediation, co-optation

¶ *What are the six essential steps in the conducting of a confrontation meeting?*
1. Climate setting
2. Information collecting
3. Information sharing
4. Priority setting and action planning
5. Social action planning
6. Immediate follow-up

After reading this chapter, you should be able to

1. discuss the nature of conflict.
2. identify and discuss the various factors that contribute to conflict.
3. discuss the various behavioral manifestations of conflict.
4. identify and describe the various audiences in conflict relationships.
5. discuss the various processes for resolving conflict.
6. explain how the strategy for resolving conflict is planned.
7. explain how a confrontation meeting is conducted.

THE teachers' union of a large city has asked the local board of education for certain across-the-board increases in pay and fringe benefits. The board has refused to meet these demands, which it considers excessive, and has made an offer that the union leadership considers unacceptable. Having failed to come to some agreement by midnight of the day before school is to open, the union votes to go on strike and to remain on strike until a satisfactory agreement is reached.

Conflict between groups, cultures, factions, institutions, and individuals can be viewed as a natural outcome of the structure of society, with its built-in goal and value conflicts. Individual goals may be *incompatible* with group goals; goals of a particular group may be incompatible with those of society. The goals of labor are often incompatible with those of management. Invariably, the sensing of incompatibility leads to frustration, anger, and sometimes revolt. When such anger or revolt occurs, a society may lose its ability to function either temporarily or permanently. Consequently, conflict should be resolved as quickly and efficiently as possible.

Conflict is resolved when antagonists or parties to the conflict are *motivated* to span lines of communication. Such motivation is cultivated through the process of mediation in which skillful negotiators, through an understanding of conflict environments, are able to temper hostilities and induce rational responses to problems and provocations. In this chapter, we will discuss how public communication enhances the effectiveness of mediation and resolution.

In order to resolve conflict effectively, we should *first* try to understand the nature of conflict; *second*, we should be aware of how conflict is caused; *third,* we should be able to detect the manifestations of conflict; *fourth,* we should be aware of the various audiences that prevail in a "conflict" arena; *fifth,* we should be able to formulate or set up various processes for "managing" the conflict in order to "hold off" the revolt; *sixth,* we should be able to plan *a* particular strategy; and *seventh,* we should launch the strategy. If these seven concerns are given sufficient attention, a considerable amount of success would be ensured. We shall discuss each of these concerns of the public communicator separately.

The Nature of Conflict

To understand the nature of conflict, it would be useful to look at the phenomenon of conflict from *three* perspectives: (1) as a type of clash; (2) as a process of some sort; and (3) in terms of the *irrational bases* that give conflict its disturbing, upsetting characteristics. All three views would be a proper and practical framework for public communication.

CONFLICT: A CLASH

Simons provides a very good definition of what is involved in a clash precipitated by conflict. According to his definition, *"social conflict is a clash over incompatible interest in which one party's relative gain is another's relative loss."*[1] Simons points out that conflict is *not* merely a misunderstanding between two or more parties; *nor* is it merely a semantic confusion or a communication breakdown. The clash, brought on by conflict, presupposes something *more than* a disagreement or difference of opinion. As a matter of fact, when people treat conflict as if it were merely a disagreement or a communication breakdown, the conflict tends to increase rather than decrease.

Conflict between blacks and whites, integrationist and segregationist, Jews and Arabs, tax assessor and taxpayer, labor and management, and so on, involves much more than disagreements and breakdowns. Conflict involves *differences in value orientations, personal animosities,* and more importantly, a *competition for scarce resources,* and the perception that *the vested interests of one party is being threatened by the other party.* When the clash is precipitated by differences in values, personal animosities, competition for scarce resources, and perceptions of threat, those of

1. Simons, H., *Persuasion: Understanding, Practice, and Analysis* (Reading, Mass.: Addison-Wesley Publishing Co., Inc., 1976), p. 250.

us who attempt to mediate and resolve the conflict may discover that the modes of public communication outlined thus far in this book may not be enough to effect a resolution. That is why this chapter is necessary, for it will outline strategies that are uniquely related to the conflict environment.

CONFLICT: A PROCESS

Conflict may be viewed as a process of changes in the relationships between elements of the environment and members of the environment. The elements of the environment may be quality education, job status, occupational roles, decent housing, policy changes affecting student grades or teacher-evaluation, and the like. The members of the environment are individuals who see themselves becoming increasingly dissatisfied. Whatever the elements or the parties involved, the process of change contributes to changes in the relationships between the parties who compete for these elements. *Conflict continues until the process of change is modified or until one or more of the parties or groups disintegrates or disbands.* The restoration of cooperation among feuding parties does not, however, necessarily mean that conflict has been resolved; it may only indicate that overt, disruptive behavior has once again become routine. A good example of this would be the *apparent* de-escalation of the civil rights movement of the sixties. Is the conflict really over? Did the scarce resources—jobs, good education, increased occupational status—eventually become plentiful for minorities. Or is it that the behaviors of the revolution—marches on police stations, demands for curriculum changes, insistence on gaining access to choice neighborhoods—have now become routinized?

Conflict, then, is a process of two broad classes of changes: (1) a change that precipitates the conflict relationship; and (2) a change in response to conflict that either leads to resolution or disintegration. From this perspective, two key areas require close analysis: the causes of conflict, and the behaviors resulting from conflict. We shall make this analysis shortly. However, we must yet look at the third perspective on conflict from its irrational bases.

CONFLICT: ITS IRRATIONAL BASES

People often complicate the picture of what is really involved in a particular conflict because they frequently depart from rational, reality-based behavior in their individual struggles against one another or in their participation in group struggles. Throwing a brick through a window, looting a store, or burning a school bus

—all irrational behaviors—eventually lead to a complication, obscuring, or confounding of a problem. Distortion of information, hostility, and other factors all enter into the interaction between personal and social forces within a society. The group process provides a ready mechanism for giving expression to conflict; it provides a sanctioned voice as well as an umbrella. For example, an *individual* who stands before an embassy shouting: "Death to the Fascists!" may quite easily be forced to desist, as he may be apprehended for creating a public nuisance or for being crazy. However, if a group of individuals stood before the embassy and shouted: "Death to the Fascists!" no arrests may occur. In other words, the group will be allowed to voice its dissatisfaction and it will serve to protect, as an umbrella, whoever needs to shout. Whereas individual aggression is not socially sanctioned, group aggression may receive support from the immediate social environment.

In the 1960s and early 1970s, many Americans celebrated and condoned the looting and burning that attended the Black social protest. What is *irrational*, here, is that it is quite usual to find that antisocial acts are often given full social approval by the very people those acts are perpetrated against. When this occurs, the protective agencies of government are stymied in the effort to curb violence and mete out penalties in that the audiences become increasingly fuzzy.

With this understanding of the nature of conflict—the fact that (1) it is more than mere disagreement; (2) it is an intricate process of changes; and (3) it is characterized by irrational, perplexing bases—we are ready to discuss the causes of conflict.

Inputs Creating Conflict

Conflict is generated by the process of changes that occurs in the *roles* people take in society, the *issues* contributing to the happiness or unhappiness of their lives, people's *perceptions* of the environment, their *expectations*, their involvement or noninvolvement in *decisions*, their *goals* in relationship to the goals of others, and the quality and quantity of *communication*.

ROLES

The behavior of all parties, groups, or agencies must be integrated with the needs of the entire society in order to achieve maximum efficiency and harmony. Roles—their assignment and subsequent enactment—are a means of bringing about the integration and coordination. Any deviation from the role is likely to be a major source of social conflict.

Each role in society represents a normative model of conduct that defines the expected contribution of persons occupying a given slot to the achievements of the goals of society. For example, we have expectations of what is "normal" in the expression of the role of father, mother, college professor, student, policeman, and so on. This model of conduct or expected pattern of behavior embraces two basic factors: (1) rights, and (2) obligations.[2] For example, with regard to *rights*, a society or governing agency has the "right" to anticipate certain behaviors or performances from its citizens, and the citizens have the "right" to anticipate certain behaviors or performances from the society that surrounds them. *Obligation*, on the other hand, refers to the commitment that the surrounding society or governing agency must make to its citizens with regard to the performance expectations held by those citizens. The obligation, then, is that certain role behaviors must be exchanged. For example, citizens must pay taxes and the government must provide a good quality of life; the citizens expect such behavior. Deviance in the performance of obligations will lead to a struggle for "rights," and conflict will emerge. If people's children are not provided with good schools, they will picket or petition for the "right" to have good schools. Conflict ensues when either one of the parties denies the existence of either the "obligation" or the "right," or both. In short, conflict occurs when the roles that should be enacted are not enacted, and the obligation to be fulfilled is not fulfilled.

ISSUES

The term *issues* relates to the scarcity of some resource that is desired by two parties. Frequently, in a labor-management conflict, we hear someone say: "The issue in this case is 'good working conditions.'" In that conflict, "good working conditions" represent the scarce resource. Boulding has written that:

Only when there is scarcity in the economist's sense can there be issue conflicts, for the only thing that conflicts can rationally be about is the distribution between two or more parties of some good which is both scarce and valued.[3]

2. Sarbin, T., "Role Theory," in Gardner Lindzey (ed.), *Handbook of Social Psychology*, Volume I (Reading, Mass.: Addison-Wesley Publishing Co., Inc., 1954), p. 226.

3. Boulding, K., "The Economics of Human Conflict," in Elton McNeil (ed.), *The Nature of Human Conflict* (Englewood Cliffs, N. J.: Prentice-Hall, Inc., 1965), pp. 172–173.

Groups or subcultures within a system that is characterized by cooperative, nonconflicting relationships have presumably reached an agreement on the distribution of valued goods, services, or resources. But, when those goods, services, or resources are perceived by one group as becoming scarce, while its availability to other groups persists, an *issue conflict* will result. For example, if a group sees itself as getting *no* good education, but it also sees another group as receiving good education, there will be the emergence of conflict in the society. As a matter of fact, the most common *issue conflict* involves what we call "territorial prerogatives," such as good housing, good education, respect for neighborhoods, civil rights, and so on.

PERCEPTION

Perception is the process by which people select and interpret environmental stimuli. The interpretation need not, however, be congruent with reality. Perceptual errors are common occurrences. We must understand that the environment is constantly bombarding us with a tremendous variety of information; it is literally impossible for any of us to take in, assimilate, and organize all of this, even on a fairly circumscribed matter.

Different groups or cultures within a society are likely to have unique perceptions of reality based upon predispositions, attitudes, or values which, in turn, are determined by their roles, personality attributes, and the numerous environmental conditions facing them. Thus, two or more different groups within the same system may observe the same phenomenon in exactly reversed terms. For example, an artist was commissioned to paint a mural to adorn the wall of a civic center. The work, upon completion, evoked mixed responses. One group of citizens viewed it as representative of a celebration of women; another group viewed it as being outrageously pornographic and demanded that it be removed. If there are differences in perception, it is conceivable that there will be differing bases of action in response to the same situation. Such behaviors are, therefore, likely to frustrate and produce conflict. In the case of the civic center mural, the building was firebombed.

EXPECTATIONS

When a group expects that society or government or management will not treat them properly, the "expectation" generally materializes into reality. Why? Because perceptions constitute the framework in which expectations are verified. Merton described the perception-expectation tandem in terms of people's failure to distinguish between *perceived impediments* and *actual impediments*.[4] The notion of "the self-fulfilling prophecy" provides an excellent example of the significance of the distinction. The process of the self-fulfilling prophecy begins with a fear of disaster or mistreatment. This fear may not be supported by overt threat; the threat can be largely imagined. A group of people reacting to a perceived threat may take some "retaliatory" action, which, in turn, may result in a conflict situation.

For example, at a newly integrated school, a handful of white students who had been attending that school, *expected* that the recently enrolled black students would glare at them intensely, insolently, and hatefully. *That was the expectation!* The reality however, could be one or more of several circumstances: (1) that most newcomers tend to stare or gaze more intensely at people and things in their new environment; (2) that the black students *would not really glare*, but merely look for signs of welcome or approval; and (3) that the blacks would not even look at the whites.

Reality notwithstanding, one morning the ringleader of one of the gangs of white students on campus calls his group together and admonishes them to "keep your eyes on dem black dudes! If they glare at you . . . jist glare back at 'em. We ain't takin' no stuff offa dem. Dis here school belongs to us!" As the blacks *stare*, the whites *glare*. The blacks, now "perceiving" hostility, also begin glaring at whites. The prophecy or expectation is fulfilled—the school is caught up in conflict, and is on the brink of revolt.

DECISIONS

When two or more groups feel the need, or actually attempt to control decision-making activities within the system, conflict can arise. Unilateral demands for decision-making power or responsibility within what has been considered the domain or prerogatives of another group may induce conflict. For example, a citizens group's attempts to "assist" the residents of four untidy, ill-kept houses in the vicinity, by coming around—uninvited—on a Saturday morning and pruning the hedges, picking up trash, mowing the lawn, and sweeping off the driveway. The four "nonconforming" residents, unwilling to accept the neighbors' involvement in *their personal* decision-making process, may resist the effort of the citizens group, and thus create a conflict situation.

4. Merton, R., *Social Theory and Social Structure* (Glencoe, Ill.: The Free Press, 1949), pp. 179–195.

GOALS

Each group or subculture in a society normally joins together with other groups in an interdependent vertical relationship so that it can serve its constituents better and receive more efficient services as a result of its participation in the system. For example, the group of people that comprise the community of Lakewood joins with several other communities—Long Beach, Artesia, Bellflower, and so on—to form a larger, central administration called the County of Los Angeles. Despite this coalition, each community or group has its own goals, and has ideas of the best methods for attaining them. No member-community of the County of Los Angeles is, however, free to pursue its own course of action without some regard to the impact of its action upon other communities in the total system. Nevertheless, a number of maverick communities, hellbent on doing their own thing, often with incompatible goals while operating within the same system, would indicate a potential for conflict between the communities.

COMMUNICATION

Communication, like roles, is a means of coordinating the behavior of groups in a system or society. Ineffective communication leads to uncoordinated behavior that is likely to precipitate conflict. Of course, many communication problems are due to selective perception, as we we have previously discussed. Inadequate procedures for communication are also a prime reason for communication breakdown. In some instances, so much secrecy and "tight" dissemination of information is maintained that suspicions and rumors become prevalent. Aside from efficiency considerations, the desire for increased information, when not satisfied, is likely to spawn considerable intra-, and intergroup antagonism and conflict.

We have seen that conflict is likely to be caused by five basic input factors—*roles, issues, perception, goals,* and *communication.* An awareness of these basic causes is as essential to the formulating of plans or strategies to resolve conflict, as is an awareness of the manifestations of conflict. We shall discuss a few telltale behaviors next.

Behavioral Manifestations of Conflict

Once conflict exists, overt behavior may follow. The variety of possible behaviors falls under one broad general category that we call the *exercise of power.* Every behavior or action that is generated by conflict is calculated to exert power or irresistible influence in order to bring about change or resolution. Some conflict behavior is pathological, that is, largely irrational and destructive to the group and its surrounding elements, whereas other behaviors such as resolution behavior, is functional. Resolution behavior usually involves both a willingness to curb the erratic, pathological behaviors and a skillful exercise of power by all parties in the conflict relationship.

The first reaction to frustration is an attempt to remove its cause. In a social system or a society, an effort by one component or a group to change the behavior of other components or groups is the exercise of power. Robert Dahl draws the connection between conflict and power as follows:

Let one person frustrate the other in the pursuit of his goals, and you already have the germ of a political system. For the one may then try to change the behavior of the other. If he does so by creating the expectation of sizeable rewards or deprivations, then relations of power come into existence.[5]

The point that Dahl makes is that the exercise of power is a major conflict response as well as a cause of conflict. Some of the behaviors that represent the exercise of power in conflict relationships are: *threats, coalitions,* and *symbolic activity.* Let us look into the characteristics of each of these three behaviors.

The utterance of threats, when friction and frustration exist is generally considered to be a pathological response to conflict. We say that *threatening* behavior is pathological because threats tend to elicit threats, obscuring the real crux of the problem. There are many dimensions to the links or interdependencies between a group and other groups in a society or community. The linkage may involve cooperation and coordination in sharing schools, library facilities, roadways, sewage disposal, emergency services, parks, and so on. A conflict can arise over any *one* of these facilities—for example, the use or misuse of parks—whereas relationships involving the others are routinely continued. However, when one party attempts to coerce another by issuing threats in the hope of influencing its participation or nonparticipation, the conflict may spread to other matters. Thus a conflict that arose over the scheduling of activities at the village park may, because of the use of threats, lead to a retaliation through which cooperation in several or all of the other facilities is threatened.

To increase their potential effectiveness in a conflict situation,

5. Dahl, R., *Modern Political Analysis* (Englewood Cliffs, N. J.: Prentice-Hall, Inc., 1963), p. 72.

the parties to a conflict relationship may seek to increase their power by creating coalitions. Coalitions become possible because the attention of members of the group or collection of groups is focused on the common threat and diverted from their individual differences. Recently, a majority of independent vegetable growers who are normally engaged in competitive relationships with one another, banded together when confronted with a common threat by their itinerant farm-workers. The same kind of coalition-formation was undertaken among car dealers. Palamountain described how automobile dealers formed their powerful trade organization, the National Automobile Dealers Association, in response to manufacturers' policies that tended to limit dealers' profits.[6] He also described actions by similar coalitions in the drug, oil, and grocery trades.

The exercise of power in reaction to potential, anticipated, or actual conflict also takes the form of increasing the flow of symbols.[7] Symbols represent values commonly shared by group members and those who potentially could exert some control over the outcome of the intergroup conflict relationship. Symbols and symbolic behaviors constitute the essential language of the conflict environment, and may take the form of both nonverbal and verbal activity.

Simons[8] has provided an excellent analysis of the use of symbols as the language medium of conflict. He contends that the nonverbal language of protesters provide a rather reliable index of degrees of militancy. He argues that moderates tend to dress and behave in accordance with conventional, societal norms. Militants, on the other hand, tend to flaunt those conventions by smoking marijuana in a beseiged administrator's office, burning the flag, firebombing crowded buildings, and the like. The same type of discrepancy between the behaviors of moderates and militants would be observed in the use of verbal symbols. Earlier in this discussion, we suggested that symbols represent values commonly shared by group members. We could see immediately how this sharing of values prevails within a group of militants, or within a group of moderates. We also may be able to see immediately how a protest group of moderates may reflect the values of the society

6. Palamountain, J., *The Politics of Distribution* (Cambridge, Mass.: Harvard University Press, 1955), pp. 107–158.

7. Lasswell, H., and A. Kaplan, *Power and Society: A Framework for Political Inquiry* (New Haven, Conn.: Yale University Press, 1950), pp. 103–105.

8. Simons, H., op. cit., pp. 277–283.

that surrounds it. But do militants also express values that are shared by its surrounding society? Yes, they do. But according to Simons, militants express those values in ways that call into question other widely-held values. As far as the overall distinctions in the verbal behaviors of militants and moderates are concerned, Simons suggests the following:

In general, the militant tends to express greater degrees of dissatisfaction. Whereas the moderate tends to ask "How" questions, the militant asks "whether" questions. Whereas the moderate sees "inefficiencies" in existing practices, the militant sees "inequities." Whereas the moderate might regard authority figures as "misguided" though "legitimate," the militant would tend to regard these same figures as "willfully self-serving" and "illegitimate." Whereas both might pay homage to law, the militant is more apt to derogate man-made laws in the name of "higher" laws. For many moderates, American participation in the Vietnam war became inadvisable because "we could not win." For many militants, the basic question was whether we *ought* to win. Moderates began to ask whether Vietnam was vital to our national security. Militants asked whether national security was as important as our obligation to international law.[9]

Through symbolic activities—verbal attacks and appeals, nonverbal symbols and gestures, and direct action—dissidents and protestors are able to conduct what is called *combative persuasion.* They threaten, cajole, harrass, disrupt, provoke, intimidate and coerce wrong-doers. Much of this type of behavior becomes pathological or dysfunctional because of the resistance that it provokes in people to whom it is directed. What is overlooked is that symbolic activities must remain true to the essential basic sources of dissatisfaction that aroused the conflict in the first place. Symbolic activity is effective only when it serves to dramatize the issues, enlist additional sympathizers, and pave the way for negotiated settlements or resolution.

To summarize, we have explained the three behaviors that are likely to be performed by those who protest the emergence or arousal of some significant conflict. The behaviors—threat, coalition-formation, and symbolic activity—are generally directed toward the adversary in the conflict relationship. However, many a protest would be short-lived if the protesters were only concerned with sending messages toward those parties responsible for the wrongs or mistreatment. Generally speaking the conflict audience is much larger, and we shall demonstrate how this occurs.

9. Ibid., p. 280.

The Audiences in Conflict Relationships

As we pointed, leaders of protest groups would err considerably if they were to be so obsessed with harassing the "enemy" that they neglected other audiences that might lend support or sanction to their demands. In this section, we will describe those *other audiences* briefly.

Figure 5.1 presents a simple model of the various audiences that are drawn together for maximizing gains in the typical "conflict-audience mix" involving two competing groups. The model describes five pairs of messages, with the leadership of each group directing "comparable" messages to mutually-shared audiences, and their own special-interest audiences. All in all, five audiences are utilized by each of the two antagonists. (Count the arrows that emanate from Leader A, and those from Leader B).

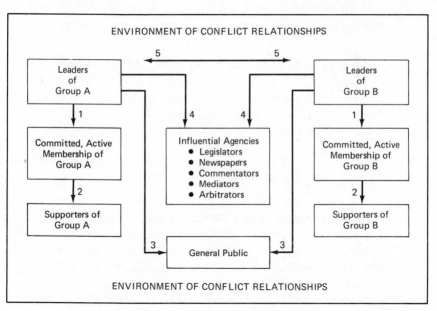

FIGURE 5.1. Leaders' message inputs and their audiences in an environment of conflict relationships. [Adapted from Herbert W. Simons, *Persuasion: Understanding, Practice, and Analysis* (Reading, Mass.: Addison-Wesley Publishing Co., 1976), p. 258.]

Let us look at each of the message inputs.

Message Inputs to Supporters. In most types of major conflicts—international, diplomatic, political, racial, and industrial—between parties, there are usually sympathizers who lend support without really becoming actively involved. Sympathy is necessary, but it often becomes noninfluential unless a way is found to make that symapthy vocal and active. Not only do we need people who appreciate or feel sorrow for our grievances, but we also need people who will "come out" and testify or demonstrate their sorrow. The strategies of persuasive public communication that we have discussed throughout this book are used primarily to recruit and "indoctrinate" these supporters. If the issue is crucial or detrimental to the functions of the group, large sums of money may be involved in getting out the supporters through rallies and campaigns. Power or leverage in conflict is largely derived from the number of supporters that either side can claim *the larger and more committed the following, the larger the power base.* Consequently, the leadership of each of the two groups must instill a feeling of oneness, a sense of jeopardy, a belief in the correctness of the struggle, hostility toward the opposition, confidence in the leadership, and a clear understanding of the remedy sought.

Message Inputs to the Committed, Active Membership. The same type of persuasion used in working with the former sympathetic, but inactive support group is also used on the committed, active membership. These individuals constitute the so-called hard core of the protest. Given their commitment, much of the message inputs will be concerned with concrete definitions of what their task in the confrontation entails—picketing, boycotting, marching, petitioning, and so on.

Message Inputs to the General Public. Because every protest movement seeks to legitimize its struggle, the sympathy and support of the general public becomes a highly valued priority. The general public constitutes the most effective pressure group and so each side attempts to gain its support. Consequently, protest leaders undertake massive public relations campaigns to demonstrate how the aims and objectives of the group are congruent with the values or best interests of the entire society, and how the aims and objectives of the opposition are not. Sometimes, the leadership resorts to combative rather than amicable tactics when working with the general public. For example, public transit workers shut down the bus service, garbage workers refuse to collect trash, firemen refuse to respond to alarms, dissidents take hostages, and so on. Frequently, the imposition of such hardships on this much-needed audience sets up an indirect pressure on adversaries on influential agencies.

Message Inputs to Influential Agencies. The influential agencies to whom messages are directed by both sides, usually consist of legislators, newspapers, commentators, special mediators, and opinion leaders. In some cases, influential agents may be called upon to act as a go-between or a courier of information pertaining to changes in decisions or demands.

Message Inputs to the Leadership of the Opposition. In most instances, especially in sophisticated conflict resolution, the leadership of both factions seldom confront each other face-to-face. For example, the President of the United States and the Prime Minister of North Vietnam never actually confronted each other in the extensive, protracted Vietnam Peace talks. Communication between adversaries usually becomes very restricted, and much of the declaration of intent is conveyed through nonadversaries, allies, or neutral parties. As conflict escalates, messages ostensibly directed at other leaders may actually be meant for the ears of nonadversaries or followers as a way of confronting the rigidity, stupidity, or immorality of the opposition.[10] All the while, of course, messages can be used to gain the opposition's attention, and to estimate their willingness to negotiate or compromise.

Once the audiences have been established or identified, the leaders are ready to engage in certain resolution processes. We will describe these processes in broad, general terms; these processes *do not* represent the strategy utilized in resolving conflict. (We will be talking about the strategy later.) In the next section, we will be concerned only with describing the various processes in which any given strategy may be imbedded.

Processes for Resolving Conflict

A society or system will maintain or keep its components together in a viable network only when the various groups or subsystems are willing to remain in that society or system. A way must be found to induce disgruntled groups to continue their participation, cooperation, and contribution. Consequently, the entire resolution process is utilized for determining how many or what type of inducements could be given to a group in order to influence them to continue their contribution. One group assesses how much it can give while the other assesses how much it will be willing to take. The basic problem, then, is to achieve an inducement/contributions balance for each of the parties in the

10. Ibid., p. 259.

conflict relationship. Bakke and Argyris made the following observation:

The first problem in all organizational life is how to take an aggregate of varied individual people, with varied capacities and predispositions, and get them involved in cooperative activity which adds up to success for the organization and satisfaction for individuals concerned. In short, the problem is to *integrate* the individual participants with the organization.[11]

There are three basic processes through which this attempt at integration is negotiated: *bargaining, mediation,* and *cooptation.* One may utilize one process or a combination of any of the three.

In the broadest sense, bargaining is a process involving the simultaneous exercise of power by two or more parties in a conflict situation. The antagonists must have equal amounts of power, for there would be no point in bargaining if there were a marked imbalance of power, i.e., one party having much, and the other party having very little. However, if the parties, having equal amounts of power, attempt *only* to exercise power, conflict will not be resolved; there must be some accommodation. The parties should, however, have at least a vague conception of the amount of accommodation they are willing to make.[12] In other words, some assessment must be made concerning how many concessions you wish to make in exchange for what kinds of behaviors. The problem of bargaining is, then, one of devising a plan that will reestablish cooperation without requiring one of the parties to exceed its accommodation limit.

Bargaining sometimes takes on the characteristics of cutthroat game, and communication strategies are crucial to the process. One of the major tasks is to convince the other side that a position of a demand is solid and will not be changed. There are many devices used to make such a stance quite clear.

these include the use of an agent to communicate one's offer but without authorizing him to accept a counteroffer; demonstrating the loss of prestige one would suffer if the offer is not accepted; committing oneself by impersonal messages and being unavailable for receipt of return messages; and relating one's offer to a principle or precedent in such a way that accepting a counteroffer would involve a serious

11. Bakke, E., and C. Argyris, *Organization Structure and Dynamics* (New Haven, Conn.: Labor and Management Center, Yale University, 1954), p. 5.
12. Schelling, T., "An Essay on Bargaining," *American Economic Review* (June 1956), pp. 281–306.

violation, with the understanding that a stalemate is preferred to such a sacrifice of principle.[13]

In addition, the bargaining parties may seek to change each other's limits by making their contributions appear to be more valuable than previously perceived.

The use of bargaining to resolve conflict depends largely on the *trust* each participant in the process has in the other.[14] A nontrust relationship is generally resolved through suppression and warlike behavior. On the other hand, a trusting relationship is conducive to problem solving, whereby each party achieves benefits based on an agreement among them.

Mediation. In many conflict situations, the involvement of a third party—a specially appointed person such as the secretary-general of the United Nations; the Red Cross, etc.—is utilized to achieve a settlement. A few years ago, the Federal Government (in the person of a special mediator, William J. Ussery) *mediated* the conflict between labor and management in the steel industry.

Mediation does not necessarily resolve conflict; it is safe to assume that management and labor in the steel industry still do not see eye-to-eye on several issues. However, mediation may suspend the conflict in the interest of society. Quite often a mediator, realizing the impasse created by the stubbornness of both sides, attempts to lead the parties away from a preoccupation with their conflict *toward* a preoccupation with superordinate goals. Superordinate goals are defined as:

goals which are compelling and highly appealing to members of two or more groups in conflict, but which cannot be attained by the resources and energies of the groups separately. In effect, they are goals attained only when groups pull together.[15]

For instance, one of the most common superordinate goals is that of survival or protection against an outside threat. It's a type of a "let's forget our differences because we've got to fight the Russians" arrangement. In northern California, two warring gangs

13. Sturdivant, F., and D. Granbois, "Channel Interaction: An Industrial-Behavioral View," paper delivered to the December, 1967, American Marketing Association Professional Dialogue Session on Channels of Distribution, Washington, D. C., p. 11.

14. Loomis, J., "Communication, the Development of Trust and Cooperative Behavior," *Human Relations* 12 (1959), pp. 305–315.

15. Sherif, M., "Superordinate Goals in the Reduction of Intergroup Conflict," *American Journal of Sociology* 63 (January 1958), pp. 349–350.

were enticed into banding together in order to fight a brushfire that threatened the community. In a sense, their working together created a *mediated ceasing* of conflict; the conflict, however, was not really resolved.

Cooptation is largely used by large governmental or business agencies to reduce conflict (and not necessarily to resolve it). Cooptation is "the process of absorbing new elements into the leadership or policy-making structure of the social environment as a means of averting threats to its stability or existence."[16] Cooptation enhances any organization's chances for survival within its environment through an accommodation of potentially harmful aspects of the environment. Coopting can be either formal or informal. A formal method entails absorption of dissidents or protesters into policy-making and leadership positions. For example, during the social protests of the sixties, many blacks were coopted or absorbed into government leadership positions. In many instances, containment of conflict appears to have been the intent, rather than resolution of conflict. The informal method of cooptation entails placing dissidents or protesters on so-called "advisory" boards. Many universities, plagued by student revolts, promptly devised advisory boards from which to showcase the idea that students should stop protesting because they "were now being given some voice as to the way things ought to be." The truth of the matter is that cooptation—informal or formal—merely postpones the necessary remedy. It leads to "tokenism" and an eventual escalation of crises; the problem smoulders, only to explode later.

Of the three processes, *bargaining* appears to be the more effective in providing sound remedies. Conducted in an environment of mutual trust and respect, it appears to be more suited to resolving conflict than either mediation or cooptation. The latter two seem to provide nothing more than containment.

At this juncture, we have completed laying out the groundwork. We have tried to present a sort of "philosophy" of conflict relationships. We have discussed the nature of conflict, how conflict is aroused, some of the behaviors evident in a conflict environment, the audience at which information is deliberately directed, and some of the processes in which those messages are organized. *We are now ready for the building of strategy.*

16. Thompson, J., and Wm. McEwen, "Organizational Goals and Environment," in Amitai Etzioni (ed.), *Complex Organizations* (New York: Holt, Rinehart and Winston, 1962), p. 84.

Planning the Strategy

Conflict never goes away unless some type of *change* is implemented. Since conflict involves two or more parties, groups, or subcultures, the implementation of change would have to be negotiated by mutual consent. Negotiations depend on communication. Consequently, a carefully planned communication strategy is essential for increasing the prospects of successful change. Our communication strategy should be able to reinforce constantly the idea that the innovations to be implemented in resolving social conflict must take both *social* and *technical* changes into consideration. For example, a "good" education is a very worthwhile social circumstance; however, one will not obtain a good education (if a "bad" education now exists) unless some thought is given to technically rearranging the structure or the machinery in which education presently operates. So, conflict resolution is derived from an overhauling or ideas and structures. The strategy for achieving both the social and structural change can be planned in terms of responses to a master list of questions, which can be modified and focused on any particular conflict situation that may occur.

1. *If changes are made, what will that change replace?* Change requires people to stop doing something and start doing something else. Even if the change means that something is merely being added to ongoing responsibilities, it will still call for an additional expenditure of time, effort, money, and so on. What shifting or priorities are to be involved?
2. *What other techniques or procedures will be affected by the new idea or practice?* Any innovation, large or small, will generate a ripple effect that will spread outward to change a considerable portion of the social environment.
3. *What new materials, space, or other structural arrangement will be required to accommodate the change?* Suppose that a group of college-educated, native Americans were to go on a rampage, insisting that their demands for better, higher status jobs be met immediately. The question to be answered would be: How, and on what schedule will the physical or structural changes be accommodated?
4. *Who, besides the protesters, will benefit immediately from the change? Who will apparently not benefit at all? What will be the nature of the benefits?* These questions are very vital to counteracting any haphazardness or unnecessary haste in implementing solutions or change. Perhaps the most

destructive view of any change is that decision makers and/or dissenters will profit while everybody else must pay the price in greater effort or in disruption of set patterns.

5. *Who within the system is likely to be threatened by the change?* This is the reverse of the question on benefits. The threat may be genuine or the result of misinformation or misunderstanding. Within justifiable limits, a communication strategy will seek to provide clarification and reassurance to those whose self-confidence is threatened by the prospect of change.

6. *Once the decision has been made, and it is handed down by the relevant authority (e.g. the civil courts, university administration, municipal administration, and so on) to the various implementing or drafting agencies, what provision is made to ensure that it is understood well enough to be executed?* The social perception of the necessary or required change at the decision-maker level will be different from those at subordinate levels of implementation and execution. The communication strategy must account for loss of detail as the directives or mandates move through the system.

7. *Who will participate and/or be consulted in the decision-making process?* Although dissenters, administrators, and those who will be "forced" to adopt the required changes may all subscribe to different norms, desires, and values, some involvement by all of the parties during the deliberating and decision process would increase the changes for smooth adoption.

8. *What is the recent history of relationships between decision makers, adopters, and dissidents?* The climate of such relationships will form the context for the new effort, and an effective communication strategy will build upon past successes or acknowledge and attempt to explain past difficulties.

9. *What is the recent history of changes in the society?* Such information will help you see whether the social environment may be characterized as static or conservative, innovative or progressive. It would also provide some indication as to how easy or difficult the proposed change would be. In a static environment, even a minimal change may be seen as a major or drastic undertaking.

These nine questions constitute the foundation for the analysis of the "conflict audiences." They cannot be ignored if effective, efficient public communication is necessary to the fusion of all parties into a cooperative, coordinated entity. In the pursuit of conflict resolution, effective public communication is that which is able to draw antagonisms into a genuine concern for the discovery of proper solutions. It is that type of communication which provides an honest, unstructured, nonmanipulative exchange of ideas and feelings. *We are now ready for the strategy.*

Our plan is one that should work in any type of conflict environment. The issues may vary, but the strategy would be the same. Our strategy constitutes an action-oriented method for planning social change. In it, information on problems and attitudes is collected and fed back to those who produced it, and steps are taken to start action plans for improvement of the condition. We will present the strategy mostly in "outline" or procedural form in order to "sequence" the necessary steps. The *general* design will be presented first, and will be followed by the actual step-by-step strategy.

THE GENERAL DESIGN

The general design constitutes the overall objective that you will sketch during the drafting, or drawing-board planning. Your objective would be to get all of the representatives of the various factions together in a common meeting place for a *confrontation meeting.* With your group or audience assembled, you would then try to get them to fulfill an agenda that calls for a completion of the following six steps:

1. Climate setting—establishing willingness to participate.
2. Information collecting—getting attitudes and feelings out into the open.
3. Information sharing—making total information available to all.
4. Priority setting and group action planning—holding task force sessions to set priority actions and to make timetable commitments.
5. Social action planning—getting commitment by top authorities to the working of these priorities.
6. Immediate follow-up by the selected blue-ribbon task force —planning initial actions and commitments.

This six-step agenda should not be rushed; it is often necessary to spend a day or two hammering out the phases. Now that you have the general idea, let us lay out a specific strategy.

The Strategy for the Confrontation Meeting

PHASE 1: CLIMATE SETTING (APPROXIMATELY 60 TO 75 MINUTES)

At the outset, you must be able to communicate your goals for the meeting and your concern for an interest in free discussion. You must also assure your group that there are no penalties to be incurred for open confrontation, and that "all of the cards should be laid on the table." Sometimes (and you would have to allow more time for this!), you or your designee may want to talk about the problems of communication, the need for understanding, the assumptions and the goals of the society as a whole, the idea of sharing responsibility for decisions, and so on.

PHASE 2: INFORMATION COLLECTING (APPROXIMATELY TWO HOURS WITH A BREAK PERIOD)

The total group is divided into small heterogeneous units of five or seven people. The assignement given to each of the units would be somewhat like this:

Think of yourself as a community member who has certain needs and goals, and as a person who is vitally concerned about the total community. What are the obstacles, dissatisfying elements, or poor attitudes prevalent in your community at the moment? What different conditions, if any, would make the community more efficient and satisfying to live in?

Each unit is instructed to select a reporter to present its results at a general information sharing session to be held following a luncheon break.

PHASE 3: INFORMATION SHARING (ONE HOUR—75 MINUTES)

Each reporter writes the unit's complete findings on newsprint, which is tacked up around the room.

You would then suggest some categories under which all the data from the sheets can be located. If there are 75 items, you may be able to group these items under six or seven major categories (you may not get as many items, and you may not need seven categories; it depends on the number of people and the type of problem). Some of the categories may be: "communication difficulties," "differences in life-styles," "differences in allocation of resources," or "problems with law-enforcement."

Then the meeting takes a coffee break, during which all the data sheets are duplicated for general distribution.

PHASE 4: PRIORITY SETTING AND GROUP ACTION PLANNING (ONE HOUR AND 15 MINUTES)

The total group reconvenes for a 75 minute general session. With you, they go through the raw data on the duplicated sheets and put category numbers by each piece of data.

People are then split up into *different* five- or seven-member groups, and are charged to perform three specific tasks:

1. Discuss the seriousness of the problems and issues that affect the community. Decide on the priorities and early actions to which the group should be prepared to commit itself. (They should be prepared to share this commitment with their colleagues at a later session.)
2. Identify the issues and/or problems to which administrative agencies should give its priority attention.
3. Decide how to communicate the results of this session to the entire group.

(*At this juncture, you may decide to quit for the day.*)

PHASE 5: COMMUNITY ACTION PLANNING (TWO HOURS)

(N.B. For this session, it may be a good idea to have the authorities who actually make administrative decisions attend.) The total group, along with invited officials, reconvenes in a general session, where:

1. Each unit reports its commitment and plans to the total group.
2. Each unit reports and lists the items that its members believe the governing agencies should deal with first.
3. The administrator or potential decision makers reacts to the list and makes commitments by setting targets, timetables, assigning task forces, and so on, for action if required.
4. Each unit shares briefly its plans for communicating the results of the confrontation to their various "rank and file" members of the outside. (At the end of this phase, the total group should *select* a blue-ribbon task force of six or seven *capable* individuals to do the work in Phase 6.)

PHASE 6: IMMEDIATE FOLLOW-UP BY THE BLUE-RIBBON TASK FORCE (ONE TO THREE HOURS)

The blue-ribbon force meets immediately after the confrontation meeting ends to plan first follow-up actions, which should then be reported back to the entire group within a few days. Some timetable should also be set for periodic progress reports every four to six weeks.

The entire strategy is drafted on the assumption that compromise is possible when people negotiate honestly, openly, and in good faith. It involves the joint participation of all the major antagonists of a community, society, or organization. To be effective, there must be a knowledgeable, skillful manager who understands the dynamics of the conflict environment. We trust that the discussion that we have presented will aid you in becoming a manager who would successfully negotiate the concerns and complaints of people through conflict unto resolution.

K E Y   C O N C E P T S

Can you define and give examples of the following terms?

Conflict	Bargaining
Threat	Mediation
Coalition	Cooptation
Symbolic activity	Confrontation meeting
Combative persuasion	

P R O P O S I T I O N S

1. Conflict between groups, cultures, factions, institutions, and individuals can be viewed as a natural outcome of the structure of society.
2. Conflict is resolved when antagonists or parties to the conflict are motivated to develop lines of communication.
3. Social conflict is a clash over incompatible interest in which one party's relative gain is another's relative loss.
4. Conflict will continue until the process of change is modified or until one or more of the parties disbands.
5. Conflict is likely to be caused by five basic input factors: roles, issues, perception, goals, and communication.
6. When two or more groups attempt to control decision-making activities within a system, conflict is likely to result.
7. Every behavior that is generated by conflict will exert power or influence that is intended to bring about change or resolution.
8. Some of the behaviors that represent the exercise of power in conflict relationships are threats, coalitions, and symbolic activity.

9. The exercise of power in reaction to conflict often leads to an increase in the flow of symbolic activity.
10. Symbolic activity is effective only when it serves to dramatize the issues, enlist additional sympathizers, and pave the way for negotiated settlements or resolution.
11. The larger and more committed the followers, the larger the power base of any given party in a conflict relationship.
12. A society or system will be able to maintain or keep its components (social groups) together in a viable network only when the various groups or subsystems are willing to remain in that society or system.
13. The effectiveness of bargaining in an attempt to resolve conflict depends largely on the trust each party in the process has in the other.

Part III
Problem Analysis

Chapter 6
Environmental and Social Inputs

P R E V I E W

¶ *What was the primary function of public speaking in Syracuse in 466 B.C.?*
Swaying judges, juries, and assemblies in arguing property rights

¶ *Who were the Sophists?*
Traveling skeptics who questioned all things

¶ *What was the principal contribution of Protagoras?*
The "Father of Debate" instructed his students to successfully argue both sides of an issue

¶ *What was Isocrates' contribution to rhetoric?*
The importance of ethics and integrity

¶ *What were the classes of rhetoric as assigned by Aristotle?*
Deliberative—for the assembly
Forensic—for the court
Epideictic—for ceremonial occasions

¶ *Who were the two prominent figures in Roman rhetoric?*
Cicero and Quintilian

¶ *Who was the major shaper of rhetorical development through the early Christian era?*
Augustine, who applied rhetorical theories to moral instruction

¶ *What was the contribution of Francis Bacon?*
The analysis of common errors of inference, fallacies, and popular assumptions

¶ *What were the two antithetical movements of the eighteenth and nineteenth centuries?*
Fenelon, who regarded rhetoric as a tool for social improvement; he emphasized the importance of logic, naturalness and clarity
Elocutionists, who believed that public speaking could be re-

duced to an exact science by controlling gestures, posture, movements, rhythm, vocal quality, language, and so on

¶ *What social factors have shaped contemporary rhetorical life?* The media, politics, government, world concerns, business organizations, law, education, and consumer affairs

OBJECTIVES

After reading this chapter you should be able to

1. identify the major contributions and contributors to rhetorical development in the Greek, Roman, Early Christian, and Middle Ages.
2. discuss the impact of the mass media on the modern age.
3. discuss some of the American social and environment factors that have shaped rhetoric in this country.
4. explain the fallacy of the political statement: "different as night and day" when referring to candidates' platforms.
5. discuss the behavior of large business organizations in setting and reaching goals.
6. discuss the implications of forensic speech in law.
7. explain how the educational system prepares the students for forensic skills.

Human behavior plays a significant role in public communication at three distinct levels: the individual behavior of speakers and listeners, the group behavior of audiences, and the mass behavior of societies. We have dealt primarily with the first two levels to this point. In this chapter, we will examine the third.

Most of the members of any society share certain assumptions about the nature of reality. These assumptions are shaped by influences such as the history and traditions of society, its technological level, size, economy, governmental form, urbanization, religion, educational system, literacy level, media, and a host of others. Similarly, every society has a certain concept of the role of public communication, and recognized conventions of acceptable style and content that the public speaker disregards at his or her peril.

Although the conventions of public address may remain relatively stable for long periods, they are never static. This is why it is important that the speaker grasp the whole interrelated system of contemporary inputs with which his or her communication must be meshed. There are few spectacles more pitiable than that of the speaker who attempts to inflict upon an audience an outmoded or otherwise inappropriate rhetorical style. It is a rare modern audience that will tolerate a speaker who adopts, for example, the spread-eagle oratory of the gilded age, or the elaborate elocutionary flourishes of the eighteenth century. The public speaker who patterns his or her delivery on the great speeches of yesterday risks instant loss of rapport with today's audience.

This does not mean that the long rich history of the development of public communication is of no importance to the modern communicator. The contrary is true. Not only does the history of rhetorical theory and practice demonstrate the interrelationship between a society's needs and aspirations and its modes of public communication, but it also helps to distinguish those elements of effective communication that are, in a sense, timeless and those that are transitory.

Knowledge of the history of public communication is therefore one of the significant factors in developing an effective approach to contemporary public communication. Although a comprehensive examination of this history would occupy far greater space than we can devote in this text, it is nevertheless important to review certain high points and significant currents.

Historical Inputs

THE GREEK PERIOD

"Oratory," says Will Durant, "stimulated by democracy and litigation, became one of the passions of Greece."[1] We do not know much about the history of public speaking before the fifth century, B.C. But we do know that it was a subject of serious study for centuries. The oldest surviving book, for instance, indicates that the Pharaohs of Egypt studied effective speaking as early as 3000 B.C.

The earliest known Greek treatise on the subject, entitled "The Arts of Words," probably written in 466 B.C. by Corax of Syracuse, shows that the art of public communication had developed to a considerable degree. "The Arts of Words" was not a sudden innovation, but an intermediate step in a long rhetorical tradition that went back at least to the days of the pre-Homeric village councils, of Nestor, whose speech flowed "sweeter than honey from his

1. Durant, Will, *The Life of Greece* (New York: Simon and Schuster, Inc., 1939), p. 430.

tongue," and Odysseus, whose words fell "like snowflakes on the people." We do not know its exact contents, for no copy survives, but indirect evidence suggests that it dealt with a form of public oration that had three distinct parts: a proem or introduction designed to win the favorable attention of the listeners; a narration, demonstration, or argument, intended to instruct or convince; and an epilogue or peroration to summarize and move the audience toward a desired response.[2]

We might ask, why did an effective public speaking text appear in Syracuse in 466 B.C.? The text was a reflection of social and environmental demands. The year before a popular uprising overthrew the government, which led to the rise of a commercial class over the old landed aristocracy. It brought forth a period of intense and protracted litigation.[3] As is usually the case in political upheavals where power shifts from one class to another, all preexisting titles, rights, and privileges were thrown into doubt. It quickly became apparent that those most effective in swaying judges, juries, and assemblies would be most successful in establishing their claims to property and rights. The fortunes of many a family literally depended upon the skill of its spokesman to defend their claim to citizenship and property confiscated under the tyranny.

Thus, the earliest textbook of rhetoric of which we have any knowledge can be seen as a practical tool for adapting the existing system of communication to meet the demands of a changed social system.

The revolutionary spark struck in Syracuse flared rapidly through the other Greek cities in Sicily, carrying with it renewed interest in public communication.

The enthusiasm for graceful and effective oratory became widespread throughout Greece in the Golden Age, stimulating a general need for education in public communication. As Durant observes:

The debates in the Assembly, the trials before the *heliaea*, and the rising need for the ability to think with the appearance of logic and to speak with clarity and persuasion, conspired with the wealth and curiosity of an imperial society to create a demand for something unknown in Athens before Pericles—a formal higher education in letters, oratory, science, philosophy and statesmanship.[4]

2. Kennedy, George, *The Art of Persuasion in Greece* (Princeton: Princeton University Press, 1963).
3. Durant, opt. cit.
4. Durant, Ibid., p. 358.

This demand created a class of itinerant lecturers and tutors who became known by the term *sophistai,* which means teachers of wisdom, from which we get our words *sopistication, sophomore* ("wise fool"), and *sophist.* The Sophists traveled from city to city, attracting whatever students they could at whatever price they could command, and they naturally varied greatly in talent and integrity.

The Sophists as a group were clever and skeptical men who questioned all things, including the existence of the gods—a point that earned them little favor in the eyes of the Golden Age establishment. Two of the most famous sophists, Protagoras and Gorgias, are noted for projecting two concepts that have influenced the theory and practice of public speaking through the ages— the idea of the relative nature of truth and the deliberate appeal to the emotions as a means of persuasion.[5]

Protagoras sometimes called "the Father of Debate" developed the concept that there are two sides to every question, and encouraged his students to defend either side of a proposition with equal skill. He created what he called commonplaces, pat speeches or dissertations on popular subjects that could be delivered or inserted into an address upon any occasion.

Gorgias has been called the founder of the art of prose. Apparently a close student of the work of Corax, he emphasized the importance of figures of speech, beautiful language, and speech rhythm. He advocated and practiced a style of oratory that was lofty, ornate, and often aimed at the emotions, rather than at the reason of his audience. Plato, a bitter critic of the Sophists, portrayed him as an opportunist who was always willing to sacrifice ethical restraints in order to produce the desired response.

Isocrates, who may have been a student of Gorgias, exercised a tremendous influence upon the Greeks of his era. A man of unquestioned integrity, he emphasized the ethical responsibilities of the orator, and taught that a good speaker was first of all a good man, with a broad education and a commitment to the welfare of the community. Although he was cursed with a weak voice, he wrote numerous speeches for others. This handicap may have generated Isocrates' most important contribution to rhetoric. Beginning with the excessive ornamentation and artificiality of the Gorgias model of oratory, Isocrates evolved a natural and graceful prose style for both oral and written expression that launched the tradition of simplicity and directness in public communication.

Despite their shortcomings and diversity, the Sophists made an

5. Kennedy, George, op. cit., 50–68.

enormous contribution to the general development of philosophy and education, and to public communication theory and practice in particular. As the foregoing review indicates, their appearance on the historical scene was neither accidental nor aimless. They appeared in response to their society's need for philosophical and rhetorical tools to consolidate the revolutionary gains of the progressive commercial classes that were everywhere challenging the suffocating political power of the old landed aristocracy. The old order's power rested upon established political and religious absolutism, bulwarked by the mysticism handed down from Pythagoras and Parmenides through Plato, and eventually finding Christian-era expression in St. Paul. The Sophists continued against this tradition in another great current of Greek philosophy, the naturalistic rationalism of Thales and Anaximander. Their skeptical revolution was the philosophical counterpart of the political democratic revolution. For argument based on authority, they substituted arguments based on probability. Instead of automatic acceptance of the supposed will of the gods and the established conventions, they taught the necessity of skepticism toward all questions, including the existence of the gods no less than the ability of human beings to know the will of the gods.

Their systems of philosophy and education were a functioning part of the changing social system of the era that produced them. Because they taught concepts and rhetorical tools that were vital to the processes that were breaking up the old social and political order, they earned the bitter (and sometimes dangerous) hostility of the conservative establishment and its spokesmen by their real or imagined attacks on the basis of its authority, religion.

It is a tribute to the Sophists that when a coup brought the 500-year-old feudal oligarchy back into power in 404, the teaching of rhetoric was banned in Athens.

Plato. The contributions of the prominent critics of the Sophists are well known to us. Indeed, what we know of the Sophists themselves is often indirect, deduced from the arguments and responses of their opponents. For example, the unflattering portrait in Plato's dialogue Gorgias[6] is a principal source of our knowledge of Gorgias. In that dialogue, Plato reduced rhetoric to a form of pandering, and classed it on the same level with the arts of household and adornment. In the Phaedrus,[7] however, he treats

6. Plato, Gorgias, translated by W. R. Lamb (Cambridge, Mass.: Harvard University Press, 1925).

7. Plato, Phaedrus, translated by H. N. Fowler (Cambridge, Mass.: Harvard University Press, 1914).

the subject in a more favorable light, suggesting that it is bad speechmaking, not speechmaking in general, that is evil. Good speechmaking, on the other hand, is based upon knowledge of the truth, both about the subject matter and about the soul, and may be practiced by a good man who is an accomplished orator, for the spiritual benefit of his listeners.

Aristotle. It is probable that the most influential public communication text in history, Aristotle's *Rhetoric*,[8] was written as an answer to Plato, who had been Aristotle's teacher. *Rhetoric* is divided into the book of the speaker, the book of the audience, and the book of the speech.

In the first book, Aristotle provided the new classic definition of rhetoric as "the faculty of discovering in all particular cases the available means of persuasion." He defined persuasion as a product of the character of the speaker, the emotions of the audience, and the content of the speech. He distinguished between rhetorical (persuasive) communication and dialectical (analytical) communication, and divided a rhetorical speech into three classes: deliberative for the assembly, forensic for the court, and epideictic for ceremonial occasions. In addition, he criticized contemporary textbooks for concentrating on forensic rhetoric to the practical exclusion of the other kinds of public speaking.

Although Aristotle was a harsh critic of the Sophists as well as of Platonists, he continued their tradition of skepticism and naturalism, and has sometimes been regarded as the founder of the scientific method. Like the Sophists, he stressed the importance of arguments from probabilities.

Most of the concepts of the book of the audience should have a familiar ring to students of modern public communication. Aristotle argued that the effective speakers must first know themselves and their own limitations, and then must understand how emotions affect the responses of listeners and how the emotions are aroused. He discussed the effect of age, experience, power, and wealth on audience response, examined rhetorical reasoning and the development of lines of argument.

In the book of the speech, Aristotle attributed the necessity for skillful delivery to the shortcomings (his term is usually translated as the "sorry nature") of the audience. He appears to have considered the subject a bore and devoted little space to it, preferring to stress the factors contributing to oratorical style. He gave the

8. Aristotle, *The Rhetoric of Aristotle*, translated by Lane Cooper (New York: Appleton-Century-Crofts, 1932).

highest priority to clarity, followed by propriety and liveliness, to be achieved by realism, rhythm, and carefully chosen figures of speech. He defined statement and proof as two essential ingredients of a speech and described effective development of the speech's three conventional divisions—introduction, body, and conclusion.

Whereas his teacher, Plato, had dealt with such eternal absolutes as Truth and Virtue, Aristotle held that such ultimate answers were unknowable and unverifiable. Consequently, he maintained that all arguments must be supported by probability. Effective persuasion, therefore, depends not on appeal to the authority of Truth, but on the speaker's ability to engage the system of beliefs, feelings, and preconceptions subscribed to by the listeners—that is, what we call audience adaptation. Aristotle did not regard rhetoric as a moral discipline. The principles he laid down were independent of the morality of the purpose they served or the speaker who used them. However, he suggested that the good would prevail in the long run, because it is stronger than evil.

The only remaining work of significance from the Greek period is an anonymous treatise of uncertain data that classifies rhetorical styles as elevated, elegant, or plain.

By the time of Aristotle, virtually all of the principles that would influence the study of public speaking for the next two thousand years had been explored. Until the development of modern communication theory, works on rhetoric consisted mainly of review and refinement of the concepts of Aristotle, his contemporaries, and his immediate predecessors.

THE ROMAN PERIOD

It was two and a half centuries after the death of Aristotle, and in another culture, before another significant rhetorical work was written. This work was the *Rhetorica ad Herennium*,[9] sometimes ascribed to Cicero. It is a plain little workbook emphasizing the canons of style and delivery, offering the earliest surviving discussion of memory, and largely ignoring speech development and organization. Essentially a survey of Greek teaching, it survived as a textbook of rhetoric down to the time of Shakespeare.

Cicero in the first century B.C., and Quintilian in the first century A.D., refined and expanded upon Greek models, and both emphasized the importance of broad education and knowledge in the training of a public speaker. Quintilian approached the sub-

9. *Rhetorica ad Herennium*, translated by Harry Caplan (Cambridge, Mass.: Harvard University Press, 1954).

ject as a teacher, and his twelve-volume *Institutio Oratoria*[10] is a full curriculum of study for the student rhetorician, animated by the spirit of his famous definition of the orator as "the good man speaking well."

Cicero, however, remained the dominant Roman influence on western rhetoric through the Middle Ages and the Renaissance, not because of the originality of his contribution (he was essentially a synthesizer of the concepts of others) but because of the eloquence and beauty of his style. In the words of Will Durant:

> He re-created the Latin language. He expended its vocabulary, forged from it a flexible instrument for philosophy, fitted it to be the vehicle of learning and literature in western Europe for seventeen hundred years.[11]

THE MIDDLE AGES

Rhetorical innovations during the Middle Ages and the Renaissance consisted essentially of renewed emphasis on one or another of the styles or elements derived from Greek teachings. Early in the Christian era, a return to the exaggerated ornamentation and tricks of delivery of the most flamboyant sophists converted popular oratory into a form of entertainment, eclipsing the practical function of public speaking as a means of persuasion and instruction. After his conversion, Augustine, himself a student and later a teacher of the artificial rhetoric of the day, applied his knowledge and skill to the development of the art of preaching for the purpose of persuasion and moral instruction, as described in Book IV, *De Doctrina Christiana*.[12]

Francis Bacon reasserted the importance of reason as the helmsman of rhetoric.[13] Among his significant contributions was analysis of common errors of inference, fallacies, and popular assumptions, which he termed the "Idols" of the Tribe, the Cave, the Marketplace, and the Theater. He regarded rhetoric as an oral and written discipline in which reason employs the imagination, overcoming irrational impulses and persuading the reader or listener in support of worthy objectives.

The scientific, rational tradition reflected by Bacon produced

10. Quintilian, *The Institutio Oratoria of Quintilian*, translated by H. E. Butler (Cambridge, Mass.: Harvard University Press, 1953).

11. Durant, Will, *Caesar and Christ* (New York: Simon and Schuster, Inc., 1944), p. 166.

12. Saint Augustine, *On Christian Doctrine*, translated by D. W. Robertson, Jr. (Indianapolis: The Bobbs-Merrill Co., Inc., 1958).

13. The primary source of Bacon's rhetorical theory is contained in his *Advancement of Learning.*

two antithetical movements in the eighteenth and nineteenth centuries. The French rhetorician Fenelon,[14] like Bacon, rejected the popular high-flown style. He regarded rhetoric as a tool for social improvement, and emphasized the importance of logic, naturalness, and clarity.

At the opposite extreme, from the standpoint of style and content, yet starting from the same respect for natural law and the scientific method, was the highly artificial system that became known as the elocutionary movement.

The elocutionists believed that public speaking could be reduced to an exact science by careful observation of the response produced by the speaker's gestures, posture, movements, rhythm, voice quality, language, and so on. The movement produced an astounding number of analytical studies designed to reduce oratory to mechanics, including meticulous classifications of speech sounds, inflection, grammar, facial expressions, and physical movements, keyed to the responses (one study described 98 separate emotional reactions) they were supposed to stimulate.

Predictably, the preoccupation of the elocutionary movement with the mechanics of delivery produced counteractions. One was a revival of interest in classical rhetoric; another a fresh look at Francis Bacon's meld of psychology and rhetoric. In general, the antielocutionists restored balance to the subject by renewed emphasis on content, clarity, and naturalness. Eventually the movement collapsed of its own weight, although even today an occasional pulpit or political platform performance betrays its lingering influence.

Contemporary Environmental and Social Inputs

Americans are a uniquely rhetorical people. From tribal pow-wow to political convention, from frontier "augurin' contest" to panel discussion, from medicine show to soap opera, Chautauqua, burlesque, fireside chat, and street theater, circuit-riding preachers and teachers, auctioneers, spielers, street-corner hawkers, folk singers, and demonstrators—all have contributed to the richness and color of a vibrant, imaginative, national oral tradition. A television network flashes to millions of viewers the picket with a hand-lettered sign marching in front of its studio. The powerful and eloquent Daniel Webster sat in the same congress with David Crockett, who related to his constituents with such stories

14. Fenelon, *Dialogues on Eloquence*, translated by Wilbur S. Howell (Princeton: Princeton University Press, 1947).

as how he once "grinned the bark off a tree" in a contest with a dead possum. The patrician Franklin Delano Roosevelt maintained his rapport with impoverished dirt farmers and jobless urban workers with homey pointed anecdotes about his Scotch terrier.

Perhaps nothing more typifies the breadth and invention of the streams that feed the mainstream of American rhetoric than the story of the Chautauqua movement, the amazing institution that for more than fifty years fed small-town America's hunger for culture, spiritual sustenance, and education with programs almost as varied and far-ranging as the audience it served.

As the foregoing brief historical review indicated, rhetoric does not develop in a vacuum, any more than any other social instrument does. It develops in interaction with the society and people it serves. Thus, just as contemporary public communication is shaped by its own past, and thus by the history of the societies in which it developed, it is also profoundly influenced by forces at work in the world in which it operates. Some of these factors in contemporary society will be described in this section of the chapter.

THE MEDIA

Plato suggested that the ideal self-governing community should never be so large that an individual could not shout and be heard by everyone in it. Even in his day, few communities met this requirement literally, and not even the smallest self-contained political unit meets it today. Yet, in a strange way, the whole world today comes as close, if not closer, to that particular ideal as did the city states of Plato's time.

The reason, of course, is the media. The enormous range and speed of modern communications equipment has the potential of creating what Marshal MacLuhan has aptly called a "global village." In the familiar example, the Battle of New Orleans was fought two weeks after the end of the War of 1812 because of the slowness of communication. Today not only news of the event, but instantaneous graphic coverage, can be flashed to any point on earth in a fraction of a second.

Where once popular knowledge of the physical appearance of national leaders was confined to sketches or posed and poorly reproduced photographs, today not only their appearance but also their verbal and corporal behavior can be observed in minute detail.

The result of the media revolution has been far-reaching, creating an aggressive preoccupation with image and packaging, intense competition for access to the media among those with a product or program to promote, and heightened concern over the problems of ownership, control, and manipulation of the media.

POLITICAL

The impact has been no less severe on rhetorical content than on style, particularly in political oratory. As the audience has broadened, so have the strokes with which the politician paints his or her program. Sharp, well-defined stands attract some listeners, but repel others. Under the circumstances there is an almost irresistible tendency for candidates to describe their positions in such deliberately vague generalities that—even if no one is strongly attracted—no one is strongly offended. As a result, when opposing candidates describe their platforms as "different as day and night," too often they are as indistinguishable as noon and midnight in the twenty-four hour twilight of the arctic solstice.

GOVERNMENT

If any aspect of modern society is more striking than the media revolution, it is the proliferation of the giant, impersonal government bureaucracy, and the steady decline of the no less bureaucratized, but increasingly ineffectual, local governing bodies. Paradoxically, as our technology has multiplied the speed and precision of communication, we find ourselves increasingly cut off from communication with and influence over our servants in government.

There are a number of reasons for this, of course, the sheer numbers the bureaucracy must serve, the pre-emption of influence by well-organized pressure groups and powerful corporate interests, the relative impregnability and inertia of the fortress bureau, and so on.

In reaction, individuals and groups have developed new communication skills and formats designed to make their voices heard and their influence felt. Their tactics have ranged from the organization of pressure groups to the creation of media events, demonstrations, boycotts, strikes, disruption, harassment of officeholders and others in positions of power, confrontation, and terrorism. Many of these exhibit considerable ingenuity and knowledge of the points of vulnerability in our highly mechanized society. One of the most interesting was the demonstration by a San Francisco student that a whole section of the city's telephone system could be disrupted by persuading a relatively small number of people to dial a particular number at approximately the same time.

Others have exhibited equal imagination in devising ways to communicate persuasively with the public or the bureaucracy, or in some cases, with both at the same time. One of the most impressive examples is Ralph Nader who, by shrewd selection of issues and skillful and knowledgeable use of the media, the courts, and legislative hearings has often achieved the seemingly impossible in commanding a desired response from both government and corporate bureaucracies.

In one other respect, the omnipresent power of the bureaucracy is an important consideration for the speaker who intends to devise an effective communication system. This is in the area of goals. Every system has an objective that it is designed to achieve, but it is a pyrric victory to achieve an objective, only to have it cancelled by an unforseen change in national direction or policy.

The modern federal bureaucracy, however, is so sprawling and complexly interwoven with every facet of our lives that a minor decision in Washington can have a disproportional local effect on the amount of money in circulation, the rate of inflation, the number, size, and quality of homes built, and so on.

Thus, no goal-oriented system is complete unless it calculates the possible effect of government action on its objectives, and how to forestall or counteract such effects.

WORLD CONCERNS

With the increasing interrelation and interdependence of the nations of the world, events at distant points on the globe impinge more and more heavily on our lives. At this level, as well as in communication, we relate to remote nations almost as if they were merely another part of our "global village."

The influence of world events and attitudes affects us not only as externals, but as shock waves that set up systematic vibrations in our own environments. The United States does not simply have economic, diplomatic, and military relations with Israel and the Arab nations; it has internal populations of Jews and Arabs, as well as companies and other organizations with strong sentimental or financial ties to one or another of the contending Near East powers. War or threat of war in that area, an oil embargo, a boycott or other such external events produce internal response in our population. Our relations with the nations of South America, with Mexico, and with Cuba, with the black and white regimes of Africa, with China—in fact, with virtually every country and political movement in the world—have a similar effect on our internal political balance.

No public speaker can expect to deal effectively with problems of this nature without recognizing that the once-clear line of demarcation between national and international politics is becoming increasingly indistinct.

BUSINESS ORGANIZATIONS

Like government, business has taken on an increasingly international flavor, with expanding interests and growing ties in every quarter of the globe. Business organizations have also adopted a strong advocacy policy, lobbying vigorously for their own interests —often in apparent opposition to the public interest. Their enormous economic and political power often enable them to attain their goals, even in the fact of widespread popular opposition. In recent years this has been particularly true in questions affecting the environment.

It is equally true in another area of interest to the goal-oriented speaker, who often desires to change existing conditions or policies. Like individuals, business organizations that are successful tend to oppose change, whereas those that are less successful are more apt to welcome it. Unfortunately, it is the successful organizations that wield the greatest power, and those hoping to create changes often find themselves struggling with both the natural inertia of things and the active opposition of powerful organizations.

LEGAL

The earliest known rhetorical instruction, you will recall, arose in response to the need for tools to defend property and rights in the courtroom. Aristotle considered courtroom speaking one of the three important divisions of the subject, giving it the name by which it is still sometimes described, *forensic* speech. In the Middle Ages, when the most popular use of public speaking was to astonish and entertain the audience, the tradition of persuasive rhetoric was kept alive by the continuing need for effective courtroom presentation.

Modern law has kept pace with the expanding bureaucracy, and, with it, the demand for professional courtroom skills, to the point that the phrase "my lawyer" is almost as common as "my doctor" in American conversation. For those who become entangled in it, the law often becomes a nightmare network of contradictory requirements and penalties. For all of us, it is a powerful, pervasive influence in every facet of our lives, and an important factor to be considered in any purposeful undertaking.

EDUCATION

Public education virtually began as speech training with the schools of itinerant sophists. Broader education received an important boost from their insistence that the orator require liberal arts instruction. In the modern world the school is the citizen's first and longest training ground for formal forensic skills. The school not only offers systematic rhetorical instruction, it also requires the student to engage in continuous written and oral expression. At the same time, it is a powerful instrument for the ongoing interaction in which the traditions and conventions of society are both transmitted and continuously reshaped.

From Aristotle's time to the present, the level of education of both the speaker and the audience has been regarded as a consideration of primary importance in effective communication.

THE CONSUMER

No individual is more honored in the abstract than the average citizen, the man or woman on the street, the voter, the consumer. At the same time, none has experienced more frustration in being heard and having his needs met. In order to be listened to, the individual must, paradoxically, join a pressure group.

Ralph Nader became an instant folk hero, and an instant subversive to business organizations and government agencies, by seriously taking up the cause of the consumer. His primary thesis was quite simple: the public has the right to demand that manufacturers obey the law by providing safe, effective, honestly advertised and fairly priced products; the public has the right to demand that its ultimate natural resource, the environment, not be stolen and destroyed for private gain or government convenience.

The response of public and private bureaucracies to individuals like Nader and to the movements they have stimulated has been twofold. On the one hand, grudging legal compliance with the demand for consumer protection when no other course is available; on the other, massive public relations campaigns to convince the consumer that his or her wishes are taken into consideration and to recast the image of the corporation as a responsible, environment-conscious public servant.

Conclusion

The foregoing is only a sampling of the major environmental and social inputs that enter into the development of the effective public communication system. They shape the behavior of speaker and audience alike, and have a strong influence on the range of response it is possible to evoke in a given audience in a given environment at a given time.

These are the kinds of factors or inputs that a professional communicator takes into consideration almost automatically in the preparation of a single address or of a campaign. They influence the definition of the overall goal and of the communication goal, target selection, audience analysis, topic selection, message, sources, style, platform behavior, delivery, and evaluation.

Although we have some new tools and concepts to work with today—communication theory, behavioral psychology, the general systems approach—and although modern environmental influences are highly complex, there is really little that is new in this basic approach. As our historical review indicates, effective communicators have always been aware that the speaker must begin from self-awareness, and proceed to the fullest possible understanding of the audience and the influence at work on it.

It cannot, really, be otherwise when the ultimate objective of public communication is to produce a specific behavior in a specific audience. In the normal situation, the speaker has, and should have, no power to coerce the desired behavior, only words, knowledge, and communication skills with which to reach into those other minds and stir up responses that culminate in a voluntary decision to adopt the desired behavior.

Perhaps, as Aristotle suggested, it is the "sorry nature" of the audience that makes the task seem so unnecessarily complicated, or perhaps it is only the lack of understanding on the part of speakers.[15]

K E Y   C O N C E P T S

Can you define and give examples of the following terms?

Sophist
"Commonplaces"
Deliberative speaking
Forensic speaking
Epideictic speaking

"Sorry nature" of the audience
Elocutionist
Semantics
"Global village"

15. Aristotle, op. cit.

1. Members of a society share certain assumptions about reality that are shaped by a wide variety of influences: history and traditions, technological level, size, economy, governmental form, urbanization, relition, educational system, media literacy level, and a variety of others.
2. The earliest textbook of rhetoric can be seen as a practical tool for adapting the system of communication to meet the demands of a changed social system.
3. The first real educators were travelling lecturers called sophists.
4. Isocrates was among the first to emphasize integrity and ethical responsibilities of the orator.
5. Aristotle divided discourse into groupings according to the occasion upon which they were delivered: deliberative speech for the assembly, forensic for the court, and epideictic for ceremonial occasions.
6. Aristotle is regarded as the founder of the scientific method, stressing the importance of argument from probabilities (enthymemes).
7. In Rome, Cicero and Quintilian emphasized the need for broad education and knowledge in the training of the speaker.
8. Early in the Christian era, Augustine developed the skill of persuasion and moral instruction.
9. Elocutionists believed that public speaking could be reduced to an exact science by careful control of gesture, posture, vocal quality, and so on.
10. The mass media have effectively reduced the size of the world to what McLuhan calls the "global village."
11. The proliferation of the media has caused politicians to avoid sharp, well-defined stands, relying on vague generalities to attract the greatest number of supporters.
12. The unmanageable size of modern government has forced individuals to band together to make their voices heard.
13. Because of the diminished size of the modern, media-linked world, nations are no longer able to act without considering the international implications.
14. Large business organizations, because of their international interests, have adopted a strong advocacy policy, lobbying for their own interests, often in opposition to the public good.
15. Rhetorical considerations have contributed to the reduction of the practice of law to the practice of persuasive discourse.
16. The entire educational system tends to act as a rhetorical primer, preparing students for effective communication.

Chapter 7
Source Inputs

After reading this chapter, you should be able to

1. identify the main elements of a source that influence public communication.
2. explain the meaning of the term *ethos.*
3. list and explain the main components of our perception of a source.
4. explain the effects of source credibility.
5. explain how a source establishes common ground with receivers.
6. differentiate between dispositional and membership group similarities.
7. explain three dispositional strategies for influencing the receiver.
8. explain when not to use similarities as a basis for influence effects.
9. define the term *status.*
10. explain how status of the source affects a receiver.
11. define the term *power.*
12. differentiate among the five types of power.

WE SPEND most of our lives listening to other people talk. We are, in fact, more often the recipients than the creators of messages. Thus, a large number of people serve as our sources of information, attitudes, and values; they may be friends, children, instructors, media commentators, social organizations, or governmental representatives. Each source is different, possessing a variety of characteristics that affect the transmission, reception, and acceptance of their message. For instance, in San Francisco a group of journalists invite a consumer advocate to discuss the issue of nuclear plant safety. A tall man in his early fifties, wearing a blue, rumpled suit leans forward on the podium, scarcely stopping to look at the papers in front of him, presenting one argument after another. He explains the existing safety standards and concentrates on potential problems. The newspapermen hurriedly scribble notes, nodding in unison with each new point.

The source holds no public office, he hasn't been employed by any company, he isn't an expert in nuclear power, but the audience listens intently. He says his figures show "coldly and with slide rule precision" that a recently released report underestimates nuclear dangers to the American public. He accuses the utility industries of scare tactics, and says they are guilty of misrepresentation. His appeal to the audience, "Stop in the name of humanity," provokes a sudden outburst of applause.

In a ghetto neighborhood in Los Angeles, mothers lean out of their windows, straining to see the commotion in the streets. Television vans are parked along the curb, their crews tripping over each other's equipment. In the center of the disturbance, unperturbed, a mayoral candidate goes from store to store. "I'm among friends," he explains into a battery of microphones. As he continues walking, the crowd grows, each person assuring him of their belief and support.

A Republican candidate, witty and boyish at sixty-five, stands before an American flag, five times his height, in a downtown music hall in Oklahoma City before 3,000 people; the scene resembles an ad for a patriotic movie.

He has built expertly toward this time, an actor squeezing a scene for maximum dramatic effect, and as the audience leans forward, sensing what is known in the theater as "a moment," he pauses. In a husky voice he says, "If we ever get Washington out of the classroom, maybe we'll get God back in."

The listeners go wild. They explode to their feet in a roaring, cheering, foot-stomping thunder of applause. One or two jump up and down and shout "Hallelujah!" like a spiritual revival meeting. A primed audience continues to cheer. The chemistry between the candidate and the Oklahomans is so perfect that an aide shakes his head, noting, "My God, he can't even swallow without being cheered."

One reporter covering the campaign calls him a cardboard candidate, "right off a corn flakes box," another regards him as a decent and accessible man; a third says he is aloof and unreachable. Mention his name to a conservative Republican and angels sing. Talk about him to liberal Democrats and they'll tell you he's the most dangerous man in America. Others talk about the "celebrity factor"—face and name recognition boosted by fifty movie roles going back to 1937—and about his carefully scripted and stage managed presentations along the campaign trail.

"His speech is the same one he's been giving all year," one critic says, "and for that matter last year and the year before, give or take a new joke. . . ."

Each man receives support because of who he is, not because of what he says. We all realize that *the identity of the speaker is as important as what is said.* The White House has a reputation that affects all its messages, just as the Jewish Defense League, Sierra Club, Socialist Party, and Teamsters all have images that affect their public communication. If we know the source is a member of the A.M.A., we have an impression of what is to be said. If the Ku Klux Klan sponsors a rally, we believe the source has certain attitudes, based on our impression of that group.

Many people have spent years acquiring the knowledge needed to label themselves professors, medical doctors, lawyers, engineers, or scientists. When they speak to us, we accept what they say whether or not we find them particularly attractive. When Daniel Patrick Moynihan argues that the United Nations is following the wrong policies, we listen because we believe he knows what he is talking about. We are accepting his expertise, not his personality.

Today many political candidates are created on television and in national publications. One candidate, for instance, is Ivy League educated, dynamic, polished, a man of inherited wealth, devoted to public service. As the campaign continues, he appears more and more on television news shows talking informally with reporters or speaking before large audiences. His voice is pleasant, his manner serious but with some lightness and humor. He has a good smile and looks like someone you would enjoy knowing. His opponents claim he says nothing, avoiding all issues. Nevertheless, the voters continue to reelect him. We all know that *the way we view a communication source affects how we respond to his public communication.* Our view of the source's appearance, personality, knowledge, honesty; our admiration, trust, and affection of the source *all* influence public communication.

The influence of a source has had many labels. In classical times, it was called *ethos.* Aristotle said of the speaker, "we might affirm that character is the most potent of all the means to persuasion."[1] In recent years, it has been called source credibility, image, charisma, status, power, and prestige. Regardless of what we call it, how we receive a message and its influence upon our attitudes and behavior depends on who the source is. Consciously or unconsciously we respond to certain characteristics of a source. Because we are unique human beings, we all can perceive the same speaker in a variety of ways, and thus respond quite differently to the same individual. Jerry Brown, Governor of California, has been called by some a very trustworthy and dynamic speaker, whereas others have found him to be dull and politically deceptive.

In this chapter we'll examine the main elements of a source

1. Aristotle, *Rhetoric*, trans. Lane Cooper (New York: Appleton-Century-Crofts, 1932), p. 9.

that influence public communication. We'll concentrate on the individual or speaker as the source; this is one major emphasis in speech communication. At the same time, we cannot lose sight of the fact that the source interacts with the message, receiver, and environment. Actually, the source and message are indistinguishable. The reputation of the speaker is part of the message. A well-organized, documented address, for example, produces more confidence in a speaker's expertise. We will attempt to identify those source elements that influence all of us.

Perceptual Inputs

An intense young man is making a speech before a college audience; he fires away at auto manufacturers. "Bumpers, doors, fenders," he proceeds down a list, "must be repaired at an exorbitant expense." He accuses the industry of creating a multibillion dollar replacement market. He suggests that auto makers are guilty of massive thievery. He asks that the audience join him in developing new tougher federal automobile regulations. The man is Ralph Nader.

His words provoke a sudden outburst of cheers from the audience. The lanky six-footer wearing a loose gray suit moves away from the podium, to the front of the auditorium stage. A question period begins. "When are you going to run for President?" a student asks. "I'm less interested in who is to be President," he replies, "than who is to become president of General Motors!" This response brings another roar from the students. The audience has found its hero in a young lawyer, fighting the giant automobile corporations. The influence of this one man has been aptly characterized in biblical jargon by the Public Affairs Council:

And it came to pass that to that land of fiery creatures which was called Detroiticus there came an advocate. Of little fame, but of great determination was he. And he spake unto the Council of the Greats saying unto them, 'For ye have loosed upon the land a plague of Things and these Things do maim and even kill my brethren, and these Things ye have called Corvairs. Yea, though ye are great and I am humble, I do call upon ye to remove this plague from the land. And this call I make for the Kingdom of Consumers.'

And the advocate, he called Nader, returned to the capital city where he caused to be written new laws; laws which would aid and comfort his people, the Consumers. Thus did he show the way for the Not so Greats, those called Consumers, to petition their Supreme Leaders to act against the Greats whose Things do foul the air and waters, and who take tool in exchange for their fruits of the lemon tree.

Many of the Not So Greats joined together under the banner of the advocate, and they became known across the land as Nader's Raiders.

This is a man who within a few months in the late 1960s became the idol of countless college students. Students were the largest group he attracted. On most campuses, students could be found espousing his rhetoric. Some of them even went to Washington to work with him on investigations of government and business. They were dubbed "Nader's Raiders," and the label stuck. By 1971, he was chiefly responsible for at least six major consumer laws.

What made this unassuming man the influential figure he is today? Why does he continue to command the respect of students and consumers alike? Why are we influenced by his statements to the press and in college auditoriums? A complete answer to these questions is obviously quite complex and beyond the scope of this text or chapter, but part of the answer lies in our image of this individual. He is a man who works twice the time on the job as the average man or woman; a man who has taken all his money from court settlements, lecture fees, and book royalities to form a nonprofit law firm called Public Interest Research Group. His initial success in battling General Motors makes him appear like David fighting the mighty Goliath, an individual willing to fight despite great odds against him. Although he is really a rather shy individual, he appears forceful to his opponents and to those he addresses throughout the country. Others, many of whom dislike what he stands for, even admire his quick mind and capacity for hard work. Most Americans view him as sincere, honest, trustworthy, intelligent, and knowledgeable. This perception of Ralph Nader has assisted him in becoming a very influential spokesman for the American consumer.

It is our image of the source that influences us, not what the source is really like. Our perception of any source is a combination of characteristics formed by past, present, and future expectations of that source. Since the time of Aristotle, the audience's view of a source has been recognized as a multidimensional construct. In *Rhetoric*, Aristotle listed the components of ethos as good sense, good character, and good will toward the audience. He believed these three qualities (inputs) of the source induced an audience to believe the speaker apart from the proof he might use to support his statements.

We will now examine the essential components of our perception of the source in a public communication system. The components serve as input variables to make the speaker more or less acceptable or unacceptable to us in a speaking situation.

COMPONENTS OF OUR SOURCE PERCEPTION

For the last twenty-five years, social scientists from psychology, sociology, and speech communication have attempted to explain the way we perceive a source; to identify the components of our perception. Surprisingly, only two major components stand out: *expertness* and *trustworthiness*.

Expertness relates to the impression we have of the source's competency or training, as it relates to the topic of the message. Henry Kissinger, for instance, would possess great expertise when speaking on foreign affairs. Our perception would be based on knowledge of his service as Secretary of State. Your speech instructor would possess great expertise on public commentation because of his or her formal education. A fellow student could appear knowledgeable because she has read extensively on the topic. There also are times we see a source lacking in expertise, for example, a basketball player espousing political views. The basketball player's expertise is confined to one topic—the game of basketball.

There are times when we transfer our perceptions of a source from one topic to another. During the late 1960s, Dr. Benjamin Spock was a leading critic of the United States' policies toward Vietnam. Many citizens considered him an expert, not based on his experiences with foreign policy, but because he had established a reputation over thirty years as this nation's most influential pediatrician. *A source should always be evaluated in relationship to the topic*, but this is a difficult task for untrained communicators.

Trustworthiness relates to the impression we have of a source's honesty or sincerity, and it relates to the source's use of valid arguments and statements. When Ralph Nader pledges to help the American consumer, we trust him; his previous activities provide a basis for our belief. Physicians and college professors are often granted an implicit degree of trust, regardless of previous actions and statements. As children, we may have accepted our parents' punishment because we believed they were just and fair. On the other hand, most Americans view politicians as untrustworthy. There is a general belief that their public statements are not totally candid. This mistrust also plagues car salesmen, Pentagon officials and, too often, law enforcement personnel.

Expertness and trustworthiness are independent perceptual components. For instance, Henry Kissinger was viewed by most Congressmen as knowledgeable, yet dishonest in his dealing with them on Middle Eastern policies. Jacques Cousteau, on the other hand, is viewed as both honest and knowledgeable when he warns us of our destruction of the oceans' flora and fauna.

Four other perceptual components appear important, but they are not as significant in our overall perception of a source: (1) dynamism; (2) sociability; (3) coorientation; and (4) charisma.

Dynamism relates to the impression we have that a source is dynamic. We generally think of this component in respect to a speaker's delivery. A dynamic source would be viewed as energetic, extroverted, active, aggressive, and decisive. A communicator described as meek, hesitant, timid, or passive would not be seen as dynamic. Billy Graham, Ronald Reagan, and Jane Fonda are all extremely dynamic sources. It has been suggested that dynamism, although an independent component, may operate to heighten or dampen our perception of a source's expertise or honesty. Billy Graham's trustworthiness, for example, may increase because of his speaking style.

Sociability relates to our impression of the source as being cheerful or sociable. Television show hosts like Mike Douglas, Dinah Shore, and Merv Griffin strive to create this impression with their viewers. We expect to see this component among speakers attempting to solicit money for a charity or in conversations with friends.

Coorientation relates to the impression we have that a source stands for a group we like, represents our values or is just someone we want to hear. This component exists when a physician listens to the President of the American Medical Association, when George Wallace talks to his Alabama constituency, or when our best friend appeals to us for a small loan.

Charisma is used to describe extraordinary merit, grace, genius, or power in a source, which brings about a direct personal allegiance by receivers. A communicator who is thought of as being convincing, logical, believable, intelligent, whose opinion is respected, whose background is admired, and in whom the listener has confidence could possess charisma. John F. Kennedy and Martin Luther King possessed this component for a majority of American listeners.

Only six major perceptual components are presented here; in fact, the structure of our perception of a source is far more complex. One study, for instance, suggested twenty-eight different components. In real situations, perceptual components are hard to isolate. They are not dependent on objective attributes, but rather on our personal interpretations of the source. They are dependent on the perceptions of individual receivers, and not necessarily on any actual characteristics of the source. The President of your educational institution will be perceived differently by faculty and students; the governor of your state will be viewed differently by legislators, educators, union members, and his or her own family.

Because our interpretation of the source is related to the message and environment, it isn't surprising that our perception of the same source will vary over time, topics, and cultures. For example, a· biology professor will be perceived one way when teaching a class in college, another when discussing the value of topless bars in Ames, Iowa. Richard Nixon, for example, was perceived in 1972 by many Americans as very knowledgeable, honest, dynamic, and so on. By 1974 following the exposure of Watergate events and subsequent cover-up, he was looked upon by many of the same people as deceitful and insincere. Even during a single communication event our perceptions of a source may change. McCrosky, Larson, and Knapp suggest· that our perception of the source passes through three stages: (1) antecedent; (2) situational; and (3) terminal.[2] *Antecedent* credibility is our perception of a source before the presentation of the message. It is determined by our knowledge and past experiences with the source. For example, if the speaker has been honest with us, and if he has a national reputation on the topic. The second stage, *situational* credibility, is the perception derived by the source during the actual communicative event. A source who we believe to be knowledgeable might actually show only a superficial understanding of the topic and thus our view of this expertise will change during the speech. The last stage, *terminal* credibility, refers to the perception of the source we take with us following the event; it becomes the antecedent credibility in our next encounter with that source.

The different perceptions we have of a source create a framework for influencing our behavior toward the source. Based on our perceptions of a source, we assign a specific degree of credulity or acceptability to the source. We call this phenomenon source credibility. The degree of believability, acceptability, or source credibility may range from high to low. The more acceptable a source the higher his source credibility and vice versa.

Before we examine the effects of source credibility, we must see

2. McCrosky, J. C., C. E. Larson, and M. L. Knapp, *An Introduction to Interpersonal Communication* (Englewood Cliffs, N. J.: Prentice-Hall, Inc.), pp. 84–85.

how the perceptual components relate to source credibility. We say that a source who is perceived to be very trustworthy, honest, dynamic, or sociable, possesses *high* credibility, whereas a source who is viewed as very untrustworthy, dishonest, undynamic, or unsociable has *low* credibility. Because the components are independent, a source can be viewed as having high credibility on one component and low credibility on another. For example, Jane Fonda speaking on foreign policy might be viewed as having high credibility on dynamism and trustworthiness components, but low credibility on the expertise component. The higher the credibility of a source the more acceptable or influential he or she will be in a public communication situation.

SOURCE CREDIBILITY EFFECTS

The importance of source credibility must not be underestimated. Kelman and Hovland had three groups listen to the same speech favoring lenient treatment of juvenile delinquents. Three different introductions were used: one identified the source as a judge, highly trained, well informed, sincere, and an experienced authority on juvenile delinquency; the second identified the source as a member of a studio audience. No information about his expertness or trustworthiness was provided; and the third introduction identified the source as a self-centered, former juvenile delinquent who was in trouble with the law. The group hearing the communication from the judge, (high credibility) was more favorable toward lenient treatment than those listening to the juvenile delinquent (low credibility).[3] There is little question that low credibility sources are not as influential as high credibility sources. For example, when, prior to its presentation, a message is attributed to a low credibility source (untrustworthy), the receiver may ignore the source's appeals. A receiver's willingness to accept a speaker's suggestions depends upon *both* how well informed and how sincere he believes the communicator to be. It is very difficult for the average receiver to separate the major factors of credibility. They seem to interact, and their interaction determines the total source's effect on the communication situation. Some receivers, however, separate the components of credibility well enough that they have differential effects. A receiver may lower the source credibility of an expert because they believe their motives are open to suspicion. We may feel that a congressional candidate is an expert on domestic affairs, but that he

3. Kelman, H. C., and C. I. Hovland, "Reinstatement of the Communicator in Delayed Measurement of Opinion Change," *Journal of Abnormal Social Psychology* 48 (1953), pp. 327–35.

supports welfare reform merely to get reelected to public office. On the other hand, an untrustworthy source could increase his source credibility by clearly showing knowledge and understanding of the topic. For instance, the same congressman proposes the same domestic legislation in a nonelection year or when it may lose him votes.

What about the long-term effect of source credibility? It appears that the different effects of high and low credibility sources disappear over time. This phenomenon has been called the "sleeper effect." Kelman and Hovland found that over a period of time receivers often disassociate the source of a message from the message itself. The acceptance of the judge (high credibility) decreased and acceptance of the juvenile delinquent (low credibility) increased.[4] We remember what is said but not who said it. Thus, time can diminish the impact of source credibility upon a message. Historians have seen this occur time and time again. Legislative proposals espoused by low credibility sources and rejected by the populus have over time gained favor and become part of our national framework, for example, social security, prison reform, and so on.

The actual influence of a source is determined by the relationship between the source and the message. For instance, the organization of a message affects source credibility. A disorganized message can reduce the source's influence upon a receiver. It may be that disorganization makes the source appear less knowledgeable or trustworthy. On the other hand, an organized message can increase source credibility.[5] In Chapter 12 we will investigate how to properly organize a message for listeners.

The delivery style of the speakers will also affect source credibility. It has been found that the speaker's vocal style conditions the receiver's perceptions of the source. When a speaker uses a conversational style, he is seen as more trustworthy, but less dynamic. Expertness does not appear to be affected by delivery style.[6] This is a fortunate circumstance for many college instruc-

4. Ibid.

5. Sharp, H., and T. McClung, "Effects of Organization on the Speaker's Ethos," *Speech Monographs* 33 (1966), pp. 83–91; Baker, E. B., "The Immediate Effects of Perceived Speaker Disorganization on Speaker Credibility and Audience Attitude Change in Persuasive Speaking" *Western Speech* 29 (1965), pp. 148–161.

6. Pearce, W. B., and B. J. Brommel, "Vocalic Communication in Persuasion," *Quarterly Journal of Speech* 58 (1972), pp. 298–306; Pearce, W. B. and F. Conklin, "Nonverbal Vocalic Communication and Perceptions of a Speaker," *Speech Monographs* 38 (1971), pp. 235–37.

tors. The more effective speaker will be one who has high initial source credibility and uses dynamic delivery. We will investigate how to properly deliver a message in Chapter 13.

The amount of source credibility an individual has is a function of the receivers, the topic, the speaker's presentation of the message, and the situation at hand. The actual influence depends on the receiver's perception of the source. We will now explore how we might modify or control the perception others have of us as a source.

Source-Receiver Identification

Most speakers, because of training or experience, attempt to establish a *common ground* with their receivers. They *identify for the receiver their real or apparent similarities*. This action is taken to overcome differences that exist between them; differences that could work against the source's communicative goal. A candidate for office, for instance, will overcome status or wealth differences by showing how he's "just one of the folks." A speaker may assert a similarity of beliefs, attitudes, intentions, and values toward issues, people, or objects. A source may emphasize similar schooling, socioeconomic class, religion, sex, occupation, or club memberships. We can place source/receiver similarities into two broad categories: (1) dispositional, and (2) membership group. Let's examine each category.

Dispositional similarities concern the beliefs, attitudes, and values we share with our receivers. Statements establishing common dispositional ground may be relevant or irrelevant to the topic being discussed or the primary communication goal. When a car salesman approaches you on the car lot and begins complimenting the clothes you're wearing, he's using an irrelevant similarity. It may enhance his image, but it has nothing to do with his main topic, automobiles, or your goal to buy a car. When this same man remarks that he also likes a car that needs little maintenance, the appeal is relevant to the goal of selling you a car.

We will comment on three strategies that use dispositional similarities to influence the receiver. They are called the (1) *yes-yes*, (2) *yes-but*, and (3) *assumed-we* approaches. The goal of the "yes-yes" and "yes-but" strategies is to establish receiver agreement on the source's terms. We attempt to get the receivers agreeing to our basic ideas or arguments prior to making our influential pitch.

The "yes-yes" approach begins with the source identifying a number of acceptable ideas or arguments that are used later to support the source's primary goal. For example, a car salesman would handle a customer in the following manner:

SALESMAN: You're looking to buy a used car?
CUSTOMER: Yes, I am.
SALESMAN: If you're like most people, you want a car that gets good gas mileage.
CUSTOMER: That's right.
SALESMAN: I'd guess, too, that you don't want to be bothered with servicing the car regularly.
CUSTOMER: There's no question about that.
SALESMAN: Like most people you don't want to go into hock over the car.
CUSTOMER: You said it.
SALESMAN: Now, here's the car for you—a 1959 Edsel.
CUSTOMER: Oh!
SALESMAN: It gets 15 miles per gallon, needs service twice a year, and will only cost you $25.

The "yes-but" approach begins with the source raising the opposition's arguments, which we agree with, and then offering a series of "buts" intended to set the stage for the source's main goal. The source establishes an aura of open-mindedness prior to attacking the opposition. Our car salesman would handle a customer this way:

SALESMAN: You're looking for a new car?
CUSTOMER: Yes, I am.
SALESMAN: Let me show you this winner. I'll tell you—you'll get only 18 miles per gallon.
CUSTOMER: That's right.
SALESMAN: You'll need service every 6,000 miles.
CUSTOMER: There is no question about that!
SALESMAN: The car will cost approximately $4,000.
CUSTOMER: That's what I've heard.
  BUT . . .
SALESMAN: The service can be performed at your local garage . . . The $4,000 investment will last at least five years . . . you'll be able to use regular gasoline . . .

The "assumed-we" approach begins with an assumption that the receivers are a collective group rather than a collection of unique individuals. This method places source and receiver in the same in-group and individuals who differ into a generalized "they." Robert Roth uses this strategy in a news commentary directed toward individuals who had seen the antiwar demonstrations of Spring 1971, in Washington, D. C.:

In the first weeks of protest activity, we were proud of those young people who came here to show their government that the peace movement was not dead. . . . We were particularly proud on the final day of that first week when uncounted thousands gathered to voice a massive demand for peace now.

We were proud of the protesters. They were orderly, decent, well-behaved.

We were proud of our police. They handled a difficult situation with a minimum of fuss.

And we were proud of ourselves. We had put up with the inconveniences inevitably caused by the presence of the demonstrators, in a spirit of tolerance which was shared even by those who disagreed with the protesters' goal.

We felt pretty good about it.

But then, after a week of uneasy anticipation, came a new wave of demonstrators. . . .

They were deliberately and outrageously disorderly, disruptive, destructive and provocative. . . .

Who, we asked, did these kids think they were? Why, having made their point in the first demonstration, and made it well, didn't they go home? What right had they to interfere with honest people who had work to do and families to feed?[7]

A source may also establish common ground with the audience by emphasizing similarity in group membership.

Membership group similarities concern both voluntary and involuntary groups. For instance, a source may identify the common sex, race, or origin. These group memberships are involuntary, that is, the source cannot control his/her membership and they often carry observable characteristics. The source may also point out similar memberships in the A.M.A., Elks, Teamsters, economic class, occupational or a religious group. These group memberships are within our control or voluntary associations.

Membership group similarities may serve as a form of indirect suggestion. The receiver infers similarities on the basis of the membership group. For example, "we Phi Beta Kappas are all intelligent." A receiver may even imply group similarities by the source's choice of language, dress, and the like. Science professors, jazz musicians, airplane pilots, and CB radio enthusiasts all have a special language that is quickly identified as constituting membership in that group. Certain groups even foster a distinctive use of language. Many Jews, for example, will use Yiddish terms in the

7. Roth, R., Violent demonstrations bring sorrow to the capital, *Philadelphia Sunday Bulletin* (May 9, 1971), in H. Simons, *Persuasion: Understanding, Practice, and Analysis* (Reading, Mass.: Addison-Wesley Publishing Co., Inc., 1976), pp. 154–155.

course of a conversation. Professor Higgins in *My Fair Lady* attempted to change Eliza Dolittle's dialect and language in order to provide an external sign of membership in a higher social class. He was successful in getting British society to infer incorrectly her social class and origin.

Advertisers have used group appeals for years. Cadillac Seville, Schweppes soft drinks, and Gucci leather goods are marketed toward people of real or imagined high status. They often use testimonials by people similar to the audience they seek to sell, such as housewives, market shoppers, satisfied car owners, and so on.

A source also may use both irrelevant or relevant group similarities. When a candidate for President speaks before the American Legion pointing out his service during the Korean War, he is establishing an irrelevant group membership. The membership has no *real* relationship to the Presidency. On the other hand, the same candidate could establish his military service as a relevant appeal if he talked about funding for our nation's defense.

When the source and receiver share similar experiences, speak the same language, belong to the same groups, and hold many beliefs, attitudes, and values in common, it increases the receiver's understanding of the source. How does this real or perceived similarity affect the source's power to influence? We know that a receiver's attraction for a source increases as dispositional similarity between source and receiver increases. The similarities may work as positive reinforcements for the source. Membership group similarities, on the other hand, appear to be less significant determinants of attraction.

Whereas we can link source-receiver similarity to source attraction, there is little evidence that source-receiver similarity affects the receiver's perception of the source's honesty, objectivity, or intelligence. Simons suggests a weak positive relationship between attitudinal similarity and the receiver's perception of the source's trustworthiness. An even less dependable relationship exists between membership group similarities and source trustworthiness.[8] The relationship between similarity and source trustworthiness is dependent on the receiver's perception of the membership group identified by the source. Receivers belonging to the same group as the source may find the source more worthy of respect or trust than dissimilar, nonmember sources. However, because of the receiver's knowledge of his group, he might recognize that sources of dissimilar groups have greater competence and dependability than his own group members.

8. Simons, H., op. cit., pp. 155–167.

We might ask if source attraction is as significant in determining a receiver's attitude toward a position advocated by the source as respect and trust for the source. Source credibility studies indicate that attraction (dynamism and coorientation) play a considerably smaller role in the evaluation of the source than expertise or trustworthiness. In turn, attraction to the source plays a smaller role in affecting attitude change. Thus, emphasis on source-receiver commonalities, especially membership group similarities, may not always have great influence value.

At times, in fact, it may be more advantageous to point out differences between source and receiver. A physician, speaking to a lay audience on the subject of oral contraceptives, should be more successful in emphasizing the difference between herself and the audience. A source sharing the audience's lack of expertise might be perceived as sincere, but not believed. Actually, some receivers do not value themselves or the groups with which they are affiliated; Americans of Polish extraction may not admit their origins, educated blacks and Chicanos may adopt white stereotypes of their uneducated brothers, and Jews may manifest antisemitism. Receivers who reject their membership group will be more receptive to individuals who show or emphasize differences rather than similarities. It would appear that a dissimilar, but more prestigious source is a more influential communicator. Simon states "that while similarities may lead to attraction, the relationship between membership group similarity and image of the source is *strongest for those source components least significantly related to attitude change*.[9] Sources should be similar to the audience, but also different enough to increase their credibility.

ROLE-STATUS DIFFERENCES

The perceived status differences between a source and receivers' roles also may act as an agent of source effect. Every day we assume a number of roles. In the classroom, we play the role of student; at work, the follower; at parties, the clown; in groups, the leader; at home, husband, wife, parent, son, or daughter. Each role has a perceived status.

A person's status is usually defined, formally or informally, by a set of rights and duties. The fraternity president, for example, is given formal rights and duties by his organizations national and local constitution. Informally, the president may be allowed to dominate the group's decision making. *Status refers to our posi-*

9. Simons, H. W., N. N. Berkowietz, and R. J. Mayer, "Similarity, Credibility, and Attitude Change: A Review and Theory," *Psychological Bulletin* 73 (1970), pp. 1–15.

tion or rank in relation to others. The president of a university has higher status than a dean at the same institution. Each role is given a relative rank in a hierarchy of prestige. We could rank the roles at an educational institution as follows:

RANK	ROLE
1	President
2	Vice-President
3	Deans
4	Associate Deans
5	Department Chairpersons

The higher the rank of a person's role, the higher the status in most situations. When two roles are compared, such as ours and a speaker we're listening to at the time, we make a judgment of the source's status; it will be higher or lower than ours. For example, if the source is a college instructor, that individual will be accorded a higher status than yourself (student). If you are a college senior and the source is a freshman, you may see the source as having a lower status than yourself. The status of the source is always related to the status of the receiver with whom he/she is interacting; like credibility, status is the result of a receiver's perception.

A source may be perceived as having higher status in one role over another. A physician will be accorded higher status by a patient in his office; however, the same physician would be accorded a lower status at a P.T.A. meeting that the patient is also attending. In this example, the circumstance interacts with the relationship between source and receiver to determine the source's status.

A source's status may result from the message topic. Let's say we're listening to a speech instructor discussing source effects. We would perceive the instructor as having a higher status than ourselves. But if the instructor were discussing the difficulty involved in accomplishing a top-spin lob, it's reasonable to assume we would lower his status.

How important is the perceived status of the source? Generally, the higher the status we are willing to accord the source, the greater the likelihood we will be influenced by that individual or group. We are influenced by the higher status of others, even though that status may be unrelated to the issue we are considering. Our physician, for example, may suggest a course of action for improving the recreational facilities in our residential area. Because we see that role as commanding high status in our society, we might perceive the plan, if espoused by such an individual, to be worth pursuing. Even if we know nothing about the source except its status relative to ours, we may concede to decisions by a higher status source. For example, we may vote to support the Women's League of Voters' suggestion that all public officials make (a) full disclosures of fiscal resources even if we lack any first-hand knowledge of the organization or its means of support. Bettinghaus suggests that the status an individual appears to possess is not responsible for influencing the receiver. But the perceived status differences between source and receiver may lead the source to be perceived as worth listening to, believable, or knowledgeable.[10]

SOURCE POWER

The *control or authority a source possesses over a receiver* can be called the source's *power*. Like source credibility, similarities, and differences, the source's power develops from the relationship between source and receiver. A student (receiver) will accept the influence of his instructor (source) because he wants to achieve an A in the course. The source's power in this case is derived from his control of grading process.

The source's power may, however, be limited to a narrow range of activities. The instructors may dictate how we study for an exam or act in the classroom, but they can't tell us what to eat or whom to date. In addition, power relationships are not one-sided. Both receiver and source have a degree of power; the source may have more power, equal power, or less power than the receiver. A student, for instance, can exercise power over an instructor's control of classroom grading by contesting the final grade to a departmental grade appeals committee.

According to French and Raven, there are five types of power: reward, coercive, referent, expert, and legitimate.[11]

1. *Reward Power* The source's power is based on the ability to grant or withhold reward from a receiver. If you can give me a trip around the world or get me a promotion, you can exert reward power over me." The amount of power is determined by our perception of the ability or willingness of a source to grant our reward. A friend might suggest that if you study with him, you'll get an A on the exam. This student may

10. Bettinghaus, E. P., *Persuasive Communication*, 2nd ed. (New York: Holt, Rinehart and Winston, Inc., 1973), pp. 107–108.

11. French, J., and B. Raven, "The Bases of Social Power," in D. Cartwright (ed.), *Studies in Social Power* (Ann Arbor, Mich.: The University of Michigan Press, 1959), pp. 118–149.

assist you in preparing for that exam, but he or she doesn't possess the ability to give the grade. In this case you might seriously consider the value of working with this individual.

2. *Coercive Power*   The source's power is based upon the ability to withhold or bestow punishment or penalties. An instructor may threaten to fail students unless term papers are submitted by a certain date. However, the degree of power will be determined by how the source has used punishment in the past. Thus, if the instructor doesn't really fail students who submit late papers, it is doubtful that the threat will exert much power over the student.

3. *Referent Power*   The source's power is based upon the receiver's identification or liking of the source. A student may admire how well organized a teacher is for class, gives reward and punishment fairly, and reads widely on a variety of subjects. Consequently, their liking of the source increases. Students may try to emulate their teacher's behavior and work as hard for the course as does their teacher.

4. *Expert Power*   The source's power is based on receiver's belief that the source has greater skill, information, or knowledge in an area than he or she does. College instructors possess expert power over students. The instructor's expert power comes into play when students are told to interpret certain concepts and theories in a certain way. When the students accept the instructor's suggested interpretations, it is an indication of expert power.

5. *Legitimate Power*   The source's power is based on a given right, by agreement, to dictate the behavior of receivers. University policy may specify that instructors enforce a certain dress code for students. It may require that shoes be worn, or that females not wear bikinis to class. This power rests on the receiver's acceptance of a social structure, illustrated by our example.

If a source intends to use its power to influence a receiver, *what type of power is best?* Reward and coercive power are often dependent upon the presence of the source to produce compliant behavior. The receiver must believe that the source can and will provide either a reward or punishment for certain behavior. Collins and Guetzkow argue that coercive power is not as efficacious as reward power, but in terms of inducing compliance in an actual situation, positive *or* negative sanctions seem equally effective.[12]

12. Collins, G., and H. Guetzkow, *A Social Psychology of Group Processes for Decision Making* (New York: John Wiley & Sons, Inc., 1964).

Receivers' public expressions and behavior will be influenced more than their private attitudes, beliefs, or values. A crucial point to remember, however, is that our public statements in time may be internalized and accepted, particularly when they conflict with our private ideology. Scott and Mitchell suggest, however, that the more a source must use reward or coercive power, the less likely that their authority will be accepted as legitimate power.[13]

Referent power is a most important and effective basis of power, because the referent source can exercise power when not present or even when no deliberate influence is intended by the source. Any power attempt is costly and the most efficient and economical way of gaining compliance is by the receivers' voluntary, willing submission. Because referent, expert, and legitimate power may spontaneously motivate the receiver's actions, they would be less costly than reward or coercive power. These three types of power are more likely to influence the receivers' private attitudes as well as public opinions.

Improving Source Inputs

How can we improve our ability to influence the receiver? What strategies might we employ to shape our listener's perceptions? How can we raise our credibility levels? The answers to these questions are neither simple nor foolproof. However, we make the following suggestions:

1. It is the goal of every speaker to be perceived as a high credibility source, rather than a low one. Sometimes, however, our background and past behaviors, if known by our audience, can result in low credibility. To avoid such an occurrence, we should eliminate references or introductions concerning ourselves that might be counterproductive. Receivers rarely assign low credibility to unfamiliar sources; most receivers will remain open-minded until they have seen and heard our ideas. If after our talk we are rated low, we want to know it's the result of the communication event and not of our past history.

2. The Bible says "it is better to give than to receive." The source should not be seen as the primary beneficiary of his own ideas. It is always superior to appear altruistic, as if one were doing something for the good of others and without reward. Let's assume that you would like to change the grad-

13. Scott, W., and T. Mitchell, *Organizational Theory: A Structural and Behavioral Analysis* (Homewood, Ill.: Richard D. Irwin, Inc., 1972), p. 219.

ing system in college. Rather than suggesting that your grades would have been higher or better under your plan, you would indicate how it would benefit the audience. Furthermore, you might point out that a new policy, while not benefiting you, will help future students. A politician speaking on tax reform could show how new laws would increase his taxes, but decrease those of his constituency. This action should enhance the sincerity or trustworthiness of the source. We know that a low credibility source is more influential when arguing against what appears to be in their best interests. For instance, a low credibility student speaking to university trustees might argue for higher tuition. Although increased tuition places a financial burden on the student, there would be an indirect benefit of increased revenue providing better teachers, equipment, and a wider range of course offerings.

3. The people we associate with affect our credibility. We always want to be associated with high credibility sources. We should strive to show the receiver our relationship to individuals or groups possessing high credibility. Ideally, some of their credibility will rub off on us. To increase our expertise dimension, for example, we might indicate our membership in Phi Beta Kappa or Phi Kappa Phi, national honor societies with selective membership requirements in hopes that the audience will perceive us as being very intelligent. Instructors often drop the name of a past mentor or friend who is a leader in the area being studied in class. Some speakers like to cite highly credible sources who espouse similar ideas; others merely throw in quotes from a variety of high credibility sources. Academicians are forever using quotes from famous philosophers; politicians seem to have a catalog of quotes from our founding fathers.

This strategy is no more apparent than in a political campaign. In fact, candidates frequently have an agency or staff members poll their constituents to determine which individuals or groups have the highest credibility. The candidate then identifies himself in the speech with these individuals or groups either as a friend, member, or supporter of their views. In 1960, John F. Kennedy was fond of quoting Thomas Jefferson and of identifying the New Frontier approach with Roosevelt's New Deal.

We could also increase our credibility by showing how we are different from low credibility sources. On campuses where there is a rift between administration and faculty, instructors will often try to show how the ideas differ from the central administration. In the late 1960s, many radical and liberal speakers tried to disassociate themselves from the establishment. In recent political campaigns, many candidates have attempted to show that they aren't part of the Washington bureaucracy.

4. Visual aids that can be used to supplement and clarify your message may enhance your credibility. Visual aids will probably benefit speakers who are initially perceived as having low credibility. How often have you said, "one picture is worth a thousand words," or "seeing is believing." We often feel that seeing something is more believable than just hearing about the same event. When a friend tells us about the two ton great white shark that got away, we will consider it just another fisherman's tale, unless we see pictures of the creature. Visual aids properly used lend credence and clarity to our message and provide an additional basis of support to strengthen our acceptability. Visual aids also may increase our audience's retention level.

5. Our message should appear organized to the receivers. Organization will be of particular benefit to the moderately or low credible source. However, the organization pattern must be one the receivers can easily follow. In most situations we should avoid overly detailed organizational patterns. Lawyers are sometimes trapped into using very complex and detailed patterns to present their cases. This approach not only delays jurors who are not accustomed to patterns involving a morass of data, but also reduces the lawyer's credibility. Receivers listening to an extremely detailed presentation also may become suspicious of the source's motives.

6. If we are attempting to raise our credibility and/or power, it may be advantageous to show how we differ from the receiver. It is very difficult to establish our expertise by being too colloquial. We should indicate early in our talk any direct or indirect experiences that we have which make us more knowledgeable on the topic. Students might point to books and articles they have read; businessmen might use examples from their offices.

7. We should never promise to reward or punish our receivers for voicing certain opinions and showing specific behaviors unless we can deliver. If we make promises that are subsequently not fulfilled, we decrease our power and future power attempts may prove to be wasted energy on our part. We also should be consistent in our use of reward or coercive

power. If a source were to reward on one occasion but not another, the receiver would become unsettled. Once again, if receivers are unsure of your response to their behavior, they may not be influenced by your power attempt.

KEY CONCEPTS

Can you define and give examples of the following terms?

Ethos
Credibility
Components of our source
   perception:
   Expertness
   Trustworthiness
   Dynamism
   Charisma
Source credibility
   Antecedent credibility
   Situational credibility
   Terminal credibility

Dispositional similarities
Membership-group similarities
Status
Power:
   Reward
   Coercive
   Referent
   Expert
   Legitimate

PROPOSITIONS

1. The way we view a communication source affects how we respond to its public communication.
2. Credibility is a set of perceptions we have of a source.
   a. The five major components of credibility are expertness, trustworthiness, dynamism, coorientation, and charisma.
   b. Credibility is a multidimensional construct.
   c. The credibility of a source will vary over time, topics and culture.
3. Source credibility refers to the communicator's influence or impact in the public communication system.
   a. Source credibility will vary over topics, receivers, time, and situations.
4. Receivers tend to accept the influence from sources they perceive to be competent and/or trustworthy.
   a. A high credibility source will generally be more influential than a low credibility source.
5. The delivery style of the source affects source credibility.
6. An organized message can increase source credibility.
7. The real or apparent similarities between source and receiver can provide a basis for source effect.

a. Dispositional similarities are more influential than member-ship-group similarities.
   b. Source-receiver dissimilarities will sometimes be more influential than their similarities.
8. The higher the status we accord the source, the greater the likelihood we will be influenced by that individual or group.
9. A source's power can be used to influence a receiver.
   a. Reward and coercive power depend on the presence of the source.
   b. Coercive power is not as efficacious as reward power, but its sanctions seem equally effective.
   c. Referent, expert, and legitimate power would be less costly than reward or coercive power.
   d. Referent power is the most important and effective basis of power.

Chapter 8
Message Inputs

P R E V I E W

¶ *What are message inputs?*
The elements of a message that influence public communication

¶ *What is a message?*
What the source says or writes in a public communication situation

¶ *What is the form of the message?*
The organization of the source's message

¶ *What are the major functions of a message introduction?*
Identifying what is to be discussed and why
Identifying what is not to be discussed
Defining key terms
Providing background information
Identifying the message form

¶ *What is the primacy-recency problem?*
Determining if message arguments presented first (primary) or last (recency) have the greatest message effect

¶ *What are the major functions of a message conclusion?*
Summarizing the message
Making a direct appeal for change

¶ *What is the content of a message?*
The information and appeals contained in a message

¶ *What are three types of message appeals?*
Factual
Emotional
Humorous

¶ *What is message-sidedness?*
The number of different positions on a particular message topic

¶ *What are two types of audience participation?*
Active
Passive

¶ *What are message distractors?*
Anything that diverts the audience's attention during the presentation of a message

¶ *What is delivery?*
The way a message is spoken and presented to an audience

O B J E C T I V E S

After reading this chapter, you should be able to
1. identify the main elements of the message that influences public communication.
2. define the meaning of the term *message*.
3. explain the effect of message organization on receiver retention, comprehension, and change.
4. identify the functions introductions can serve for the message.
5. differentiate between primacy and recency effects.
6. differentiate between implicit and explicit conclusions.
7. identify the functions conclusions can serve for the message.
8. explain the effects of evidence on receivers.
9. distinguish between the types of message appeals.
10. explain how message appeals effect the receivers.
11. differentiate between one and two-sided messages.
12. explain the relationship between message-sidedness and receivers.
13. differentiate between one-sided and two-sided messages.
14. define and explain the term *distractors*.
15. explain the effect of message presentation on the receiver.

THE Ford Granada moved slowly through the crowded Los Angeles freeway traffic. Gertrude Stone, the silver-haired and brilliant president of *Women for Israel,* was driving with her program chairwoman, Bessie Colodzin. They were on their way to the regional fund raising dinner at the Beverly Hilton and Gertrude's mind was on the address she was to deliver.

Her goal was to raise one million dollars for a new research wing at the Medical Center on Mt. Scopus in Israel.

"You've spoken before this particular group, Bessie. Who will be willing to give the most support," she asked.

Message Inputs

Bessie, past regional director of the Los Angeles area, answered thoughtfully: "Well, I know that the Sharon Chapter is always willing to pitch in and do their best, that is, if they know what you really want. They're a great group of workers."

"Oh, I know that!" replied Gertrude impatiently. "But what do they want?"

"Look, they'll do the job if they understand the value of our goal," Bessie responded.

"What do they know about the hospital?" She paused for a moment, thinking to herself, "I'll need to begin with some background on the project, follow with a listing of the latest medical research at the Center—before I ask for their assistance."

A sales executive arrives at the Thrifty Supermarket offices for a meeting on his latest product, *Instant Lunch*. The home office staff and managers from each of the thirty markets were assembled in the conference room awaiting his promotional routine. Sitting in back of a rectangular table in front of the gathering he began:

"Gentlemen, it goes without saying that I have for you today one of the most outstanding new products ever to be prepared for the average shopper."

The introduction caused a perceptible shudder throughout the managers, but the sales executive failed to notice their reaction. He continued by telling the managers how he expected them to introduce his new product. His comments were directed primarily to a small cluster of men located at the far end of the room. His remarks were peppered with such expressions as "You see, men" and "You know what I mean." Each time the managers winced. Eyes darted back and forth. Papers were shuffled.

The meeting completed, the salesman, by then aware that something was amiss during his talk, asked a friend in the group, "Something seemed wrong. Did I do something out of line?"

"Oh, really it's nothing. Don't worry, for goodness sake," his friend explained. "It's just that—er—the managers weren't familiar with the product."

"But they know what to do, don't they?"

"I guess so, but you assumed too much. They rarely push products they aren't sold on."

A young, attractive woman representing the Better Business Bureau arrived to address a homeowners cooperative on the topic of consumer savings. She began by identifying herself with the audience and defining her terms:

Everyone listening to me talk tonight is a consumer like myself. We know a consumer is one who consumes, that is, uses up goods and services. We all are restricted by the amount of money we have to spend. We face many problems in determining how to spend our money in a way that gets the most out of it.

She proceeds by examining the plight of American consumers and a method for solving their problem.

. . . while I have called the consumer bewildered, others have referred to him as a "boob" . . . while these harsh descriptions are not entirely deserved, they do serve to illustrate the weakness of the consumer's bargaining position when making a purchase. The less affluent the consumer, the more valuable he or she becomes . . . We require low prices, but overpay for inferior merchandise. We must buy economically, yet frequently have available only the most uneconomical sizes and quantities. We require substantial information, yet this is the commodity we most seriously lack . . . "Let the buyer beware" is still the rule of the marketplace.

One way we can all help ourselves is to form a cooperative. A consumer cooperative is a business enterprise organized by consumers who make a modest investment and whose pooled funds are then used to provide the goods and services for which it was organized . . . Profits, economies, and savings derived from efficient management and quantity buying are returned to the membership of the cooperative. The "profits" thus earned by the cooperative are divided on the basis of purchases made and services used by the members. . . . While much remains to be done in the United States to organize cooperatives more effectively, nevertheless, it is one way in which we can protect ourselves from the law of the jungle which prevails in the marketplace. It is perhaps the best way to guarantee we will get a dollars worth for a dollar spent.

The crucial element in the public communication situation was the message in each of the previous examples. The *message*, or *that which the source says or writes*, is a necessary element for any communication transaction. It is the vehicle by which contact is made between source and receiver within a specific environmental context. Messages are composed of symbols, verbal and nonverbal, that elicit particular meanings and responses from receivers. These symbols must have shared meaning for both source and receiver if the message is to be understood by all involved parties. Our sales executive in an earlier example assumed that his receivers knew what he was talking about. It was a fatal mistake in this situation; having potentially disastrous effects upon the sales of his product.

Because the message is only one element in our public communication system, its form, content, and method of presentation are related to the source, receiver, and environment. A Sierra Club representative explaining the problems of offshore oil drilling to a social club might focus on how oil spills spoil the landscape. Delivering the same message to a business organization, the man might launch into statistics on the cost of cleaning up after accidents. To school children, he might point out the fearful toll that oil leaks can take on local wildlife. The message must fit into the total system for it to have an effect on the receiver. Imagine a situation in which a parent is talking to his local PTA. He leans on the table, hands trembling, voice quivering, and shouts, "Friends, I'm troubled. The Governor has said he intends to provide school support, but you know how that always ends up. Will you join me in writing to our state senator, urging him to support our cause." A number of messages have been communicated by the speaker. The quivering voice and trembling hands are non-verbal symbols that may indicate to the receiver that he is tense, nervous, and disturbed. The verbal message provided the apparent reason for his distress and a desired response by the audience.

For his appeal to be successful, the audience must correctly interpret the nonverbal and verbal symbols. In addition, the audience must understand the meaning of the total message. For example, the speaker states "to provide school support, but you know how that always ends up." The audience must share the meanings for these two ideas for the message to make sense and provide justification for the response.

Because all messages are related to the receivers, it is critical that it be adapted to their particular interests and needs. Gertrude Stone, for instance, was concerned with providing the kind of information required to engender support from a particular group in her audience. The representative of the Better Business Bureau clealy identified her needs with those of the audience and provided a method for meeting those needs.

In this chapter we'll investigate the main elements of a *message* in the public communication system. Three basic message areas are separated for analysis: the organizational characteristics, or the form of a message; the ideas and arguments presented, or the content of a message; and methods for expressing the content. We should recognize that although we talk about three distinct message areas, they are not perceived as being distinct by most receivers. Each single area has an impact on the other elements. In turn, the message, although discussed separately from environment receiver, and source, never occurs without the presence and effects of these public communication elements. As we examine each message area we will identify the input variables affecting the public communication system.

Form of the Message

You are sitting around a table in the student cafeteria and talking with classmates about a lecture you've just heard in the campus auditorium. The lecture is the teacher's primary message. In response to his message you might suggest, "he really sounded disorganized." Other students may express displeasure over his failure to tie the message together or put forth his arguments properly. All three responses are expressing concern over the organizational characteristics or form of the message. Messages are composed of a number of symbols, but meaning is derived from the ordering of symbols into sentences, paragraphs, chapters, arguments, summaries, and so on.

Why should we be concerned with the form of our message? Why not provide receivers with the information we feel is necessary, and leave it at that? Some people assume that providing a message without consideration of its form will still produce the desired effect. Unfortunately, for many speakers this rarely occurs. Merely telling the receiver the facts doesn't necessarily influence their beliefs, attitudes, intentions, or behavior.

Does it really matter whether or not a message is presented in an orderly fashion? In general, an orderly presentation of a message will be more influential, better understood, and will help the speaker appear more reliable. Whereas minor disorganization seems to have little impact on a message's influence, major dislocations (transposing introductions, transitions, and conclusions) weaken the effect of a message. And the receiver's retention of the message is affected by the arrangement of material; the more disorganized the message, the less retained by the audience.[1]

INTRODUCTION

Most speakers and teachers of speech communication tell us that a proper introduction is the prerequisite for achieving a de-

1. Baker, E. G., "The Immediate Effects of Perceived Speaker Disorganization on Speaker Credibility and Audience Attitude Change in Persuasive Speaking," *Western Speech* 29 (1965), pp. 148–161; Jones, J. A., and G. R. Serlousky, "An Investigation of Listener Perception of Degrees of Speech Disorganization and the Effects on Attitude Change and Source Credibility," Paper presented at the ICA convention, Atlanta, Georgia, 1972; Applbaum, R. L., and K. W. E. Anatol, *Strategies for Persuasive Communication* (Columbus, Ohio: Charles E. Merrill, 1974), p. 73.

sired message effect. Like the overture of a Broadway musical, it primes the audience. It can also relax listeners, grab their attention, or make them receptive to influence attempts. Does a speech really need an introduction? Surprisingly, there is little evidence that supports the necessity of an introduction. Although the evidence is scarce and inconclusive, the effect of an introduction appears to relate to the source and the receivers' involvement in the topic. Well-liked sources, for instance, will be more influential if they announce their intent to persuade, whereas disliked sources will be less influential if the audience is immediately informed of the intent.[2] Allyn and Festinger found that when receivers were told that a message would clash with their views, they changed to a lesser extent than if they had not been informed of the message's position.[3] Although we lack information on the effect of introductions, it is clear that they can serve a number of functions.

1. *Identifying what is to be discussed and why.* Many speeches fail to reveal their purpose until the very end. When this occurs, audiences tend to lose interest, may misperceive the actual goal, or may begin to suspect the speaker's motives. It's difficult even for the most intelligent listener to follow a detailed presentation without some recognition of the message's purpose. The introduction should clearly identify the topic of the speech and the goal of the speaker, whether we want our audience to gain information, change a belief, or take some action. Rather than saying, "We should all do something about the energy problem," we might say, "All of us have the responsibility to find and implement a plan for decreasing our dependency on foreign oil reserves."

2. *Identifying what is not to be discussed.* Too often, audiences expect from the speaker more than her or she ever intends to deliver. It is important, therefore, that the speaker note those areas of the topic that will not be covered. A speaker discussing the oil importation problem might say, "I'm not going to advocate that we stop all imports—there's no question that we cannot meet our country's needs solely on our reserves. However, what I am going to discuss is a plan for

2. Mills, J., and E. Aronson, "Opinion Change as a Function of the Communicator's Attractiveness and Desire to Influence," *Journal of Personality and Social Psyhcology* 1 (1965), pp. 173–177.

3. Allyn, J., and L. Festinger, "The Effectiveness of Unanticipated Persuasive Communications," *Journal of Abnormal and Social Psychology* 62 (1961), pp. 35–40.

decreasing dependency on foreign oil and increasing the use of alternative energy sources."

3. *Defining key terms.* In most instances, the speaker is more knowledgeable than the audience on the speech topic. If an understanding of the speech rests on certain terms or concepts, it is crucial that the speaker define them in order that the audience can follow the speaker's line of reasoning.

A speech teacher, for example, may define nonverbal communication as "all source and receiver messages, except the production of verbal messages, performed in a communication context." Because this definition is quite abstract, it may be necessary for the instructor to provide students with examples. For instance, "When people talk, they often shift forward and backward, wave their hands or pocket them, frown in disbelief or wink, stammer hesitantly, or speak in solemn tones. All of these behaviors communicate some impression to the participants in a communication situation. Because the messages are not transmitted with the use of verbal language, we call them "nonverbal communication." Definition by example provides clarity and an experiential basis for understanding key terms.

4. *Providing background information.* A speaker may wish to introduce historical material on the topic prior to presenting his or her main ideas or arguments. If the audience is unfamiliar with the topic, the speaker should provide the background information necessary for educating the audience. Background information also can establish the need for change or existence of a problem.

5. *Identifying the message form.* If the speech is complex or presents a number of arguments, the speaker might provide an overview in the introduction. This will assist the audience in retaining the main ideas or parts of the speech. The speaker might say, "Today, I intend to present five major arguments against offshore oil drilling in the United States" or "I will begin with a historical background of oil drilling in America, turn to five disadvantages of offshore drilling, and follow with a discussion of legislation needed to stop oil drilling of our coasts."

Once we have introduced the message topic, our task of informing, changing, or reinforcing the receiver has begun. The functions described for introductions are needed once again as we proceed through the body of the speech; new terms will need to be defined and additional background material will be necessary. Transitional statements and internal summaries will be needed to remind the audience of what is being discussed or not discussed and how the message is to proceed. Main headings will be needed to clearly identify the new sections of the message.

We now turn our attention to the positioning of information or arguments in the body of our message.

ORDERING OF INFORMATION

Let's imagine we have a message that is to be presented before a group of students. This message contains a number of important pieces of information that we want the students to remember. Hopefully, the information will provide the impetus for change. Where do we place the information or arguments? When receivers are not interested in our message, the major arguments should be placed first to arouse or maintain their interest. If the arguments are at the end of the message, disinterested receivers may lose all motivation or may simply not listen. When the audience is interested in the message topic, however, it is better to place the arguments last.[4]

If we are presenting a message that utilizes both sides of an issue, do we present the side we favor first or last? This is called a primacy-recency problem. We are concerned with whether the message arguments presented first (primacy) or last (recency) have the greatest effect. Cohen remarks that "the advantages of one order over the other depend on the particular conditions under which the communication is presented, including the predispositions of the audience and the type of material being presented."[5]

In a review of primacy-recency literature, he set forth the following generalizations:

1. When speakers are presenting two sides of an issue, there is no advantage in speaking first, because a variety of conditions (time, audience, place, and so on) may determine the more influential speaker.
2. When listeners are publicly committed to one side of an argument, the second side is not likely to change their position. This intransigence may be based on a need to save face. Changing positions might make one appear inconsistent, suggestible, or even dishonest.

4. Karlins, M., and H. Abelson, *Persuasion: How Attitudes and Opinions Are Changed* (New York: Springer Publishing Co., Inc., 1970).
5. Cohen, A. R., *Attitude Change and Social Influence* (New York: Basic Books, 1964), pp. 8–9.

3. When a speaker presents both sides of an issue, we usually are influenced more by the side presented first. If there is activity between presentations, or if we are warned by the speaker of the possibility of being misled, then what is said last seems to have more effect.
4. If listeners do not become interested in a subject until *after* receiving information about it, they may have difficulty retaining and applying that information. On the other hand, if they are already interested in the subject, they will carefully store and be able to apply that information. If you know you're going to Europe, you will eagerly absorb details from a lecture on Europe. But if you find out about your trip *after* the lecture, much information will have eluded your grasp.
5. Attitudes change more if desirable, acceptable ideas are presented before less desirable ones. If, early in the message, a source presents ideas that are agreeable to us, the audience is more likely to be responsive and accept what follows. However, if he starts off with points that disturb us, we may become critical and are likely to reject subsequent ideas, even if they are sound and agreeable.
6. The pro-con order is more effective than the con-pro order when used by an authoritative source whom the audience respects. We are more favorably influenced if she begins with arguments supporting her position and *then* presents those counter to her position.
7. The last heard argument is *more* effective when there is a long delay between two messages, and testing immediately follows the second message.

In a similar vein, a source should present a problem to an audience before solutions are presented. The need-plan order is more effective, both in the short run and in respect to delayed effects, presumably because it is more interesting and better understood.

Cohen states that "taken as a whole, the findings regarding primacy and recency seem to rule out any universal principle of primacy in persuasion."[6] Rosnow and Robinson make the following statement regarding the possibility of either a law of primacy or recency:

Instead of a general law of primacy or recency, we have today an assortment of miscellaneous variables, some which tend to produce primacy (primacy-bound variables), other of which, to produce re-

6. Cohen, op. cit., pp. 9–16.

cency (recency-bound variables). Still others produce either order effects, depending on their utilization or temporal placement in a two-sided communication (free variables). Nonsalient, controversial topics, interesting subject matter, and highly familiar issues tend toward primacy. Salient topics, uninteresting subject matter, and moderately unfamiliar issues tend to yield recency. If arguments for one side are perceived more strongly than arguments for the other, then the side with the stronger arguments has the advantage—'strength' being the free variable. Another free variable is 'reinforcement.' When incidents that are perceived as rewarding or satisfying are initiated close in time to a persuasive communication, opinions tend to change in the direction of the arguments closer to the rewarding incident. When an incident is dissatisfying, or punishing, opinions tend to change in the direction of the arguments farther in time from it.[7]

CONCLUSION

We've all had the experience of listening to a speech when the speaker suddenly stops talking and sits down, leaving us hanging in mid-air, or heard a speaker who concludes his presentation with the remark, "In summary, I have presented five key points for discussion. . . . Thank you." These concluding remarks and actions are both abrupt and unsatisfactory. All speeches need a proper eading.

The proper use of conclusions is no less a situational phenomenon than an introduction or argument placement. Their effectiveness is related to the message topic, receiver characteristics, and type of conclusions. There are two basic types of conclusions: *explicit* and *implicit*. Implicit conclusions leave the audience to infer the proper action or belief based upon ideas presented in the speech. Explicit conclusions, to the contrary, spell out the specific actions or beliefs desired by the speaker. Research suggests that when dealing with educated audiences, such as a group of college students, and the message is simple, it is best to use implicit conclusions. Some receivers will view an explicit statement as propaganda and become hostile or suspicious of the message and speaker. However, conclusions should be stated explicitly when the message is complex and receivers are either less intelligent or initially unfavorable to the message's point of view.[8]

What major functions can a conclusion perform for the message? First, the conclusion can *summarize the message*. A conclusion is extremely helpful in tying together the main ideas or arguments presented by the speaker. They can remind the audi-

7. Rosnaw, R., and E. Robinson, eds., *Experiments in Persuasion* (New York: Academic Press, Inc., 1967).

8. Applbaum, R. L., and Anatol, K. W. E., op. cit., pp. 91–92.

ence of the major points in the presentation and restate the speaker's primary and secondary goals. Second, the conclusion can *make a direct appeal for change.* The conclusion of a speech is the ideal place to ask for change by receivers, that is, to take some action or adopt a certain belief. Be forewarned that although speakers who ask for greater change produce more than those who ask for less change, the actual change is generally less than that requested by the speaker.

In this section, we discussed the organization of a message, including information on introductions, conclusions, messages, and the ordering of information. In the next section, we will examine the content of the communication—the specific information that the source transmits to the receiver. We will attempt to discover what types of information have the greatest influence on the receiver.

Content of the Message

If the organization of a speech is the cement, its content represents the building blocks of our message. Yet how often have you heard a friend bemoan the failure of politicians to discuss the issues? How often, after listening to a speech, have you walked away and remarked, "Gee, she sounded great, but I don't think she said anything."

When presenting our message to an audience, we must be just as concerned with *what* information is contained in the message, as *how* we order that information. The proper use of information, evidence, or appeals must be viewed in the context of a public communication system. Message content interacts with message organization, the speaker's mode of delivery, characteristics of the receiver, and the situation.

We will limit our discussion of message content to the use of evidence, message appeals (emotional and factual and humorous), and one-sided and two-sided messages.

EVIDENCE

Two very difficult decisions a speaker must make are: (1) *what* evidence should be used in the message and (2) *how much* evidence is needed to achieve the speaker's goal. From numerous research studies on the effect of message evidence, we can arrive at some very general conclusions that should help us in making our decisions.

Evidence in a message seems to be related to the credibility of a source. A less credible source gains credibility by inclusion of evidence. Students, for instance, when delivering classroom speeches, should be careful to provide enough documentation to lend credence to their position or goal. Students are rarely viewed as credible sources by either teachers or fellow students. A teacher, who is a high credibility source in the classroom, would not need as much evidence to support a position. A speech teacher, for example, could make conclusions regarding the use of evidence in speeches without citing research studies, and would be quite influential. A highly credible source will lose credibility, however, if evidence is not included following another presentation on the same subject that included evidence.

The amount of evidence needed in a message is related to the message topic. If we are listening to a speaker trying to convince us that we should have yearly medical checkups, the topic will need little evidence for support as we are quick to recognize the value of medical checkups. If the speaker is trying to convince us that we should not support the building of nuclear power plants, evidence on this topic seems essential. Most of us have little prior knowledge or evidence on this subject. If listeners are familiar with the evidence presented, they will be more influenced by it. For example, if we have just finished reading articles arguing against the building of nuclear power plants, we would be more receptive to a speaker who cited that very evidence than if we had not been previously exposed to the articles.

The acceptance of evidence will be influenced by whether we perceive the evidence as reliable. If we are listening to a speaker using evidence on a specific topic, that evidence must appear relevant to the topic, and must be presented by a credible source to be accepted (for instance, Ralph Nader using the accident record of the Chevrolet Corvair to establish the problem of automobile safety). If we do perceive the evidence to be irrelevant, or to come from an unacceptable source, we are inclined to discount the speaker's message. In 1973 presidential aides used Nixon's statements as evidence to indicate that a Watergate coverup did not exist. A majority of Americans found both source and information unreliable and unacceptable.

The effect of evidence also seems to be influenced by the delivery of the source; poor delivery lowers the impact of evidence. The beginning speaker often fails to recognize that merely gathering a sufficient amount of evidence is not enough to achieve one's goal. We must also be concerned with how the evidence is presented to our listeners. Chapter 13 will discuss ways speeches should be delivered.

It is quite obvious from our discussion that evidence is interrelated with the source, receiver, the perceptual processes of both, the presentation of the message, and the speaking situation.

MESSAGE APPEALS

A speaker may attempt to influence a receiver by making certain appeals that he hopes will motivate the listener to accept the source's position. We will examine three very different motivational appeals: emotional, factual, and humorous.

We've all heard that it's better to appeal to the heart than to the head. Many speakers think they can be very successful if they make use of the audience's emotional response toward certain topics. Some people believe humor is a very effective device for motivating audience change or reinforcing existing beliefs, whereas others suggest that speakers should concentrate on the facts or evidence. It is not surprising that research on these types of appeals has been inconclusive. The effectiveness of appeals depends on the mood of the audience, the issue to be discussed, and the composition of the audience. One would be foolish to use humorous appeals on the topic of cancer or purely emotional appeals when attempting to get smokers to quit smoking. It appears that *no type* of motivational appeal *is always superior.*

One type of emotional appeal that has received extensive study is the use of fear as a motivational change agent. The use of fear in public communication has not been uncommon throughout history. More recently, however, it has been used frequently as a political strategy. In the presidential campaign of 1964, one classic television commercial for Lyndon B. Johnson attempted to suggest nuclear war should his opponent, Barry Goldwater, be elected. During the Republican primaries of 1976 a similar picture was painted of Ronald Reagan. In the Los Angeles mayoral race of 1974, the incumbent attempted to scare voters into voting against his opponent by suggesting that this opponent, a black man, would ruin the city. In this particular election, the incumbent's use of fear appeals was so unsuccessful that he was soundly defeated at the polls. It appears that at times fear appeals can be successful as influencing agents within a message. However, are appeals to fear generally successful? Are there different types of fear appeals? When are they successful or unsuccessful?

Over twenty years ago, Janis and Feshback laid the cornerstone for modern research on fear appeals by examining three types of such appeals and their effect in producing change among groups of high school students regarding dental hygiene. One group received a strongly threatening lecture that included the possibility of cancer among the consequences of poor oral hygiene. The second group received a mildly threatening lecture that condemned people who neglected their teeth to nothing worse than a few cavities. The third group received a lecture of an intermediate degree of fear. Janis and Feshback found that the more threatening the lecture, the more worry students expressed immediately after the lecture. After a period of one week, however, they found that the group subjected to the least amount of fear conformed most to the message. They concluded that under conditions where people are exposed to competing messages dealing with the same topic, the use of a strong fear appeal tends to be less effective than a minimal threat appeal in producing a change in attitude.[9] We might suggest that high fear appeals produce threats that receivers are more likely to meet with defense mechanisms. Hence, they become more resistant to the high fear appeal in a message.

Low fear appeals, however, are not always the best means of producing attitude or behavior change. Leventhal and Watts exposed audiences at a state fair to high, medium, and low fear appeals on the topic of nonsmoking. In their persuasive message, they recommended that the audience stop smoking and take an X-ray at a nearby mobile unit to detect the presence of cancer. They found that audiences exposed to the high fear appeals stopped smoking more significantly than those exposed to the lesser fear appeals. However, the audiences exposed to the low fear appeals were more likely to have the chest X-ray. They suggested that the extreme fear that produced an avoidance reaction for the audience members forced them to avoid the further possibility of fear coming from the X-ray. Thus, the high fear appeal group selected an alternate method for reducing the threat—they stopped smoking.[10] It's also been found that high fear appeals are successful in modifying behavior when using the mass media, television, radio, or newspapers as agents for transmitting the message.

Many factors influence the effectiveness of fear appeals in messages. Strong fear appeals surpass weak fear appeals in effectiveness when the message is of low interest value or low relevance to the audience. The dramatic nature of the high fear appeal may make the message more interesting. Even high credibility source using a high fear message would be more effective when using a low fear message. His credibility may make the appeal more believable, or lend credence to the information provided, thus mak-

9. Janis, I., and S. Feshback, "Effects of Fear-Arousing Communications," *Journal of Abnormal and Social Psychology* 48 (1953), pp. 78–92.

10. Leventhal, H., and J. C. Watts, "Sources of Resistance to Fear-Arousing Communications on Smoking and Lung Cancer," *Journal of Personality* 34 (1966), pp. 155–175.

ing it more difficult for the receiver to discredit the influence attempt. Strong fear appeal that poses a threat to the receiver's family produces a greater change in attitude than would a mild appeal. Our defense mechanisms may not be able to cope as easily with a threat to a loved one as a threat to ourselves. Even irrelevant fear appeals may facilitate the acceptance of a message. It is suggested that this might occur because the fear appeal serves as a distractor (we'll discuss the role of distractors later in the chapter).

Fear appeals seem to be effective in changing behavior when: (1) immediate action can be taken on recommendations included in the appeal and, (2) when specific instructions are provided for carrying out the message's recommendations. Cronkhite recommends that the communicator present a specific course of action and demonstrate that it's effective and feasible whenever a strong fear is used. The source may confidently use the strong fear appeal, followed by a specific plan of action, when the receivers have a history of being able to cope with problems and when the suggested action is aggressive in nature, does not create a further threat, and does not appear too difficult. The fear appeal also should be realistic enough that the receiver cannot easily feel unconcerned, and should not present an excess of fear that might appear ridiculous rather than frightening.[11]

Humorous appeals have long been used in public communication. We know, for example, that the ancient Greeks were masters of the art of ridicule. Today most successful speakers, including politicians, advertisers, ministers, and even teachers, use humor in their messages. Jimmy Carter and Billy Graham have used humor to their advantage in persuading vastly different audiences to their positions on particular topics. However, some speakers find it very difficult to be humorous, regardless of the topic or audience. Many speakers disclaim the use of humor by defensively stating, "but I'm not a comedian." How important is the use of humor in a message?

Gruner found that humor is not an influential device in messages. However, he suggested we could use humor as a distractor.[12] If a receiver is initially opposed to the message's position, humor

11. Cronkhite, G., *Persuasion: Speech and Behavioral Change* (New York: The Bobbs-Merrill Co. Inc., 1969), pp. 184–185.

12. Gruner, C. R., "An Experimental Study of the Effectiveness of Oral Satire Modifying Attitude," *Speech Monographs* 32 (1965), pp. 145–65; Gruner, C. R., "A Further Experimental Study of Satire as Persuasion," *Speech Monographs* 33 (1966), pp. 184–185; Gruner, C. R., "Satire As a Reinforcer of Attitude," Paper presented as SCA, Chicago, December, 1972.

Message Inputs

may distract the audience's attention and thus be more influential than a serious message. On the other hand, humor directed at a position we hold may not be very amusing to us. In fact, such humor may create a boomerang effect, causing us to react against the speaker and his position.

It has also been suggested that humor may operate as an attitude reinforcer. Because we laugh at those individuals or groups with which we do not sympathize or identify, we enjoy humor directed against enemy groups and least enjoy humor ridiculing the groups we identify with. Likewise, when we hold specific attitudes, humor directed toward the opposite position will lend support to our. position and reinforce our beliefs. Political spokesmen are masters at satirizing the issues espoused by their opposition.

Humor does have an impact on the credibility of a source. A humorous source may be rated as more trustworthy than a serious one. Thus, a low credibility source might utilize humor to raise the audience's perception of him and, therefore, improve his chances to influence the audience to his particular position.

ONE-SIDED AND TWO-SIDED MESSAGES

We're listening to a woman argue against future construction of nuclear power plants. She points out several problems, such as poor plant safety regulations, disposing of radioactive wastes, and catastrophic disasters resulting from reactor malfunctions. After presenting her position, she asks that we vote for a new proposal that would limit power plant development. Notice that our speaker has presented only one side of the topic. Do not confuse message-sideness with the ordering of arguments. Each message topic has a number of arguments that may be used in some order during the message. We must choose the number of positions on a topic to be presented prior to determining how the arguments will be ordered.

How effective will a speaker be if he or she, presents only one side of a topic? Because most topics have at least two sides, we must decide whether to include more than one alternative in our message. In making a decision, we would suggest that if the audience initially favors the position taken by the message, the one-sided message will be most effective. Politicians, for example, generally avoid discussing an opponent's position when talking to members of their own parties. One-sided messages are generally more effective with less-educated receivers. It may be that they aren't familiar with both sides, or that they already favor the position advocated by the speaker. In fact, one-sided messages tend to be more effective if the audience is in agreement with the speaker's position.

On the other hand, two-sided messages appear more effective when the audience is opposed to the position presented. This forces the listeners to compare the advantages and disadvantages of each side and, thus, observe the value of the speaker's position. Two-sided messages also make a listener more resistant to counterarguments. The counterarguments will not catch receivers by surprise and so, they should be able to ward off any attempts to change their positions. Should your audience be familiar with both sides of an issue, the message effect can be weakened by avoiding one of these sides.[13]

If we were addressing an audience of college students or graduates, it would be best to use a two-sided message. Although results of the findings are inconsistent, it appears that two-sided presentations will be more effective with better educated individuals, regardless of their initial positions.

Presentation of the Message

A tall, slender young man strides to the front of the class. From the pocket of his levis he pulls a set of crumpled index cards, places them on the table to his right, and begins to talk. He directs his speech primarily to those students in the back of the room, disregarding the displeasure shown on the faces of classmates in front. He presents the message in a very conversational manner, talking to the students as friends. His speech is well organized and thoroughly researched; the message is clear and forthright. Yet, when the students are asked to evaluate his speech, the following remarks are repeated over and over again, "He didn't talk to us," "We weren't included in the presentation," "The topic should have been handled more formally." These students were reacting to the manner in which the message was presented to them. We'll examine how message presentation effects public communication. We will specifically investigate the role of audience participation, distractors, and general delivery upon message influence.

ACTIVE AND PASSIVE PARTICIPATION

Let's assume that our communication goal is to reinforce the existing attitudes of students that the present system of grading

13. Karlins, M., and H. I. Abelson, *Persuasion* (New York: Springer Publishing Co., Inc., 1970), pp. 22–26.

standards for public speaking activities is not objective. We have several choices—we can tell the students about the inherent subjectivity of evaluating speeches, have them participate in a discussion, read about the problems of evaluation, or write an essay on grading reliability and validity. Our choices involve the audience in both active and passive participation roles. Active participation requires the audience to take part *personally* in the creation of the message, such as participating in a discussion or writing an essay. Passive participation, on the other hand, leaves the message creation and presentation to someone else—a speaker, television commentator, or book. When we listen to a fifty-minute college lecture, we're participating passively. We must ask, "Will the message have more effect if it is presented actively or passively?"

Watts found that both active and passive participation can lead to opinion change.[14] However, over time, active participants show greater persistence in retaining the opinion change. Furthermore, active participation leads to greater involvement and superior recall of the topic and position supported.

DISTRACTORS

We're sitting in a quiet restaurant with friends; the music is soft, the lights are dim. One friend asks us to sign a petition asking for a change in grading practices. The source has used distractors (meal and music) to enhance his effect in the situation.

Distraction can enhance a source's persuasive efforts. Festinger and Maccoby, for example, had two fraternity groups listen to an antifraternity message. One group viewed a film of a speaker giving the antifraternity lecture; the second group watched a silent comedy while listening to the sound track of the first film. The distracted group (those watching the silent film) were persuaded more by the message.[15]

Distractors differ in their importance as factors in effecting message acceptance. "Generally, persuasive appeals become more powerful when presented in conjunction with moderately distracting stimuli which positively reinforce the individual."[16] Food and sex, for example, act as positive reinforcements and may in-

14. Watts, W., "Relative Persistence of Opinion Change Induced by Active Compared to Passive Participation," *Journal of Personality and Social Psychology* 5 (1967), pp. 4–15.

15. Festinger, L., and N. Maccoby, "On Resistance to Persuasive Communications," *Journal of Abnormal and Social Psychology* 68 (1964), pp. 359–66.

16. Karlins, M., and H. I. Abelson, op. cit.

crease the probability of a successful persuasive attempt. On the other hand, negative reinforcements (foul odors) are generally ineffective in the public communication situation.

DELIVERY

Most of us would support the contention that at times, "it's not what you say, it's how you say it," which effects receivers. We may fall asleep while listening to a speaker deliver a message in a monotone, fail to retain the message, or not understand what has been said. The way a speaker delivers a message to an audience has a tremendous influence over the effectiveness of that effort. Heinberg found delivery to be almost twice as important as content in determining general effectiveness of introductions, and also three times as influential as content in determining effectiveness in various attempts to have an idea accepted.

Delivery encompasses the way a message is presented to an audience in addition to the nonverbal aspects, such as the source's appearance while presenting a message, facial expressions, gestures, and the like. Delivery assists in conveying the actual meaning of our message.

There is a relationship between delivery and the receiver's retention and comprehension of a message. When a speaker varies the rate, force, pitch, and quality of his voice, receivers retain more of the message content than when listening to a static, unvaried presentation (a monotone). A study by Vohs showed that good delivery of complex materials led to better retention, and increased the information-handling capacity of the listener. There is a higher comprehension of message material when the message is presented by vocally skilled sources.[17]

Delivery can influence the amount of attitude change in the listener. Although McCrosky and Arnold did not find that delivery affected immediate attitude change for live, videotaped, or audiotaped speakers, they did find that delivery affected delayed attitude change. They also found that good delivery, coupled with quality content, produced immediate positive attitude change, whereas good delivery of poor content did not.[18] Effective delivery

17. Vohs, J. L. "An Empirical Approach to the Concept of Attention," *Speech Monographs* 31 (1964), pp. 355–360.

18. McCrosky, J. C., and W. Arnold, comment on study in McCrosky, J. C. and R. S. Mehrley, "Effects of Disorganization and Nonfluency on Attitude Change and Source Credibility," *Speech Monographs* 36 (1969), pp. 13–21.

also may raise a speaker's credibility. The higher the credibility of the source, the more likely the effectiveness of the source.

It appears that delivery is an important part of effectiveness in public communication. Like other message components, the quality of delivery interacts with other parts of the public communication system. To achieve effective communication and to enhance our credibility, we should be careful to maintain quality in delivery. We will examine delivery again in Chapter 12.

KEY CONCEPTS

Can you define and give examples of the following terms?

Message
Message form:
  Primacy
  Recency
Explicit conclusion
Implicit conclusion
One-sided message

Two-sided message
Message appeals
Active participation
Passive participation
Distractor
Delivery

PROPOSITIONS

1. The information in a message does not always influence an audience.
2. Message organization can influence an audience.
  a. The organization of a message is a situational phenomenon.
3. Introductions have an effect on receivers.
  a. Introductions alerting receivers that the message will argue against their position are less effective, produce less change.
  b. Receivers change more when a well-liked source admits his or her persuasive intent.
4. The conclusion of a message can have an effect on receivers.
  a. Conclusions should be stated explicitly when using complex messages, addressing less intelligent receivers, and when receivers are initially favorable toward the message position.
  b. Conclusions should be stated implicitly when the problem is simple and receivers are intelligent.
  c. Direct appeals for receiver change should be placed in the conclusions of a message.
  d. Conclusions requesting a great amount of change produce more change than conclusions asking for less change.
5. Message disorganization reduces the message's impact, the

audience's retention of the message, and the receiver's evaluation of the source.

6. No universal rule for ordering information in public communication exists.
   a. There is no advantage in being the first communicator when two sides of an issue are presented.
   b. When a receiver makes a public response about his position after hearing one side of an argument, the second side is less effective.
   c. When one speaker presents two sides of an issue in one presentation, receivers are usually more influenced by the side presented first.
   d. Attitudes change more when desirable ideas precede undesirable ideas.
   e. The pro-con order is more effective than the con-pro order when an authoritative source presents both sides.
   f. If a time lag exists between the presentation of two sides of an issue, the side presented last has an advantage.
   g. When no time lag exists between the presentation of two sides of an issue, the first side has an advantage.

7. The content of a message will affect message influence.

8. The evidence in a message can influence an audience.
   a. A less credible source gains credibility with the inclusion of evidence.
   b. A highly credible source can lose credibility if he does not include evidence.
   c. The effect of evidence will be influenced by the message topic.
   d. Receivers are more influenced by evidence with which they are familiar.
   e. The evidence must be perceived to be relevant and acceptable or the receiver may discount the message.

9. The presentation of one or more sides of a topic may affect the receiver's acceptance of a message.
   a. Two-sided messages are more effective when receivers initially oppose the message position.
   b. One-sided messages are more effective when receivers initially favor the position taken by the message.
   c. Receivers exposed to two-sided presentations are more resistant to counterpropaganda.
   d. Two-sided presentations are more effective with better educated receivers, whereas one-sided presentations are more effective with less educated receivers.
   e. Failure to include both sides of a topic may weaken a per-

suasive attempt if receivers are aware of the opposing arguments.

10. Message appeals have an effect on public communication.
    a. The level of fear producing change is influenced by the personality of the receiver and the message topic.
    b. Fear appeals are effective in changing behavior when immediate action can be taken on appeal recommendations and specific instructions are provided for carrying out the recommendations.
    c. Humor as a distractor may produce greater attitude change.
    d. Humor may operate as a reinforcer of attitudes.
11. The presentation of a message affects the persuasive process.
12. Active participation is more effective than passive participation in producing change in the receiver.
13. Presentation distractors may enhance the effectiveness of the message.
14. The manner of delivery used by a speaker may influence his ability to influence a receiver.
    a. The quality of delivery may affect source credibility.

Chapter 9
Audience Analysis

P R E V I E W

¶ *What are the benefits of audience analysis in planning and designing public communication?*
Audience analysis helps us to determine specific objectives, choice of information, mode of presentation. It also provides some idea about audience background, attitudes, beliefs, needs, commitments, and involvements

¶ *What is ego-involvement?*
Ego-involvement is a term used to describe a person's strength of feeling on an issue

¶ *What demographic characteristics should we study in our analysis of the audience?*
Educational background, intelligence, occupational classification, age, sex, cultural and religious background, and group affiliations

¶ *What are three personality differences that influence the effectiveness of communication?*
Dogmatism, authoritarianism, and self-esteem

O B J E C T I V E S

After reading this chapter, you should be able to
1. discuss the concept of *energizer effect* in an audience.
2. explain how audience analysis enhances the effectiveness of public communication.
3. discuss the various facets or contingencies in a speaker-audience relationship.
4. discuss the various facets or contingencies in an audience-message relationship.
5. explain the three ways in which audiences may be classified or viewed.
6. discuss the various strategies that may be utilized in dealing with various types of audiences.

7. discuss the concept of ego-involvement and its relationship to latitudes of acceptance, rejection, and noncommitment.
8. discuss the demographic characteristics of audiences and their various impacts on responses to messages.
9. discuss the personality differences that may prevail in audiences and show how those differences affect communication.

In 1968; a political candidate for a congressional seat, sensing "that the American people were fed up with the war in Vietnam," declared before an audience that he would devote himself to the "dismantling of the military-industrial establishment" if he were elected. He suggested further that "every war-mongering general should be reduced in rank," and that "American soldiers who took part in killing innocent women and children be charged for the crime of murder if and when they returned to the United States."

The audience, upon hearing his point of view, began to jeer and boo the candidate, and subsequently hurled wadded up paper and paper cups at him. The candidate later told news reporters that he was completely surprised by the reaction because "the people in that part of the state are usually *liberals*, politically."

Regardless of what he thought their political orientation to be, the unfortunate candidate should have *analyzed* his audience beforehand. An analysis of the audience would have shown him (1) that most of his audience would consist of military veterans and retired officers, (2) that a considerable segment of the audience earned their livelihood through the large military base in the area, (3) that the vast majority of the people supported the American involvement in the war, and (4) that the county had the distinction of being first in the nation as far as the number of draftees was concerned.

In retrospect, the candidate erred, not because he dared to reveal his convictions, but because, by failing to understand his audience, he was unable to implement a proper strategy for effective public communication.

Effective public communication is achieved through a skillful intermeshing of numerous inputs. Thus far, we have looked at the social, environmental, source, and message inputs as crucial elements in the public communication process. The final input element is the *audience*. Obviously, public communication would be pointless if no audience existed. Consequently, the audience is central to public communication, and the source's success depends on how the audience receives, perceives, and interprets information. So, it is important for us to understand how audiences are constituted, and how they behave toward sources and messages.

An audience is *not* a passive collection of people who merely wait to perform at the behest of the speaker. On the contrary, the audience is dynamic—ever changing, sometimes resistant, sometimes receptive, and is characterized by a drive toward unification. Mortensen views this drive as a sort of *energizer effect*.[1] The energizing influence works upon both the source and the audience itself. It leads to a quickening of the senses and changes the emotional state of the source. In some instances the speaker's performance is facilitated, and in other instances it is frustrated. The *energizing effect* also induces a state of heightened alertness or physical readiness on the part of the speaker. Thus, it is more proper to view the audience as a psychological entity that exerts a major influence on the speaker's preparation and performance and on the total context of public communication.

What about the audience's influence on its members? Apparently, the influence is the same as that exerted upon the speaker. Upon coming together in an audience, individuals find themselves merging into a sort of *psychological mix*. The psychological mix results in what various researchers have referred to as mental unity, mental contagion, collective oneness, polarization, or social contagion. Whatever the term, the point is this: the behaviors of individual audience members tend to act as cues or stimuli for the behavior of others. As Mortensen puts it, "in large audiences individuals tend to wait for the audience to react before doing so themselves."[2] Acceptance or rejection of an idea may begin with a few members and radiate or ripple through the entire audience. Thus, the speaker must be able to implement strategy derived from the *analysis* of that audience in order to hasten acceptance or slow down resistance.

This chapter deals with a very vital step in planning for public communication, namely, audience analysis—the collecting and analyzing of vital information about the audience. Audience analysis will help you to determine your specific objective or goal, your choice of information, and your mode of presentation. For example, audience analysis will provide some idea about your audience's familiarity with the issue, their knowledge of you as a source, their attitudes, beliefs, and needs, as well as their educational, cultural, and economic backgrounds. This kind of information pro-

1. Mortensen, D. C., *Communication: The Study of Human Interaction* (New York: McGraw-Hill Book Company, 1972), p. 279.
2. Ibid., p. 281.

vides you with a proper perspective on the audience. Because one of the strategies of effective communication begins with a speaker's ability to meet the audience on a common ground before suggesting discrepant points of view, it is reasonable to infer that your sense of what constitutes common ground will be derived from the fruits of your collection and analysis of your potential listeners. Marie Hochmuth Nichols stresses the need for and the nature of audience analysis as follows:

the speech-maker must compose his speech from the available potentials in his audience. He aims to link his propositions to their value systems, and the value systems differ with age, sex, educational development, economic class, social strata, political heritage, specialized interest, and so on. The speaker is a selector. He must exclude certain arguments and include other . . . All this is determined by the audience for which the speech is designed.[3]

Before the actual confrontation with the audience, your analysis must deal with all facets of the audience you plan to address. All audiences have certain general characteristics, but each one constitutes a specific group with its own peculiar needs and idiosyncrasies. For example, the NAACP, the United Farm Workers, the Gray Panthers, the Anti-Defamation League, and the John Birch Society are all organizations of minority groups. That's their general characteristic. But you couldn't successfully make the same presentation to all of them. They are alike, yet different because of their concerns, needs, and so on. The same similarities and differences may hold true for church groups, civic groups, student groups, protest groups, consumer groups, and environmental groups. The essential thrust of your analysis would therefore entail the discovery of facts pertinent to the common and diverse experiences and characteristics of your audience, those factors that will determine attitudes toward you and your topic.

Let us look at one particular audience. We will focus on the factors that the speaker considered en route to the actual encounter.

In this instance, a group of young and middle-aged owners of new homes were meeting to listen to some information on the need to rezone a parcel of land in their community so that a community recreation center could be built. The speaker—a proponent of rezoning—discovered these facts through analysis:

1. The ages in the potential audience ranged from 25–60.
2. Approximately 65 persons would gather for the meetings.

3. Hochmuth, M., ed., A History and Criticism of American Public Address (New York: Longmans, Green, 1955), Vol. 3, p. 10.

3. The members of the audience all live in a new tract where the prices of houses range from $55,000 to $70,000.
4. Each family, except three, has one or more children.

This kind of information is quite useful, but the speaker sensed that it was not sufficient. Some other information needed to be gathered, and it would call for a considerable amount of "digging." The stakes in this kind of public communication are rather high, so a good communicator would find it necessary to carry the analysis even further. Here's what the speaker *had to* find out:

1. Is this particular audience meeting for the first time or has it met before? If so, who was the speaker? What was his or her point of view?
2. What kinds of common interests are shared among the audience? What's their attitude toward recreation and cultural activities?
3. Do they understand the consequences of rezoning? What do they know about tax modification, cost factors, traffic problems?
4. Are there some influential individuals who, upon persuasion, would be willing and able to continue the campaign? (These would constitute the opinion leader that we've talked about in other chapters.)
5. What kinds of attitudes and beliefs prevail among the people? Are they highly involved or neutral about the issue?
6. Do external groups such as land developers, planning commissions, industrial cartels, or city administrators constitute the major competition?

The speaker obtained most of the information, and did a superb job of getting his audience to eventually submit a petition to rezone. The major competition was a large residential development corporation, and once the speaker "dug in," the corporation lost its influence. Your circumstances and the stakes involved may be different from that described in our example, but the homework or analysis must be done.

Audience analysis is vital to your communication strategy. You must begin by asking two important questions: (1) what is it useful to know about the audience? (2) how do I use the information once I've got it? We can approach this question by studying *six* crucial conditions:

1. The relationship between audience and speaker.
2. The relationship between audience and message.
3. The bias of the audience.

4. The ego-involvement of the audience.
5. The demographic characteristics of the audience.
6. The unique "personality" of certain audiences.

We will study each of these conditions separately.

The Audience and Speaker: Analysis of Relationships

Circumstances would be ideal if we could always choose the particular audience with which we would like to work. However, the ideal seldom occurs, and we must work with what's available. Many times you might decide that *not everybody* in the potential audience is immediately necessary to your objective. Strange? Not at all! Remember how the three-step flow of communication operates. Recall that the opinion leaders are the keys in the process. In public communication, the speaker first appeals to the opinion leaders who, in turn, pass their convictions on to the rank and file in the audience. That's the pipeline in public communication, and you should use it whenever practical or possible. By packaging your message for key groups or special auditors within your audience, you are, in effect, multiplying your own efforts through the amplifying effects of secondary communicators (opinion leaders).[4] In many instances, writers, newspeople, and community leaders are considered to be the real audience within the larger audience.

Let's assume that your objective is to advocate a new idea in a particular community, for example, a new program for social welfare. Would it not make for sound strategy if you could at once economize your efforts and reduce a widespread mobilization of opposition by first sounding out people who are more likely to be open-minded, or favorable toward your idea? Of course, the assumption here is that you would have some kind of prior access to these people, but what if you have no guarantee of such access?

Most audiences are generally friendly, courteous, and will give you a chance to be heard. There will be a few exceptions. The reactions to certain topics, such as political issues, ideas that call for drastic change in behavior, and so on, can range from indifferences to outright hostility. It's your task to find out what's likely to occur —will the audience be objective, friendly, hostile, lethargic? Here are some questions you must ask as you make your scouting report:

1. Will the audience be willing to respect me as a speaker? Do they see me as an authority on the subject? If they don't,

4. Clevenger, T., *Audience Analysis* (Indianapolis: The Bobbs-Merrill Company, 1966), p. 33.

what can I do (during my introduction, for example,) to heighten my authoritativeness?

2. Will the audience view me as knowing the nature of their problems and as having their best interests at heart?
3. Will they see me as sharing in their basic value orientations and expressed needs?
4. Have they heard me speak about this issue before? If so, where? How many times?
5. Are my views widely discrepant from theirs?

Once you have sized up your prospective audience, you would have some general idea about how to launch your attack. If you discover that your audience has a favorable image of you, your task would be relatively easy. Rather than being confronted with the giant task of trying to win the audience, you would have the smaller task of maintaining or holding that friendly, respectable relationship. Nevertheless, your task is still one of significant challenge, for you will be presenting ideas that are not entirely acceptable, or that are somewhat contrary to the listener's prevailing ways of looking at things. You should be able to use your common ground with the audience as a launching pad for your arguments.

Suppose that your audience analysis points up the fact that your potential audience may not be inclined to view you as an authority! You'll need to find *reputable* sources of information to back you up—and you must understand the value of the term *reputable*. Don't go quoting arguments from the latest issue of *Skin Jungle* to an audience of Southern Baptists, or any other kind of Baptists for that matter. Choose sources that tie in with the value orientations of your audience. You might also try to incorporate statements, quotations, and arguments from influential people whom the audience respects. This is why research on the issue is so very important. A good rule of thumb is: regardless of the situation, always play it safe on the matter of respect and authority by using supporting comments from respected authorities.

As Andersen, Nichols, and Booth[5] correctly suggest, it is not always easy to determine how an audience will react to you as a speaker. They suggest that as you continue to participate in public communication, you will acquire more skills about how to make audiences accept you. Much of what you can do immediately must

5. Andersen, M., E. Nichols, and H. Booth, *The Speaker and His Audience: Dynamic Interpersonal Communication* (New York: Harper and Row, 1974), p. 262.

be derived from your assessment of your skills as a speaker. Our formula for successful audience-speaker relationships is brief: you must be sincere, knowledgeable about the subject of communication, identify with your audience, and conform to the audience's expectations concerning manner, dress, choice of language, and so on. Follow this advice and you will have fulfilled the first phase of the analysis. We are now ready to proceed to an analysis of audience-message relationships.

The Audience and Message: Analysis of Adaptation

Some information about your prospective audience's knowledge of the message and an estimate of their inclinations would assist you in adapting to your audience. With such information, you would be able to make crucial decisions concerning: (1) topic selection, (2) formulation of your specific purpose, (3) laying out major lines of development, (4) selecting supporting material, and (5) your choice of language. Whatever the nature of the decision, the knowledge gained from audience analysis will enable you to provide for alternative courses of action should the need arise. In other words, the information will help you to *adapt* to the audience situation. Suppose that you are planning a message dealing with wage and price controls, and that from your research on the topic you have found two authorities from which to quote. Let us suppose that the two authorities provide really good materials, support, and that they both argue that increases in wages tend to contribute to increases in prices. The fundamental question is this: which source should you use? The effective speaker's choice will be influenced by the knowledge that he or she is addressing, for example, the California State Employee's Association rather than the California Association of Manufacturers. Different audiences present different psychological mixes; you must be able to read that mix and adapt your message accordingly. There are several other considerations in trying to achieve a good fit between audience and the topic or message. Before you start your packaging, ask yourself these questions:

1. *Will the audience be highly knowledgeable about the subject?* If so, you should be prepared to cope with the bulk of the known arguments against your position. You will need strong arguments, novel approaches, and the most effective kinds of appeals. That kind of audience must be led to see how your position, if adopted, would lead to their goal

achievement. On the other hand, if your audience has little or no knowledge about the issue, you must furnish a background of information. By educating the audience on certain points, they may be less inclined to resist blindly.

2. *Has the audience already heard other speakers talk about the issue?* If they have, and if they are not highly ego-involved to begin with, your major problem will be audience boredom. Here is where the need to present the idea in a novel manner comes into play. Also, if the listeners have heard other speakers convincingly present the opposite point of view, your task becomes more difficult.

3. *How interested or involved is the audience likely to be in the issue?* This question helps you determine how to motivate the audience. How do you *get* their attention? How do you maintain it? Later in this chapter we will discuss the question of interest and involvement in greater detail. Some audiences consist of *neutrals*, some consist of *partisans*, and some consist of a combination of both. The two types present some rather interesting challenges, and we'll talk about that type of strategy in our section on "Audience Bias and Orientation."

4. *How complex or difficult is it to grasp the issue?* Some issues are easy to present; others will require all the creative strategies you can muster. Consider the problems involved in arguing about wage and price controls, the curtailment of defense budgets, or the clean air-environment initiative, as opposed to arguing for later dorm hours, the sale of beer in the union, or the need for streetsweeping in your neighborhood. The presentation of complex issues generally demands well-constructed, logically-argued graphic presentation, or, as Otto Lerbinger puts it, a cognitive design, which is built upon a collection of hard facts and sound reasoning.[6] The cognitive design is based on the idea that before you present a complex issue, you should first try to anticipate the difficulties that your listeners could possibly encounter in understanding or grasping the issue. On some matters, you may have to assume the role of teacher or educator; however, try not to talk down to people. A good rule of thumb is that *when you deal with a complex topic or issue, you will have to educate before you can motivate.*[7]

6. Lerbinger, O., *Designs for Persuasive Communication* (Englewood Cliffs, N. J.: Prentice-Hall, 1972), p. 11.

7. Bettinghaus, E., *Persuasive Communication* (New York: Holt, Rinehart and Winston, 1973), p. 32.

Whether your audience will be inclined to view an issue as being complex or simple, pleasing or upsetting, acceptable or unacceptable, will depend largely on such *demographic features* as: educational background, socioeconomic classification, sex, and so on; *audience bias,* their ego-involvement with the issue; and certain unique *personality characteristics.* We shall discuss the influence of audience bias in the following section.

Audience Bias

A useful way of viewing audiences is to classify them as *partisans, neutrals,* and *opponents.* Of course, this type of classification depends on your listeners' attitudes toward your specific goal.

We believe that this classification has special merits. First, by anticipating the *bias* of your audience—estimating your listeners' partisanship, neutrality, or opposition—your attention is brought to focus again on the very important question of *attitudes* and their impact on communication. Your own attitude is manifested in the proposition you would like accepted. Your audience's attitude toward your proposition provides you with the *bias* of your audience which, in turn, enables you to view your task concretely. An audience's bias has certain dimensions: direction, degree, intensity, consistency, and salience. The *direction* of partisans is toward your proposition, and perhaps toward you, the speaker, as well. The direction of opponents is away from your proposition, and the direction of neutrals is usually doubtful. The *degree* of partisanship, neutrality, or opposition may range from weak to strong. It is useful to know whether you have strong supporters— or strong opponents. Furthermore, among people whose bias reveals direction and degree, it is helpful to estimate or gauge the *salience* of their bias: are they more or less ready or inclined to accept your proposition? Finally, the bias of your audience suggests their orientation toward related ideas and issues. A bias would tend to manifest *consistency:* people who are against "schoolbusing" may also be against an "integrated education," and may even be against the expenditure of funds for improving the quality of education afforded the disadvantaged minorities. To estimate the bias of your audience is to develop a sensitivity to others that is difficult to acquire in other ways.

There is another good reason for determining the bias of an audience. When you know whether your audience is predominantly partisan, neutral, or hostile, you can seek answers to the very practical question: *why* does this audience have this bias toward the proposition? What causes, factors, conditions, and influences have led them to respond in their manner? Your answers will suggest valuable clues for supporting materials and arguments. Assessment of bias may give us further insights into the *quality* of beliefs prevalent in an audience. For example, are their beliefs derived from a thoughtful consideration of the problem? Do they believe strongly because of personal experience and observation? Are they the kind of people who have kept abreast of the problem through discussion and reading? Are they judicious and knowledgeable partisans, or is their partisanship due to insufficient exposure to the problem? Are they indifferent or lukewarm in their partiality, or are they in favor of the proposition because they have been conditioned by family or group allegiances? Can they be regarded as prejudiced or stereotyped partisans? Are the neutrals' doubts based on thoughtful analysis of the matter, or are they due to insufficient information, or to habitual reluctance to make up their minds? There are many people who, encountering doubt, simply cast the issue aside and turn away from it. Can the neutrals, then, be classified as reasonable doubters, ignorant doubters, or chronic doubters who generally refrain from commitment?

Because *audience bias* may generally reflect a variety of attitudes toward a speaker and the topic or issue, it is not easy to advise you what to do. Should you plan your main attack for the neutrals or the opponents? Can you afford to neglect the partisans? A reasonable answer is that it all depends on the subject, the audience, and the occasion. Your own judgment, common sense, and tact are at a premium here. At the risk of being too simplistic, we shall suggest some guidelines to assist you in your first attempts.

STRATEGIES FOR INFLUENCING NEUTRALS

Neutrals, whether well-informed or ill-informed, haven't made up their minds. We would advise you to seize the chance to guide them. If they have had too little information on which to base commitment, they should welcome information. It is easier to contend with neutrals than with opponents, a fact that political campaigners recognize quite well. Campaigns generally aim at two objectives: (1) to hold the interest and support of partisans, and (2) to swing or "pull in" those who are uncommitted or vacillating. Here are three strategies for your consideration:

1. *Focus precisely on the major objection (or objections) that has caused your audience to postpone their decision, and an-*

swer *that objection with the best argument or evidence available.* People often vacillate because there is one aspect of a situation or problem that bothers them. They say, "Yes, so-and-so and so-and-so is true, but there is still one matter I am still not sure about." They are what we call judicious doubters; they want to be sure on all vital aspects of the issue, and if there is any doubt, they reserve decision and refrain from action.

Take this objection, for example, that some members of your audience may submit: "In theory, your idea is all right and we're for it, but you simply cannot put it into practice—it won't work!" How do you deal with this response? Well, you can show them how your proposal has actually worked elsewhere. Or you might draw a vivid sketch of how it might work, with enough detail to make the plan seem dynamic and appealing. A sketch of your idea in action constitutes a strong stimulus for commanding attention and perception. As Bryant and Wallace[8] suggest "The greatest virtue of the communicator has often been considered his or her power not only to make people *understand* but to make them *see.*"

2. *Give emphasis to one aspect of the problem or to one solution, and subordinate, deemphasize, or omit other sides of the question and other solutions.* Frequently, some neutrals see no great objections one way or another, but all sides and alternatives look equally attractive; at one moment they lean one way, at the next moment, another. If this circumstance exists, you should make your solution or idea appear as attractive as possible by "forcing" or enticing your audience to concentrate upon it. You should find a way to maintain attention and to exclude competing, unfavorable ideas.

3. *In addressing neutrals, use many facts and as much evidence as is appropriate.* With this approach, you will tend to satisfy those neutrals who are undecided because of insufficient information. If you have the chance to discuss the matter beforehand with a few potential members of your audience, you should watch for such responses as "I don't know" (a sign of inadequate information?), "I just can't make up my mind" (a sign of vacillation?), and "I see what you're saying, but there's still one thing . . ." (a sign of one bothersome objection?).

8. Bryant, D., and K. Wallace, *Fundamentals of Public Speaking* (New York: Appleton-Century-Crofts, 1974), p. 319.

STRATEGIES FOR INFLUENCING NEUTRALS AND PARTISANS

Your concern for the neutrals should not lull you into overlooking the partisan members of your audience. Two strategies are helpful:

1. *Ensure that the components of your message—arguments, structure, organization, and ideas—are as interesting as possible.* Some of the ideas that you direct toward the neutrals, or perhaps all of the ideas, will be old and familiar to those partisans who are knowledgeable. Thus, your major concern would be to safeguard against boredom and possible alienation.

   In being interesting you are employing sound strategy on partisans who may be lowly or minimally committed to your orientation or point of view. Moreover, by including information for the ill-informed neutrals in your audience, you are also appealing to the minimally committed partisan, because their minimal commitment may be due to the fact that they lack any real knowledge or convincing arguments concerning the issue. You must be interesting if "conflict avoiders" and "decision procrastinators" are to be present.

2. *Avoid ideas that may tend to alienate the partisans.* Suppose you were arguing or proposing that an investigation of the price-fixing methods of the pharmaceutical industry should be undertaken, and that some of your listeners are indeed sympathetic to the idea but they do not like Ralph Nader, the foremost consumer advocate. To mention his name in support of your contention would not be beneficial to you or to your argument. Let sleeping animosities lie unless you have some good reason for waking them. You would find this especially true in addressing prejudiced partisans.

   You need not appeal to or condone the prejudice of irrational partisans. The attitudes that feed their prejudice, such as loyalty to a particular civic, ethnic, religious, political, or social group, are likely to be so broad that they will apply them automatically to almost anything said or implied.

STRATEGIES FOR INFLUENCING PARTISANS

In some instances, your entire audience may be comprised of people who are already convinced about the soundness of an idea and the practicality of a certain course of action. Such as audience is overwhelmingly partisan. May such good fortune fill all of your days! Given such partisanship, you should concern yourself with one of two objectives: (1) to reinforce the soundness of the idea, encouraging them to take action whenever the opportunity arises; and (2) to urge them to undertake a definite and specific action immediately. In either case, your main concern is to *intensify* their attitude.

We hinted earlier in this chapter that an audience's bias is merely *one* of several conditions with which the communicator should be concerned when conducting the analysis of the audience. Ego-involvement is one of these other conditions. Its impact is significant and should be discussed in some depth.

Ego-Involvement of the Audience

Ego-involvement is a term used to describe a person's strength of feeling on an issue. One of the assumptions of the theory of ego-involvement is that if you know how strong or intense a person's feelings are on a topic, you will be able to predict how the person will react to messages on that topic. If you have an intense or confident attitude about a topic, or if the topic is important or salient to you, you are said to be highly ego-involved in it. Basically, the prediction is that *highly ego-involved people are more difficult to persuade than lowly involved people.*[9]

In order to predict the persuasibility or the obstinacy of your audience, you will have to know how that audience has reacted in the past to various positions that have been expressed about a given controversial issue. Each person (1) has his or her own (firmly committed) position on an issue; (2) finds some of the other stands on the issue acceptable; and (3) rejects some of the other stands on the issue. For example, if you favor forced busing to achieve school integration (that's your firmly committed or personal position), you may also be willing to accept the idea of integration convened only in certain model or "magnet" schools (that's somebody else's position), but you will reject outright the position that an avowed segregationist might take. The range of

9. The basic notion of ego-involvement can be found in Muzafer Sherif and Carl I. Hovland, *Social Judgment*, Yale University Press, New Haven, 1961; C. W. Sherif, and R. E. Nebergall, *Attitude and Attitude Change*, W. B. Saunders, Philadelphia, 1965; and Carolyn W. Sherif and Muzafer Sherif (eds.) *Attitude Ego-Involvement and Change*, John Wiley, New York, 1967; For excellent summaries of the theory and subsequent research, see Chester A. Insko, *Theories of Attiude Change*, Appleton-Century-Crofts, New York, 1967; and Charles A. Kiesler, Barry E. Collins, and Norman Miller, *Attitude Change: A Critical Analysis of Theoretical Approaches*, John Wiley, New York, 1969.

positions your audience will accept on any given topic is called their *latitude of acceptance,* whereas the range of position they will not accept on that topic is called their *latitude of rejection.* If your message or proposal advocates a position or point of view that falls within the audience's latitude of acceptance, your listeners will perceive your position as being quite close to their own. They will be willing to buy the idea. However, if your proposal advocates a position that is within their latitude of rejection, they will actually perceive or judge your position as being more distant from their own position than it really is. These behaviors are the assimilation/contrast tendencies that we talked about in Chapter 3.

Concerning ego-involvement, Sherif, Sherif, and Nebergall[10] have drawn three conclusions about an audience's susceptibility to attitudes or opinion change. First, the more ego-involved with an issue your audience is, the more difficult it would be to change their orientations. Audiences that are highly ego-involved have small latitudes of acceptance and noncommitment and large latitudes of rejection. In short, there are very few ideas that such an audience will accept, and very many ideas that they will reject.

Second, lowly or moderately ego-involved audiences generally have a large latitude of acceptance and a small latitude of rejection. Consequently, lowly involved audiences are more susceptible to being convinced about an issue. In principle, we may now state that *an audience that is clearly highly involved in an issue is less inclined to opinion change than would the lowly or moderately involved audience.*

Third, most issues have a number of sides or positions, but most highly ego-involved people can only see their side as being correct, right, or acceptable. They reject all other sides. The less involved people are, the more their willingness to consider a number of different ideas about an issue.

The key to overcoming the problems of resistance motivated by ego-involvement and the unwillingness to make rapid change is very closely related to your ability to present attractive, interesting, goal-enchancing, and value-fulfilling alternatives. In addition, if your audience finds you credible and your message salient, you may achieve the remarkable feat of converting highly involved opponents into highly involved proponents.

In this chapter on audience analysis, we have been attempting to lay out the basic concerns of the message sender or source in

10. Sherif, C., M. Sherif, and R. Nebergall, *Attitude and Attitude Change* (Philadelphia: W. B. Saunders, 1965).

the conduct of public communication. Before planning and packaging the message, it is very important that we determine similarities and differences among our potential listeners. The more we know about their common characteristics, the easier it will be for us to make some inferences about their opinions and attitudes. In order to be effective as a source, you must seek information about those common characteristics, which may be more properly referred to as *demographic characteristics*. They constitute those features and factors that tend to draw an audience into homogeneity or oneness. Demographic characteristics are perhaps the most influential determinants of beliefs, behaviors, attitudes, values, and so on. Let us discuss a few of these characteristics.

Demographic Characteristics of Audiences

The general or common properties of an audience, such as educational background, intelligence, economic status, group affiliation, occupational classification, age, sex, cultural and religious background, and so on, are called its *demographic characteristics*. An audience analysis based upon them may be called a *demographic audience analysis*. Demographic characteristics are observable; they can be more easily defined than any of the other audience characteristics that we have discussed so far. In that they are more tangible, we can use them as a basis for inferences concerning what our specific message content, treatment, and approach should be. The categories suggested here can be applied fruitfully.

EDUCATION

You should try to familiarize yourself with the breadth and the type of education held by your audience. Conceivably, both high school graduates and college graduates hold opinions on some of the debatable problems of the day: foreign policy, inflation, unemployment, education, innercity blight, equal rights, and so on. However, in the debate and discussion on such issues, a college education may well have provided a broader base of opinions and perspectives than a high school education. Consequently, when dealing with audiences showing clear-cut differences in breadth and level of formal education, you should carefully consider the amount of information, data, and explanation needed to support your contentions. It is possible, too, that the audience of college graduates, because of their backlog of information, may be critical of more things than the audience of high school graduates. College graduates may be able to conjure up more objections; and you, knowing or anticipating the likelihood, would have to devise some strategy. Should you meet their objections head on, or, should you avoid arguments or issues that do not square with your point of view? Well, it depends on the educational level of your audience! With highly educated audiences, you'd be better off if you recognize the various sides of an argument rather than stick to one side. We suggest that you use this multisided approach whether your audience is for or against your contentions. Why? Because, the more educated the audience, the more their tendency to want to look at all sides, and also because they may already have studied the issue from several angles. By incorporating the multisided approach, you may be able to work off of what we call a kind of common ground framework—i.e. you anticipate an audience's position, honor it, and go on to develop your own.

With less educated audiences, some authorities suggest that it is better strategy to present only one side of the issue, especially when that audience is in favor of a proposition. The axiom here seems to be: why confuse them with extra information and defeat your own purpose? *We do not take that position.* Public communication is a costly enterprise—it demands hours of preparation, expenditures for materials, follow-up messages—and for our investments, we seek permanence of opinion change and longevity of commitment. You will better achieve permanence of opinion change and longevity of commitment by using a multisided approach. For one thing, by educating your audience about the alternatives, you are actually preparing them to protect their opinion should they later encounter opposing arguments. This is a part of the *inoculating strategy* that we spoke about in Chapter 5.

INTELLIGENCE

Generally, intelligent individuals should be *less moved* by persuasive messages than individuals of low intelligence. The more intelligent individuals should be *more critical* of a message than less intelligent individuals; therefore, the more intelligent person should be harder to persuade. Research demonstrates that if the message that the intelligent and unintelligent audiences receive contains unsupported generalizations or irrelevant arguments, the intelligent audience, because of their critical abilities, would be less influenced. On the other hand, if the persuasive message relies on impressive arguments with ample support, the highly intelligent audience would be influenced more.[11]

11. Secord, P., and C. Backman, *Social Psychology* (New York: McGraw-Hill, 1964), p. 169.

ECONOMIC STATUS

People who exist in the lower economic brackets are assumed to be more interested in wages and in economic security than those of higher economic brackets. They may be deeply and constantly concerned with improving their status, and are generally in a state of readiness to accept any propositions that point the way to such improvements. They believe that every American should have a chance to excel. However, many of their concerns deal with practical, day-to-day means of coping or surviving. In speaking to a group of people in a low-income neighborhood, a major objective might be merely to outline how one could become eligible for food stamps and how to get them, or how to apply for some type of job-training program. The people in some cities may be concerned about lack of transportation to and from work or the high cost of fuels for heating. Some may be concerned about the need for available hospital and medical care. You might assume that their interest in such issues as the curbing of the national debt, or the need for more dollars for manned, orbital flights, would be quite minimal. The concern of people of low economic status has to do with the bread-and-butter matters of existence.

Audiences of more moderate means might be more concerned with learning about insurance for their children's education, buying a home in a decent neighborhood, property tax assessments, profit-sharing plans, and so on.

People in higher income brackets would find matters of business prospects, the stock market, wage and price controls, or foreign relations to be of primary interest. Bryant and Wallace argue that, "enjoying economic security, having position and taking pride in it, they [higher income groups] may be eager to protect these advantages and skeptical of change and new proposals."[12] They would be conservative rather than radical. But there is yet one other side to the nature of the high economic group. We have found that many who are wealthy also tend to be concerned for the welfare of others—they often support foundations, fellowships, and various philanthropic organizations.

Whatever the status, we should try to anticipate what beliefs and attitudes prevail, and study how they may affect the objectives of our communication.

GROUP AFFILIATIONS

The desire to belong is a basic human motive. People join groups and quickly grow to identify themselves with and to accept

12. Bryant, D., and K. Wallace, op. cit., p. 315.

the goals, ideals, and beliefs of those groups. By knowing what groups appear in your audience, and by finding out something about their aims and beliefs, you can decide what attitudes are in harmony or in conflict with your opinion and you can select your supporting material accordingly.

By groups, we are referring to any organized group having a membership roll, officers, regular meetings, and so on. There are organizations to which people belong through election, initiation, occupation, residence, invitation, or identification with goals and objectives. Most of these groups are called *reference groups*, and may sometimes be informal, nonstructured groups of people. Nevertheless, the sense of identification prevails. The so-called group of middle Americans may never actually meet together under terms of structure, but to the extent each person becomes aware of norms and similarity of purpose, the group of middle Americans does become real and existent. If you have a staunch liberal view, you do as liberals do; if you have conservative political views, you probably find few liberal causes you can support.

By identifying the groups, you would be better prepared to obtain relevant background information and to slant your strategy to maximize your effectiveness.

OCCUPATIONAL CLASSIFICATION

A person's occupation is closely related to membership groups or reference groups as a factor in influencing the attitudes and beliefs of people. The groups in which people work do affect them greatly. Thus, information about the occupations represented in your audience would enable you to make some predictions about their beliefs and attitudes.

Occupational classification should tell us something about income levels, amount of education, type of education, modes of leisure activities, place of residence, group affiliations, and so on. Truck drivers would typically espouse the values of the Teamster's Union, doctors would be identified with the American Medical Association, managers would hold to orientations that may differ somewhat from those of rank and file workers. Each occupational group must be approached in terms of its vocational interests and values. You know that a farmer may see things differently than a school teacher or a owner of a small shop. Ask yourself whether the occupation of your audience is relevant to your topic?

AGE

It is said that young people tend to be flexible in their political affiliations and are inclined to be somewhat idealistic. As they grow older, they tend to become concerned about the practical operation of ideas and to develop somewhat fixed attitudes toward religious and political affiliations. These observations should provide a starting point for any analysis that you may want to develop around this demographic feature.

The age group of your audience may help you to anticipate reactions or objections to certain issues or propositions. For example, a group of college freshmen and sophomores will usually resist plans to reintroduce the draft for military service more than an older group will. Why? Because such a proposal affects them directly and disturbingly. Older people—particularly those who have already served their country—may be quite amenable to the idea, unless, of course, they have children of draft age.

Both average age and age span are important aspects of audience analysis. If you know that you will speak to a definite age group, as teenagers, the middle-aged, or the elderly, you can readily focus your material in their direction. On the other hand, if the audience is heterogeneous in age, the subject materials must be more general.

SEX

Our society is currently undergoing a significant number of shifts in the traditional view of the differences between the value orientations of males and females. The Women's Liberation Movement has turned our attention to the many ways in which women hold attitudes that are quite similar to those of men. We are becoming more aware of a similarity of ambitions, drives, needs, and frustrations that cut across professional life, political activities, and social action. Women are no longer willing to be viewed as mere husband-hunters, childbearers, and housekeepers. Among middle-class, educated women, the rebellion is even stronger.

In your analysis of the audience, you would do well to consider the self-image of your listeners—both male and female. If you are communicating with a group of women who see themselves as being liberated, the values with which they will identify and the beliefs that will be salient will be different from those of the average male and from many other women. Women who attempt to convince others of the values of liberation will need to consider the sex of their listeners and their self-image.

CULTURAL AND RELIGIOUS BACKGROUND

Some knowledge of the cultural, ethnic, and racial backgrounds is certainly essential. Naturalized citizens have a tendency to retain some ties with their native homes; second and third generations are somewhat more Americanized. When a particular background predominates among an audience, your understanding and acceptance of their heritage will greatly aid your efforts. It may not do much good for you to celebrate peaceful coexistence and Soviet good will, if you are speaking to an audience of Slavic individuals who see their relatives still existing under tryanny. People's past conditions—the way they grew up, and the kinds of attitudes and values their parents had—make up the social background of audiences and exert a significant effect on how they relate to ideas.

Many authorities believe that *social background is perhaps the strongest factor in determining attitudes.* Consequently, it may be more important to consider the listener's racial orethhic heritage, or religious background rather than his or her educational background, neighborhood, or age.

Whatever the demographic feature under consideration, information in most of the foregoing areas—educational background, economic status, group affiliation, occupational classification, age, sex, and cultural background—may be acquired by a few carefully phrased questions to the program planners or even to potential audience members. However you obtain it, you will find the information to be immensely valuable.

Whereas demographic features denote those common characteristics shared by people in any given audience, there are some features inherent in each individual that make for differences in the way they characteristically operate in communication situations. Some people are pushovers, falling for every sales pitch; others are stonewalls who seem to never give in or concede. In understanding what is happening in a communication situation, it is very helpful to know about some of these features, or *personality differences,* and the reasons for them. The final portion of this chapter deals with personality.

Personality Differences in the Audience

When you direct a message to an audience, you will find that your message is accepted by some, rejected by some, and apparently has no effect on others. Even when you confront an audience in which everyone feels the same way about the issue, you will find that after your message is completed not all people have changed to the same degree. We can say that some people are more persuasible than others. Numerous theories have been advanced to explain how a person interprets incoming messages and reacts to them. Many early theorists viewed personality variables as the primary determinants of how a message is received. We, of course, believe that an individual's personality is *not* the main or primary determinant; it would appear that the situation or context in which communication occurs also wields considerable influence. Nevertheless, some individual or personality traits do appear to constitute problems or obstacles for a speaker, and we shall discuss them here. Some of the personality differences that relate to communication are dogmatism, authoritarianism, and self-esteem.

DOGMATISM: THE OPEN AND CLOSED MIND

Milton Rokeach and his associates have conducted research to study the communication behaviors of a personality characteristic they refer to as *dogmatism*.[13] In their research, the terms *dogmatic* and *closed-minded* are used synonymously, and suggest the manner in which individuals approach people, ideas, beliefs, and messages.

An open-minded person is one who is not highly dogmatic and is able to bring various belief structures together for comparison purposes. Rokeach suggests that each individual has a system of beliefs and disbeliefs that apply to his or her different spheres of involvement, such as politics, religion, education, employment, and so on. A person who is open-minded or *not* dogmatic about these beliefs is aware of common ground between opposites. For instance, the open-minded person, while opposing the doctrines of Catholicism, still recognizes that it may, in reality, be seen to advocate the same sort of charity espoused by his or her own religion. In other words, open-minded individuals do not compartmentalize their beliefs into a kind of "good-guys-over-here" and "bad-guys-over-there" dichotomy. They are willing to be exposed to controversial material, and are even able to discuss issues and orientations that run counter to their biases.

In addition to their willingness to open up to a full discussion on the issues, open-minded individuals seem to have a more optimistic outlook on life in general; they are not inclined to put blind faith in the authorities who determine policies of governance. They believe that both policy and policy-maker may be sometimes correct and sometimes incorrect. In their view, all decisions must not be imposed as irrevocably binding, and information—regardless of the source—should be evaluated along a very broad time perspective. All of this does not mean that open-minded or lowly dogmatic

13. Rokeach, M., *The Open and Closed Mind* (New York: Basic Books, Inc., 1960).

people are pushovers or suckers; quite to the contrary, they are reflective, they carefully ponder the facts, but they do give the communicator a chance to develop the arguments.

In contrast to open-minded individuals, closed-minded or dogmatic people tend to compartmentalize their beliefs, and are extremely reluctant to compare beliefs. The more dogmatic individuals are, the more they will reject any common ground between their belief system (for example, Presbyterianism) and their disbelief system (for example, Catholicism). Those who are dogmatic or closed-minded cannot bring themselves to see any overlap between two apparently competing systems. They will dismiss as irrelevant or nonsensical any arguments that attempt to point up the ways in which both Catholicism and Presbyterianism are working toward the same objectives—whether the objectives concern charity toward the poor or teaching ethical or moral values. Anything outside of their belief system appears threatening, and they tend to reject it totally, with no willingness to compromise.

Such chronically closed-minded people are normally quite pessimistic about the world and their role in it; they are inclined to believe in the absolute correctness of certain authorities whom they happen to like. What makes it tough for the communicator is that they reject almost instinctively any idea that does not agree with the particular set of authorities in which they believe. On the other hand, if an authority that dogmatic individuals believe supports a particular position, then they will shift toward that position.

The implications of studies on dogmatism are quite clear:

1. People who are extremely dogmatic will be convinced mainly in situations where the ideas are supported by authorities in whom they place great trust.
2. People who are open-minded or not dogmatic tend not to depend on trust or the lack of it for their responses to ideas. They are generally able to evaluate ideas independent of the authorities to which those ideas are linked.
3. Because open-minded individuals seem to be better able to relate to new ideas and to make reasonable adjustments, they would respond to messages, proposals, or ideas that call for sweeping social change more easily than would closed-minded individuals. Proposals calling for abortion reform, equal rights for women, educational reform, schools, and neighborhood integration, birth control measures, and the like, would

be more easily launched among the open-minded than they would among the closed-minded.

4. Closed-minded individuals hold their beliefs very closely, narrowly, and tenaciously; they do not budge readily unless the change called for is endorsed by one or several of their authorities.

Dogmatism, then, is a trait that influences stonewalling or obstinacy in an audience. A few probing questions directed at key individuals may furnish you with some assessment as to how open or closed your potential audience might be. If any degree of dogmatism is anticipated, you should attempt to identify those authorities from whom the dogmatics take their norms. Once you have identified such authorities, your next task would be to discover the points, no matter how minor, on which you and those authorities agree. Use those points, clearly identified, to good advantage in your presentation.

AUTHORITARIANISM

Much of the work in the area of *authoritarianism* and the authoritarian personality[14] has concerned the reactions of certain kinds of people toward ethnic and religious minorities.

Basically, individuals having the so-called authoritarian personality tend to have a rather high regard for authority figures, and are inclined to comply with their directives or commands blindly. Authoritarians, by dint of their worship for and acceptance of power, usually disrespect, ignore, or slight less significant individuals. They are extremely status conscious, and adhere rigidly to middle-class values. Such people are likely to make absolute judgments, cling to old values, and resist change—unless the suggestion for change originates from an acceptable authority.

Although there appears to be some overlap between dogmatism and authoritarianism, researchers contend that there is an important distinction: whereas dogmatism cuts across several issues, *authoritarianism* appears to be manifested predominantly in response to issues pertaining to religion and race. In both matters, the authoritarian's outlook is denoted by an "us versus them" posture.

Convincing such individuals is not achieved so much through the rationality or logic of your message as much as through the sources or authorities with whom your ideas are associated. If George Wallace, the governor of Alabama, represents such an

14. Adorno, T., et al., *The Authoritarian Personality* (New York: Harper and Row, Publishers, 1950).

acceptable authority, the authoritarian will be likely to adopt Wallace's suggestions regardless of the particular issue.

According to Bettinghaus:

The persuasive communicator who wishes to secure favorable attitudes toward minority groups may find his task facilitated by making use of trusted authorities to carry the persuasive message to particular receivers. If it is not possible to make use of a trusted source such as an actual communicator, then the communicator might well be advised to design his message in such a way that these authority figures are quoted in the message as favoring the proposed attitude change.[15]

SELF-ESTEEM

A person's attitude about himself or herself also exerts an impact on the outcomes in public communication. Individuals who have low self-esteem or low self-confidence are easier to sway than those who are highly confident. Not only are low self-esteem audiences easier to convice, but they also tend to conform more to the demands of others.[16] This excessive conformity and persuasibility is attributable to the possibility that they have very little confidence in their own personal judgments and opinions. They readily relinquish their opinions when confronted with conflicting viewpoints, particularly if the source or communicator appears attractive or credible.

Although low self-esteem audiences may seem to be advantageous to you as a communicator, you must not forget that their commitment, after you have gained it, may not be enduring. Anticipating that they are prone to giving in at the drop of any and every good argument, your strategy should be geared toward *inoculating* them through the means we discussed in Chapter 5.

People with high self-esteem pose a different problem. They usually have greater confidence in their opinions, and are not threatened when confronted with opinions that run counter to theirs. The result is that high self-esteem audiences are *less* susceptible to persuasion. This does not mean that they will be inflexibly closed-minded; rather it means that they will not submit unless your reasoning is logical, and your ideas are plausible.

The three personality variables—dogmatism, authoritarianism, and self-esteem—are related to your audience's perception of you, the message, the issues, and the authorities that influence their lives. They are developed over a lifetime, and come to be cherished as well-organized frames of reference against which to assess in-

15. Bettinghaus, E., op. cit., p. 71.
16. Secord, P., and C. Backman, op. cit., p. 170.

coming data and information. These personality variables usually determine to whom a person will listen, who will be influential, what topics are interesting, and what kinds of responses should be made. Awareness of them should help you to communicate more effectively.

In this chapter, we have attempted to discuss the background against which a *profile of the audience* is constructed. We have described the general aspects of audience analysis; some of the contingencies of audience-speaker relationships, and audience-message relationships. In our discussion of audience bias, we explained effective approaches for dealing with neutrals and partisans. We also talked about the impact of an audience's ego-involvement and the lack of it; and in the last two sections, we cited ways in which audiences may be characterized in terms of common demographic factors, and also how people may differ because of certain personality variables.

All of these issues are vital to the conduct of effective audience analysis and are the *sine qua non* of successful public communication. A message must be tailor-made for a particular audience; the goodness of fit and the subsequent acceptance depend on how well you have measured the audience beforehand.

KEY CONCEPTS

Can you define and give examples of the following terms?

Audience analysis	Latitude of acceptance
Energizer effect	Latitude of noncommitment
Psychological mix	Demographic characteristics
Adaptation	Personality differences
Audience bias	Dogmatism
Ego-involvement	Authoritarianism
Latitude of rejection	Self-esteem

PROPOSITIONS

1. An audience is a psychological entity that exerts a major influence on the speaker's preparation and performance.
2. The behavior of audience members tends to act as cues or stimuli for the behavior of others.
3. An audience's bias has certain dimensions: direction, degree, and intensity.

4. Highly ego-involved individuals are more difficult to persuade than lowly ego-involved individuals.
5. The range of positions that an audience will accept on any given topic is called the latitude of acceptance.
6. The range of positions that an audience will not accept on any given topic is called the latitude of rejection.
7. If a message advocates a point of view that falls within the audience's latitude of acceptance, the audience will perceive that point of view as being close to their own.
8. If a message advocates a point of view that falls within the audience's latitude of rejection, the audience will perceive that point of view as being distant from their own.
9. Audiences that are highly ego-involved have small latitudes of acceptance and large latitudes of rejection.
10. The more educated the audience, the greater the tendency to examine an issue from several perspectives.
11. Individuals who are extremely closed-minded will be convinced mainly in situations where the ideas are supported by authorities whom they trust.
12. Individuals who are open-minded are generally able to evaluate ideas on their own merit, and do so independent of the authorities to which those ideas are linked.
13. Individuals who have low self-confidence or low self-esteem are easier to persuade than those who have high self-confidence or high self-esteem.

Part IV
Problem Resolution

Chapter 10
Developing the Communication Message

P R E V I E W

❡ *What is the first step in message development?*
Clearly defining the goal, objective, or purpose of the speech

❡ *What is the second step in message development?*
Determining the specific output we hope to create with the speech

❡ *What is the third step in message development?*
Collecting the data used to achieve the communication goal and expected outcome

❡ *What are the minimum elements that should be included on a bibliography card?*
Author's name, book title, and page number; for a periodical, the name of the publication and the date

❡ *What are the two functions of the introduction in a speech?*
To predispose the audience to listen to you and to focus attention on the subject

❡ *What is the purpose of the conclusion?*
To finish the speech and to focus the audience upon the primary goal of the message

O B J E C T I V E S

After reading this chapter, you should be able to
1. discuss the importance of setting clearly defined goals or objectives.
2. explain the importance of establishing clear and concise communication outcomes.
3. identify the key sources of information that can be used in the preparation of a speech.
4. identify the various note-taking procedures for cataloging information.

5. discuss the conceptual steps involved in topic development.
6. identify the various introductory techniques.
7. discuss the functions of the introduction and conclusion of a speech.

JIM BLACKBURN, public relations director for an electric company, has a delicate public communication problem. His company intends to construct a nuclear power plant on the coast near a local university. It is expected that opposition from campus environmentalists will develop when the plan is announced.

The environmentalists believe nuclear power plants create unacceptable risks and potentially damaging pollutants. The power company believes that protecting the public against pollution and hazardous installations are important goals, but that society's energy needs cannot be met without nuclear power. They believe that plans for a nuclear generating plant are safe and realistic, and that the environmentalists' views are one-sided, extreme, and ill-informed.

A conference on *Industry and the Environment* is to be held on campus. Jim has been asked to present his company's viewpoint. In addressing this problem, he begins by considering two inputs in the development of the message—his communication goal (general input) and the expected outcome (specific output) or desired behavior by the audience.

He begins developing the message by formulating his general communication goals. He wants to modify the cognitive systems of his college audience. Because his audience can be expected to be neutral or unsympathetic, he will need to define and plan his expected outcomes very carefully. His outcomes will result from attaining his communication goal. Thus, Jim seeks through the modification of cognitive systems the acceptance of his company's environmental views and approval of the nuclear power plant. The behavior or output he seeks in this case would be to convince the campus audience not to picket plant development or write to legislators urging them to prevent plant construction.

Having selected the communication goal and identified the expected outcome, Jim is prepared to develop the topics or main areas of his message. His audience analysis indicates that he must begin by counteracting biased information. He wants to present the "other side" and draws upon information in the company's files to show differences of opinion among experts concerning the sources and extent of environmental damage involved in nuclear power plants.

He next attempts to raise doubts about the validity of the opposition's information. Business and industry exist because they supply society with needed goods and services. Thus, he shows that fulfilling this responsibility involves environmental trade-offs; for example, you must kill oysters to acquire pearls. His company and his audience must likewise accept nuclear power plants in order to achieve needed energy sources.

The previous topic establishes the third area, promoting an understanding of the actual risks and damage to the environment by nuclear power plants. He describes his company's experience and programs, indicating efforts to make the production of electrical power safe and pollution-free, the growing scarcity of conventional sources of power for generating electricity, the uncertainty of other power alternatives, and the exaggerated nature of fears about nuclear accidents. He shows the predictable effects of a cutback in power generation on business, industry, employment, available consumer goods, and home conveniences. And, finally, he attempts to convince his audience that his company should be permitted and encouraged to proceed with its plans to develop nuclear-powered electrical generating facilities.

Once formulated, Jim's goals and outcomes provide the basis for developing the topical areas of the speech. The selection of topical areas leads to the collecting and recording of data upon which to base his talk. At this stage in the development of the message, additional practical considerations emerge. Information may be plentiful on some topics and sparse on others. He will need to seek supporting evidence, or possibly abandon a particular topic. He will be allocated only so much time to speak and can devote only so much time to preparation. These factors will weigh heavily in shaping the speech.

Jim recognized from the beginning that it would be difficult to gain support for his company's position. However, if he has done a workmanlike job of preparing and structuring his message, and his delivery is adequate, he stands a chance of modifying the cognitions of his audience by shaking the convictions of some members and improving the image of his organization with most of them. If he is successful, the audience will not voice opposition to the building of the power plant.

In this chapter we will examine the foundations of speech development. We will begin by defining communication goals and expected outcomes. This section is followed by a discussion of how the public communicator collects and records the data needed for construction of the message. Finally, we examine how one develops the topic.

Communication Goals and Outcomes

DEFINING YOUR COMMUNICATION GOAL

There is no single task more important for the public communicator than defining the specific goals (objectives) of public communication. In setting communication goals it is easy to overlook the fact that limitations imposed by time and resources are important in achieving that goal. A public communication is not prepared in a vacuum. We have a limited amount of time to devote to the preparation of the speech and at times a limited source of information. For example, Jim Blackburn might be inclined to take on the goal of convincing residents of a beach town that high-temperature cooling water discharged from his company's proposed nuclear plant into the ocean will not ruin the local fishing. Since nobody knows what the effect of the water discharge will be, Jim might propose that his company set up a pilot project to study the effect on marine life. The study could produce a number of results. It might show that hot water has no appreciable effect on fishing, is beneficial to fishing, drives out some fish and attracts others, or that it decreases and destroys the fishing potential of the area.

Negative results from such a project would render achievement of his particular communication goal impossible. If another approach can not be found, Jim might have to abandon his original goal for lack of supporting information. It might just as easily prove impractical for other reasons. For example, the company might reject the proposal as too costly. But without any information regarding the effect of water discharge upon the environment, Jim cannot possibly achieve his primary objective. Thus, in selecting goals and desired outcomes, it is important to select those that are achievable within the limits of available time and informational resources.

The purpose of establishing clearly defined goals is to make our task easier and more effective. Beginning the development of public communication by defining the primary goal or goals helps to organize our time and bring together all the materials necessary for achieving those goals. It assists us in selecting goals that are achievable.

Our first step in the development of a message is to arrive at a clear definition of the goal or objective of the speech. Having established the goal of our message, we proceed to clearly delineate the desired outcomes. The communication goal is the general objective the communicator is attempting to accomplish. On the other hand, the desired outcome refers to the specific objective of the communicator's speech. For example, a speaker addressing a group of parents on school integration may have as his or her communication goal a change of attitudes and behavior by an audience. The desired outcome might be for the audience to accept the principle that school integration is desirable and, thus, write letters to the school board supporting this position.

The communication goal must be specific. One way to define your public communication goal is to identify the basic response you would like to receive from your audience. For example, you may identify your goal as providing information, changing the listener's cognitive system, inducing resistance, resolving conflict, and so on. However, public communication goals are not mutually exclusive. For example, the primary goal of a classroom lecture is to transfer new information from the source (teacher) to the audience (students). At the same time the professor might have a secondary goal of persuading students (changing their cognitive system) to accept a particular orientation to the subject matter being presented. Teachers of speech communication will often inform a student not only of the correct procedures for developing a public message but also attempt to have the student adopt those procedures in future message development. Similarly, it is difficult for a public communicator to achieve the resolution of conflict without providing information and changing the cognitive systems of listeners.

DETERMINING EXPECTED OUTCOMES

We have suggested that a person will be more effective as a communicator if he or she defines the goal of the presentation in terms of the desired response from the audience. In addition, the process of clearly identifying your goal(s) is designed to focus your energy on resolving problems that must be solved if your goal is to be achieved.

We begin with a recognition of the overall goal of our public communication, that is, to modify cognitive systems, induce resistance, resolve conflict, and so on. We next focus on the specific outcome of the public communication—determining the specific output we hope to create. For example, the audience will picket the school board or vote for a nuclear power plant. When the speaking situation and topic are assigned by others, the speaker is obliged to select the outcome given to him or her by others. However, if speakers are provided with a context but not a topic, most professionals will defer selection of the topic until they have determined precisely what response they hope to achieve. For example, the Sierra Club invites you to speak at a conference on protecting endangered animals. The outcome of the public communication is to motivate the audience to promote legislation. Given the purpose of the conference, the pre-set expected outcome, and freedom to select your own topic, you want to demonstrate the danger to society when the balance of nature is upset by the disappearance of a species. The task might be easier if your topic were an animal closely associated with society, for example, dolphins, one on which you have information and one about which you have strong personal feelings.

It is important to be very specific regarding the outcome you desire. It is not enough to say, "I want the audience to go away knowing more about dolphins than when they arrived," unless your entire purpose is to provide general information about the dolphin, and even in that case you will undoubtedly feel it is more important for the listeners to learn certain facts about dolphins. You may want to specify your outcome as, "I want the audience to remember there are only X number of dolphins left alive in the Pacific Ocean; they all live in an area of only X square miles; they perform functions Y and Z in the balance of nature; and they are threatened with extinction by casues A and B." Or, where expected outcomes precede topic selection, "I want listeners to speak out in their own communities for protection of endangered species."

With a specific description of your public communication outcome, you are on your way to developing a strong, coherent, structured, and effective message. In the preceding example, you know from the outset that you will require data on the need for the proposed legislation, its benefits if adopted by your audience, and a detailed description of the action that is required to gain adoption of the legislation. You also will need a strong appeal for action on the part of your listeners. The type of research and message structure should be shaped in terms of your communication goal and expected outcomes. Thus, your message will become an entity in it own right, with a form that follows its function, rather than a copy of some textbook model.

Data Collection

Many people are generally unaware of the total amount of published information available on almost any subject. Once you begin your topic research, you will probably discover that finding relevant material is not a problem. In fact, the inexperienced speaker often has to exercise considerable self-discipline to avoid being overwhelmed by the sheer bulk of available material.

In general, it is a good idea to begin by reviewing the information you already have on the topic. You might try roughing out a brief essay on the topic, relying entirely on your own knowledge, imagination, and speculation. You may discover that you really do not have a great deal of research to do; in any event, you will gain valuable clues to the areas in which you will require additional information.

A little reflection will often call to mind acquaintances or colleagues who may have special knowledge or insight with respect to the subject, or who can refer you to others who have such information. Your own library may provide unexpected sources of data. A home encyclopedia can often give you at least an idea of the scope and limits of the topic. Many home encyclopedias are sold with a "special research report" service, providing the owner with topical reports on request. These are sometimes quite helpful, and are usually accompanied by a very useful bibliography.

The most valuable tool any researcher has is the public or college library. Too often we fail to appreciate—or even to realize —the enormous range and volume of information this remarkable institution puts at the disposal of even the most remote community. Today, the most unpretentious small town library is a part of an interchange system that can literally reach around the world to secure virtually any available publication or item of information. Library reference personnel are universally eager to use their skill and training in ferreting out difficult-to-locate information. It would be hard for a researcher to find a more valuable ally than a member of the local library reference staff.

The first time you approach your library as a researcher, it may be a good idea to pretend you have never been in a library before. You may be surprised to learn how much you didn't know about it until you begin to rediscover it. Your first approach will probably be to the card catalog, that crucial index to all the books on the shelf. Take time to study the examples demonstrating how the index works. Many modern libraries are experimenting with new indexing techniques, but whether the one you use is arranged in card trays, loose-leaf binders, or on microfilm, almost all systems list each book alphabetically in at least three ways—by *author's name*, by *title*, and by *subject*.

The general shelves, or "stacks," are only one facet of the library's information treasury. Many libraries have special collections of pamphlets, leaflets, photographs, film, filmstrips, slides, recordings, and the like.

Particularly for the speaker on current and recent events, the library's periodicals collection can be equal in importance to its books. Most libraries have current and back issues of a wide variety of general and specialized periodical publications. The key to finding articles bearing on your subject is the cumulative *Readers Guide to Periodical Literature*, which indexes the contents of more than a hundred publications by author, title, and subject. A few minutes spent in learning to use this valuable guide will pay off in faster, more thorough, more current research for years to come.

The *New York Times Index* lists all articles printed in one of the world's most thorough daily news publications. In addition to directing you to press accounts of events bearing on your topic, the *Times Index* can be very helpful in pinpointing the dates of events you want to follow up in other publications.

Your library will also have one or more excellent general encyclopedias, such as *Britannica* or *Americana*, and special compendia such as the *Encyclopedia of the Social Sciences, Encyclopedia of World History, Encyclopedia of Religion and Ethics*, and a score of others of larger or smaller scope, devoted to such diverse subjects as the Bible, art, music, food, science, and football.

If your library has a reference desk, it can be of enormous assistance in providing information on reference materials available to you. Probably one of the first works you will be directed to will be a research reference, such as Gates' *Guide to the Use of Books and Libraries*, or Winchell's *Guide to Reference Books*.

Normally, your library also will have material, including current indexes, from the U. S. Government printing office. In addition to the *Congressional Record* and reports of various committees and commissions, government publications cover every conceivable subject, from solar energy to raising earthworms.

If you have determined that a particular book you need is not on the shelves of your local library, that is not necessarily the end of your search. Many libraries have efficient interloan arrangements with other libraries, thus effectively offering the patrons of each library access to the complete collections of a number of libraries. Where all such efforts fail to produce the book you want, your librarian can often direct you to a college, university, or private library in which it can be found.

There are a number of relatively inexpensive general and special-purpose reference works that you would do well to acquire for your own desk. These include an annual, such as the *World*

Almanac, any one of a number of collections of topical anecdotes and aphorisms, and a quotations reference such as the perennial standard *Bartlett's* or George Seldes' *Great Quotations.* In addition to being a valuable composition tool, Roget's *Thesaurus* contains a useful collection of quotations arranged as footnote commentary on his major headings.

As suggested earlier, if you make full use of the sources readily available to you, the chances are that you will find yourself with more material on your hands than you know what to do with, and your problem will be one of selection, elimination, and condensation. This is, of course, far more likely to produce a rich, provocative speech than having to stretch inadequate material to fill the allotted time.

It also has its hazards. If you are really interested in the subject, you may find yourself devoting time to exploration of all the facets and side issues, to the point that you neglect the crucial task of making the fruits of your research your own by selecting and digesting the pertinent details so that they serve your purpose.

This is the point at which you will begin to appreciate the wisdom of defining your goals and expected outcomes in the first stage of message development. When you begin to feel overwhelmed by the sheer mass of available material, take time out to review your goal and desired outcome. If, as suggested earlier, you have begun your research with a brief, general overview of the topic, such as an encyclopedia article, it may be helpful to check your memory or notes on it to help restore your perspective in determining the relative weight to assign to various subtopics.

With your overall goal and the general boundaries of the topic well in mind, you can return with renewed confidence to the task of selecting the material you will actually use. Often you will find yourself regretfully eliminating fascinating material, either because it is not really germane or because it does not significantly contribute to achieving your desired outcome.

The more research you do, the more you will learn to rely on your taste and judgment in selecting materials. To a certain extent, you will learn the craft of judging books by their covers, that is, making snap judgments on their value by a quick check of publisher, copyright date, jacket blurbs, table of contents, index, bibliography, and perhaps a sample page or two. Authors' qualifications can often be checked in *Who's Who* or one of the myriad biographical dictionaries such as *Cyclopedia of World Authors, Directory of American Scholars,* or *American Men of Science.*

Fortunately, most speeches you will be called on to develop won't require a massive research effort. Usually the reason you are asked to speak on a particular topic is that you already have some knowledge on it. If that is the case, you will probably be interested only in checking for recent books and articles on the subject. Most of your research will take place in the periodicals section, and your principal reference will no doubt be the *Reader's Guide to Periodical Literature*. It is also sometimes worthwhile to check for recent developments in the *World Almanac* and annuals published each year to update some encyclopedias.

Periodical policy varies considerably from library to library, but it is a good idea to assume that you will not be able to check out the issues you want, and so will have to do your reading at the library. Most libraries now have photocopying equipment, enabling you to make relatively inexpensive duplicate copies of pages you expect to quote or refer to extensively.

RECORDING YOUR DATA

For the most part you will probably rely on the standby of researchers through the ages—handwritten notes. Here again, you will probably have to develop some workable compromises between extremist tendencies. On the one hand, you may find yourself placing too much faith in your memory and taking such sparse notes that they are incomprehensible by the time you need to use them. On the other extreme, it is possible to wind up with such voluminous notes that your speech becomes a patchwork of undigested quotations rather than your own production.

There is a great variety of note-taking and note-filing systems, each with its unique virtues. The important thing, of course, is for you to find a system that is comfortable and convenient for you. Probably the most universally employed is the debater's system, in which each point, fact, reference, quotation, and citation is listed on a separate file card. The cards are arranged in the order desired for a particular presentation, or are filed according to some simple system for easy access as they are required.

A remarkable amount of energy has been devoted to proving the superiority of 3" x 5" cards over 4" x 6" cards (or vice versa) for speaker's notes. Although the 3" x 5" cards are easier to handle and less obtrusive, 4" x 6" cards allow you to write larger or include more on a card; the final decision depends on which you find more convenient. Regardless of the dimensions of your cards, notes should all be kept on cards of the same size. Major points, quotations, or statistics that you use repeatedly can be typed on cards of the same size so that the material getting the greatest use is not only more durable, but easier to locate in the pack.

In any case, it is a good idea to have the separate items on separate sheets or cards so they can be combined in any order you wish. It also is a good idea to begin your notes a half inch or so below the top of the card so you can write in a heading later. In order to save the time wasted in recopying, make your original notes as clear and legible as possible. Clearly indicate direct quotations by the use of quotation marks, and omission of material by a series of dots. (It is customary to use three dots to indicate an omission that occurs within a single sentence and four when one or more periods are contained in the material omitted.)

It is extremely important to record the source of each quotation, fact, or idea on the same card on which it is recorded. For a book source, this should include at least the author's name, book title, and page number; for a periodical, the name of the publication and its date should also be included. This will be helpful in case you wish to return to the original source to verify the accuracy or add to your information. However, its most important function will be its contribution to your credibility. Nothing reduces a speaker's authority so quickly as the inability to authenticate his or her assertions. If the source is on your notes, you add to the impression that you have your material constantly at your fingertips.

It is also helpful to keep a separate bibliography card on each source, giving more detailed information. In the case of a book, this should include the name of the publisher, date of copyright, edition, and any notes you may wish to record to remind you of special qualities or of your reactions to the work. Also, you will find it helpful to develop the habit of making a note of the library call number of the book on the bibliography card, as well as the library or branch in which it is located. You should keep your bibliography cards with the material you take to the platform for instant access in case you are challenged on your sources.

In the same way that careful definition of goals and outcomes eases the task of research, good research and notes will help you in sequencing, proportioning, and interconnecting the individual topics you develop into your finished speech.

Topic Development

Topic development will occupy the body of your speech, comprising 80 per cent to 90 per cent of the total, with the remainder devoted to the introduction and conclusion. Your task at this point is to bring together the fruits of your spadework—your analyses of goals, desired outcomes, audience inputs, environmental inputs, source inputs, message inputs—in such a way that the listener will be carried from his or her present state of knowledge, belief, or action to conformity with your communication goal and expected outcomes.

Obviously, the accuracy of your audience analysis becomes critical at this stage. You will need to visualize your listeners and to gauge as accurately as possible the conceptual distance between their viewpoint at the beginning of your speech and the position that would represent the fulfillment of your goal and expected outcomes. Refer to Chapters 3, 4, 5, and 8 for specific message strategies to develop your topic.

Your task is to articulate the main arguments or headings that logically lead your audience from their present position to the one you advocate. Suppose, for example, you want to persuade an audience of *laissez-faire* conservatives to accept temporary wage and price controls in the interests of combatting inflation or meeting a military emergency. Your primary arguments might be:

1. Responsible conservatives have always been willing to make any sacrifice necessary to preserve freedom.
2. Sometimes, as when we accept military service, this has meant temporarily giving up the enjoyment of some of our freedoms in order to preserve the basic conditions that make all our freedoms possible.
3. The present emergency presents us with such a choice.
4. If we do not accept temporary controls now, we will lose all of our freedoms permanently.

These arguments become the principal divisions or headings of your speech. Obviously, each argument will require the support of facts, analogies, examples, and so on. In Chapter 11 we will examine how to structure or organize the material in your speech. Once the data is collected and the speech is organized and structured, only the finishing touches need to be applied. These consist of the introduction and conclusion, transitions to smooth the movement from one point to the next, strengthening inadequately supported points with additional facts or arguments, and deciding on details of delivery, style, and platform behavior.

The introduction to your speech has primarily two functions: to predispose the audience to listen to you with interest and confidence, and to focus its attention on the subject. Humor is the perennial standby for establishing rapport with audience. This does not, however, mean that audiences respond well to conventional jokes, particularly those that are in their dotage, are long and complicated, or begin with opening lines such as "It seems there were these two Scotchmen. . . ." A clever epigram or quotation, a "one-liner," or simply a good-humored comment on the occasion, the weather, or the audience, if appropriate, is a far better ice-breaker than a labored story. A personal anecdote demonstrating the speaker's ability to laugh at himself is almost always well received. At the same time, audiences love to demonstrate their ability to laugh at themselves.

A word of caution, however. When speaking before a professional group, such as lawyers or doctors, it is a good idea to refrain from telling your favorite "lawyer" or "doctor" story—the chances are good that it's a chestnut in the profession, however fresh and hilarious it may seem to you.

Although it is the most common introductory technique, humor is not always appropriate, and there are other effective ways of establishing common ground between the speaker and the audience. Often the speaker can accomplish the same purpose by calling up a memory, experience, aspiration, interest, or danger he or she shares with the audience.

The second objective of the introduction is to establish the purpose of the speech. A remarkable number of experienced speakers neglect this important step, with the result that they are often well into the body of the speech before the audience recognizes the direction it is taking. Quite often the best way to establish the purpose is simply to state it in as straightforward a manner as possible. This does not mean that it is always wise to reveal at the outset the conclusion you intend the audience to draw. In Chapter 8 we suggested that when your objective is to persuade an audience to alter its point of view significantly, a premature announcement of this fact may serve only to arouse unnecessary resistance. The speaker who hopes to persuade an antiregulation audience to accept temporary controls, for example, might state the purpose this way:

I want to talk to you tonight about a danger that threatens us all. A danger that forces us to face hard choices if we are to preserve the economic foundations of our free society. It is the danger of inflation.

The conclusion is a brief statement that functions as a recapitulation and a structural device to give the speech a workmanlike sense of completeness. It also serves to signal the alert listener that the speech is ending, sometimes by its unmistakable tone and form, sometimes by the simple inclusion of a phrase such as "In conclusion . . . ," or "To summarize. . . ." It is important that the concluding section be as brief and clear as possible and, usually, that it include a strong recapitulation or emotional exhortation, a call for action, or relevant instructions. (For detailed suggestions on developing introductions and conclusions, refer back to Chapter 8.)

In this chapter, we have concentrated on the structural devices and construction processes that are employed to shape your public communication. As indicated in the opening section of the chapter, much of your success will depend upon the clarity with which you define realistic goals and expected outcomes. Your speech will hinge on these fundamental elements. A clear concept of goals and outcomes greatly simplifies the succeeding task of efficient research and data recording, organization of material, and topic development. In Chapter 11, we will examine ways to structure the message.

KEY CONCEPTS

Can you define and give examples of the following terms?

Communication goal
Expected outcome
Data collection
Reference source

Topic development
Introduction
Body
Conclusion

PROPOSITIONS

1. There is no single task more important for a public communicator than defining the specific goal(s) of the public message.
2. The first step in message development is to arrive at a clear definition of the goal(s) or objective(s) of the speech.
3. The second step in message development is to determine expected outcomes or specific outputs we hope to create by our public message.
4. In preparing a speech, it is useful to determine the desired audience or output.
5. The third step in message development is the collecting and recording of data for the speech.
6. Topic development will carry the listener from his or her present state of mind to a new state that conforms with your goal(s) and expected outcome(s).
7. The speech introduction should predispose the audience to listen to the speaker, and it should focus attention on the subject.
8. The conclusion should "finish" the speech and should focus on the intended outcome of your message.

Chapter 11
Structuring the Message

P R E V I E W

¶ *What are seven basic organizational patterns?*
Chronological
Relationship
Motivational
Topical
Spatial
Problem solution
Contrast

¶ *What are five basic types of supporting materials?*
Definitions
Examples
Citations
Narration
Statistics

O B J E C T I V E S

After reading this chapter, you should be able to
1. describe the chronological organizational pattern.
2. describe the relationship organizational pattern.
3. describe the motivational organizational pattern.
4. describe the topical organizational pattern.
5. describe the spatial organizational pattern.
6. describe the problem solution organizational pattern.
7. describe the contrast organizational pattern.
8. identify five types of supporting materials used in a speech.

DR. JONES, the school district superintendent, began his speech as he did every year on the first day of school, "I welcome you back to the start of what should be a most fulfilling year of work with our youngsters." The teachers in the audience yawned, expecting the usual pep talk. Yes, it was going to be another of those talks. "This year," he continued, "will be a challenge in light of the massive cutbacks in school services."

"What cutbacks?" Lee David, a debate coach, whispered.

"Who knows?" responded Dixie Chien, a French teacher. "What's he bracing us for, anyway? I wish I knew what this is all about."

The first questions any listener wants answered are: why am I here? why should I listen? what will I gain from listening? We, as speakers, must provide satisfactory answers if we wish to have receptive and active listeners. We must successfully establish the speech *purpose* and satisfy our audience's initial cynicism or malaise. Such was the problem with Dr. Jones's speech. The faculty expected that his purpose would be a simple pep talk for the opening of school. However, he indicated that the school year might present new problems without being specific as to their precise nature. Thus, his faculty was confused and hostile. The teachers did not know why they should listen or what ideas Dr. Jones was trying to convey. Although the information would have been equally disturbing, the audience would not have been nearly so hostile had Dr. Jones said, "My purpose this morning is to inform you of cutbacks and to propose specific measures to assist our working effectively within our financial boundaries." The faculty would then have a clear idea as to Dr. Jones's message.

Once we have successfully established the speech purpose, we must guide the listener through the body of our speech. Adequate structuring of a communication message is crucial. Upon reading a message, we usually have time to reread and ponder unclear points; not so with oral-verbal communication. If we are unclear, our speech will be disjointed and we will lose our audience immediately. Remember that our audience rarely has a copy of the speech to read and study. It is our responsibility to create a clear progression from point to point to insure attention and comprehension. When the basic skeleton of our speech is structured, we can then increase listener comprehension and acceptance by supporting our statements.

In this chapter, we will examine the major elements of speech structure. Organizational patterns will be described, enabling us to fit the most appropriate pattern to the selected topic. Included are specific outlines illustrating the organizational patterns. Finally, we will discuss the use of supporting materials, the information that transforms the "skeleton" outline into a speech.

The old adage that every good story has an effective beginning, middle, and end certainly applies to speech structuring. In order to begin any speech, we must provide a purpose for the listener. This will then avoid a potential source of confusion for the audience. For instance, if we begin by saying, "home mortgage interests are inhibiting the purchase of new homes," the audience doesn't know what to expect of the speech. Let's compare the former statement with, "I am going to discuss five major reasons for the decline in home ownership." From this statement, we immediately expect to learn about the decline in home ownership. We know why we are listening and we know the speaker's goal. Combine this statement with a few interesting points regarding the topic and an introduction emerges. We have oriented the listener, who knows what to expect of the message.

Organizational Patterns

We must always keep in mind that it is the speaker's responsibility to guide the listener through a speech. There are a number of organizational patterns to choose from, each varying in its suitability for the topic and purpose. We will now examine the patterns that assist us in structuring our speech.

We will describe the chronological, relationship, motivational, topical, spatial, problem-solution, and contrast patterns. Accompanying each description is an outline for a hypothetical speech to illustrate each pattern. Many speech teachers require students to prepare full sentence outlines that are easy for the instructor to read and evaluate. However, such an outline is difficult for the speaker to use when presenting the public communication. Often the inexperienced speaker will read such an outline. In order to avoid reading the speech afforded by a sentence outline, we suggest the use of topic outlines when presenting a speech.

CHRONOLOGICAL OR TIME SEQUENCE

This pattern begins at an appropriate point in time and moves forward through a series of events. The pattern never jumps haphazardly from event to event, but allows the *ordering of time* to determine where the events are placed. Thus, time is our common denominator. If we were to speak about "Coal Mining in Pennsylvania," for example, time would *not* be the common denominator for all aspects of the speech and another pattern would have to be chosen. However, if our topic was "A Day in the Life of a High School Speech Teacher," the speech could easily be organized according to time progression. An example of an outline using chronology as an organizational pattern follows. Some subsections are longer than others. We usually strive toward a balanced outline, but this rarely occurs because detailed information is necessary in some instances and would be obviously dull or inappropriate in others. In this hypothetical case, our *audience* is a group of college speech majors, who are beginning student teaching. Our *purpose* is to inform the students of the varied daily tasks and activities of a high school speech teacher. Our *organizational pattern* is that of chronology or time sequence.

"A Day in the Life of a High School Speech Teacher"

I. Morning Pre-Class Activities
  A. Meeting with school principal
    1. Discuss upcoming debate tournament at home school
      a. Rooms needed
      b. Cost
    2. Complete teacher poll concerning interest in classroom debate exhibitions
    3. Meet with students
      a. Re-work outlines for upcoming speech contest
      b. Review rules
II. Classroom Activities
  A. Basic speech classes
    1. Show examples of poor organization by playing tapes for students
    2. Review organizational patterns
  B. Debate Workshop
    1. Hear presentation by affirmative team
    2. Class critique
    3. Develop research for weak points
  C. Communication Theory Class
    1. Display picture for class inventory of individual perceptions
      a. Students fill out in and discuss perceptual differences
    2. Receive reports from committees concerning field research projects.
III. After School Activities
  A. Faculty Meeting
    1. Principal discusses cut-back in services for forthcoming year
      a. Proposed cut backs in debate budget
      b. Proposed cut backs in areas not directly related to speech
  B. Debate Society Meeting
    1. Treasurer's report concerning funds for upcoming awards night
      a. Cost of trophies and pins

b. Cost of food

c. Cost of room rental

2. President's report concerning forensic points earned by new members

TOPICAL SEQUENCE

Some subjects are best organized by considering the parts constituting the whole. All the parts relate to each other because they are all part of the same family. For instance, if we were to speak about "Amateur Theatrical Production," the topical approach would be highly appropriate. We would break down the elements of play production and treat each as a separate organizational category. The important point to remember when using the topic sequence is that each subsection must be a part of the whole, or the main subject. In the following sample outline the speaker chose only four of the major roles in theatrical production. Because all four roles relate directly to the speech title, a good way to begin is to inform the audience that four major roles will be discussed. In this respect, the speaker has provided the psychological set "four" for the audience to anticipate and follow. In this hypothetical case, our *audience* is a group of novice thespians joining a newly formed dramatics group. Our *purpose* is to inform the members of the many facets comprising a dramatic production. Our *organizational pattern* is that of topical sequence.

"An Amateur Theater Production"

I. The Director

A. Casts the play

1. Chooses actors appropriate for each role

a. May typecast

b. May want to cast experienced actors

c. May cast actors who have great amounts of time to rehearse

B. "Blocks" the play

1. Communicates the play's mood through positioning of actors

C. Develops characterizations

1. Works with actors' experimental and emotional resources

D. Sets timetables

1. Rehearsal schedules

2. Deadlines for memorization

3. Deadlines for lighting sequences

4. Deadlines for costumes

II. The Actor

A. Responsible for memorized lines

B. Responsible for characterizations developed with the director

C. In amateur productions, may have to supply or help with
   1. Props
   2. Make-up
   3. Costumes
   4. Scenery
III. The Stage Manager
   A. Oversees all of the crew's work
      1. Scenes are set properly
      2. Light cues are correct
      3. Sound cues are correct
      4. Props are distributed to appropriate actors
   B. Oversees actors during production
      1. Gives cues to go onstage
IV. Publicity Manager
   A. Oversees all advertising
      1. "Places" posters in local stores, and elsewhere
      2. Invites cast members to visit local organizations for support
      3. Places ads in appropriate newspapers
   B. In amateur productions, often oversees ticket sales as well
      1. In charge of box office
         a. Advance sales
         b. Group sales
         c. Door sales

SPATIAL SEQUENCE

In this pattern, we use space as the common denominator for organization. Speech topics involving geographic locations are especially suited to spatial sequences. For instance, if we were to orient incoming college freshmen to the locations and offerings of our campus's dormitories, we could easily organize our information by discussing dorms on the campus's east side or west side, or on-campus/off-campus living. In this way, our audience once again has a psychological set, or listening goal, this time determined by geographic location. In the following example, the topic is "Touring Southern California." With such a broad topic, a precise organizational pattern is crucial and the speech could have been approached in many ways. This particular speaker chose to orient listeners by beginning in one geographic section and working north from the original point. The advantage to this pattern is that listeners not only learn about the topic, but can visualize their locations as well.

In this hypothetical case, our *audience* is a group of New Yorkers taking a Southern California tour. Our *purpose* is to inform our tourists of the many places they will visit. Our *organizational pattern* is that of spatial sequence.

I. Southernmost Section of Southern California
  A. San Diego Area
    1. San Diego Zoo
    2. Sea World
    3. Old Towne Missions
    4. Balboa Park Shakespearean Festival
  B. San Juan Capistrano
  C. San Clemente
  D. Newport Beach
  E. Huntington Beach
II. Middle Section of Southern California
  A. Long Beach Area and West Orange Country
    1. Disneyland
    2. Knott's Berry Farm
    3. Queen Mary
    4. Long Beach Harbor
  B. Los Angeles Area
    1. Farmer's Market
    2. Century City
    3. Los Angeles Music Center
    4. Chinatown
III. Northernmost Section of Southern California
  A. Hollywood Area
    1. Grauman's Chinese Theater
    2. Universal Studios
    3. Hollywood Bowl

MOTIVATED SEQUENCE

Alan H. Monroe developed the motivated sequence, which is helpful in problem-solving and persuasive endeavors. The speaker indicates that an area of difficulty exists and that the speaker has a program for dealing with the difficulty. There are five basic steps that the motivated sequence follows:

1. Attention
2. Need
3. Satisfaction
4. Visualization
5. Action

In persuasive speeches especially, we may want to move our audience to adopt specific action. Our efforts would be futile, however, if we did not first indicate a need for action. For such endeavors, the motivated sequence provides the framework to move our audience toward specific action. We are not merely persuading our audience to believe in a certain way. We want listeners to act upon their beliefs as well.

In the following example, the speaker, a condominium owner, wanted to organize the other owners against the company providing services for the complex. The owners had endured problems and inconveniences and were disgusted. The speaker's *audience* was composed of condominium owners, the *topic* was "Let's Get Our Money's Worth," the *purpose* was to persuade other owners to withhold payment of services, and the *sequence* was motivational.

"LET'S GET OUR MONEY'S WORTH"

I. Attention
   A. Prices for services are rising
   B. Owners can't afford additional raises
   C. Owners can't do maintenance work themselves
   D. Owners can't afford to live elsewhere themselves
II. Need
   A. Discussions with the company failed
   B. Company gave no guarantees
   C. Company breached contract
   D. Letter-writing campaign failed
III. Satisfaction
   A. The group shares a common problem
   B. Individuals acting as a group can accomplish more
   C. United action is the last resort
IV. Visualization
   A. Other developments refused to pay same company
      1. Successful
         a. No raises for a year
         b. Improved service
   B. Eighty per cent of owners agreed to pay strike in a circulated questionnaire
V. Action
   A. All owners should refuse to pay association dues
      1. Meet with company
         a. Monies will be withheld until the following have been accomplished
            (1) Fixed swimming pool
            (2) Fixed front gates
            (3) No further raises for one year until the contract is up for renewal

CONTRAST

This pattern explores *differences* and *similarities*. Individuals often learn effectively by being able to compare one thing to another. We, as speakers, become teachers and should use tools to insure listener comprehension. Contrast is often an invaluable aid in teaching others. It is an especially good pattern to use for informative speeches, although it can be employed to structure arguments as well.

The following outline provides structure for an informative speech given by a physical education teacher about the various Olympic events. The contrast pattern was appropriate because although the two events had so much in common that they could easily be compared, there were also significant differences. The *audience* is a group of college students, the *purpose* is to inform, and the *pattern* used was that of contrast.

"GLAMOUR SPORTS OF THE OLYMPICS: FIGURE SKATING AND GYMNASTICS"

I. Similarities
   A. Both have competition for men and women
   B. Both use knowledge and training in dance forms
      1. Athletes study dance
      2. Points awarded for grace as well as athletic skill
   C. Both use music in some events
      1. Athletes use musical selections to bring out individual personalities
   D. Both have compulsory and optional events
      1. Compulsory routines are always first and scores are added to optionals to determine standings
II. Differences
   A. Selection for Olympics
      1. National skating champions automatically go to the Olympics
      2. Special trials held in gymnastics
   B. Grouping
      1. Team medals awarded in gymnastics
         a. Individual competition after team awards
      2. Pairs medals awarded in skating
         a. Individual skaters may or may not compete as pairs
   C. Scoring
      1. Scale of 0–10 in gymnastics
      2. Scale of 0–6 in skating
   D. Equipment
      1. Skaters need only ice, boots and blades
      2. Gymnasts use several pieces of apparatus
         a. Men
            (1) Rings
            (2) Horse
            (3) Horizontal bar
            (4) Parallel bars

b. Women
(1) Vault
(2) Uneven parallel bars
(3) Balance beam

RELATIONSHIPS

We can approach the use of this pattern by thinking of our subject matter in terms of cause and effect. In persuasive endeavors, especially, we often want to show disastrous effects of a given course of action. "Do you want to contribute to *this?*" We've seen such appeals on TV, showing pictures of nuclear fallout, air and water pollution, and malnourished children. Each is the effect of such monsters as unsafe nuclear testing, industrial waste, and war, and the impact of these messages is intense.

Speeches can be organized either by presenting the action and its effect or by concentrating on the effect if the cause is well understood by our audience. The following outline illustrates the organizational pattern of *relationships* by describing undesirable effects of smoking. Our *purpose*, naturally, is to convince an audience of smokers to stop.

"STOP SMOKING—NOW"

I. Effects of smoking on the individual
  A. Lung Impairment
    1. Tars and nicotine change color of lungs
    2. Shortness of breath
    3. Increased risk of lung cancer
    4. Chronic cough
  B. Threat to Heart
    1. Increased risk to heart attack
  C. Unpleasant odor on hair and clothes
  D. Psychological Dependency
    1. Smoking may be a screen for serious psychological problems
  E. Physical Dependency
    1. Difficult habit to break
    2. Expensive habit to keep
II. Effects of smoking on others
  A. Impairs health merely by inhalation of smoke
  B. Smell makes others sick
  C. Smoke clings to others' clothes and hair
III. Effects of smoking on the environment
  A. Smoke discolors walls and furniture
  B. Stale smoke give homes a poor odor
  C. Careless smoking causes fires

PROBLEM SOLUTION

John Dewey proposed a five-step approach for problem-solving discussions. Although Dewey's reflective thinking process is a theoretical description of how the mind analyzes a problem, it is also a superb procedure for organizing a problem-solving speech. Because we spend considerable time communicating in an attempt to solve problems, Dewey's five-step reflective thinking process is most assuredly worthy of our study. The procedure has a further advantage because it provides a system of checks, enabling the speaker to move on in his problem solving only after he has accomplished specific goals.

The following outline employs Dewey's five steps: define the terms; define the nature of the problem; establish criteria to judge possible solutions; generate possible solutions; select the solution which best meets the criteria. The outline serves as a basis for a discussion concerned with a problem common to most campuses —parking. We can see from the outline how it would be difficult for a group using Dewey's approach to jump to erroneous conclusions.

STUDENT PARKING PROBLEM

I. How shall we define the terms?
   A. What do our terms mean?
      1. By "permissible" we mean that all student parking areas will be open to all students with appropriate car stickers at all times
      2. By "guarantee" we mean that all students who pay a parking fee will have a place to park
      3. By "on campus" we mean all parking areas within the college's designated areas and not on residential streets or in commercially-owned lots.
   B. What limitations shall we place on our discussion?
      1. We are not to be concerned with the parking needs of anyone other than the student
      2. We are not to be concerned with off-campus parking
II. What is the nature of the problem?
   A. What are the causes of the college's poor parking facilities?
      1. Are there too many students attempting to park on campus?
         a. Is it necessary that all students drive to the campus?
      2. Are available spaces limited?
         a. Number of spaces on campus
         b. Number of parking permits sold
   B. What are the effects of the college's poor parking facilities?
      1. Are some students unable to find parking?
         a. Number of students without parking

2. Do some students park in illegal areas?
    a. Number of students receiving parking tickets
       (1) Reasons students give for parking illegally
III. By what criteria must we judge any possible solution to the problem?
  A. How should the solution be financed?
    1. The solution should be funded by student fees
    2. The solution should not raise student fees by more than five dollars
  B. Is the solution practical?
    1. Authorities must be able to implement the solution
IV. What are the possible solutions?
  A. Increased bus service to the campus
  B. Incentives for not driving to the campus
  C. An underground parking facility
  D. A high-rise parking facility
  E. Car pooling by students
V. Which solution best meets the criteria?
  A. Car pooling by students

Supporting Materials

Once we have the skeletal structure of our speech, communication of purpose and clear organization are generally provided. However, a speech needs more than a mere progression of ideas for it to accomplish its purpose. Even with the most appropriate organizational pattern, a speech may fail. One reason for this is that an audience will not accept your arguments merely because you say they're legitimate. At times your information is not conveyed clearly. And, at other times your topic is of a highly controversial or emotional nature and "cold facts" are not sufficient to affect your audience.

Supporting materials enhance the speech skeleton with the necessary *definitions of terms, examples, citations, narration,* and *statistics.* Such materials are not only recommended, but they are vital to a successful speech. Specific types of supporting material are appropriate to different speech situations, depending on the speaker's goal. We must decide which supporting materials to use and where to place them in a speech. The following section will describe the different types of supporting material and their use.

DEFINITIONS

How futile it would be for us to try to convince an audience to adopt the Free Lunch Plan if our audience didn't know what it was. Or, suppose Dick Button was analyzing the World Figure Skating Championships and he told us that Russian skaters use their "edges" superbly. Would we know that he was referring to use of the blade? Without definition, he could not communicate effectively to a vast audience.

There are several types of definitions, including the one you're most familiar with—the dictionary definition.

Conventional definitions revolve around rules that establish which language symbols to attach to an object, situation, or concept that we all agree upon. For example, when an umpire says "first down" during a football game, the players and spectators understand that the offense has moved the ball to a specific yard line. The term has been defined by the rules of football. *Descriptive* definitions are descriptions of the phenomenon contained in the term. If we were to define the word *fear* by using a descriptive definition, we would enumerate the qualities inherent in a fearful reaction. *Prescriptive* definitions imply or describe what ought to be. For example, a prescriptive definition of a teacher would list the qualities a teacher ought to have. "A good teacher has a tolerant disposition, enjoys his work, and can communicate subject matter effectively."

We must always be sure to define terms that might be unfamiliar to our audience. Sometimes background material is necessary, and at times a short definition may suffice. Technical terms must be defined; what seems apparent to us may be unknown to others. We will reap an additional bonus by being precise in our terms; our audience will respect our knowledge, trust us, and will want to listen.

CITATIONS AND QUOTATIONS

One result of effectively using supporting materials is the respect we gain from our listeners. Citations and quotations also serve this end. Suppose we are trying to convince an audience to pass legislation favoring the "right to die." To merely discuss the reasons why we are in favor of it would be foolhardy. An intelligent audience's reaction would certainly be, "who are you and what experiences have you had to make you expert on such a subject?" However, an audience's reaction would be far less hostile if we cited supporting opinions by doctors, religious and governmental leaders, and individuals who had endured the experience of watching a terminally ill person suffer endlessly.

Our audience would be more likely to accept a speech embellished by "expert" testimony. Quotations should be used in such cases, but we must beware that the quotations are from legitimate sources and that we don't read quotes endlessly, as to bore listeners.

EXAMPLES

Using examples is a superb way for us to communicate complex or unfamiliar concepts. When a listener is given examples, he will usually extract their meaning in his own way and avoid abstractions that may prove cumbersome to an understanding of the speaker. Suppose a school principal told members of the faculty that they should use verbal feedback during student conferences. The principal's message would be enormously enhanced if he then said, "For instance, when a student makes a statement, it is helpful to respond by repeating the statement and asking if that was what the student meant." In this way, the faculty has, through an example, received a clear indication of what the principal is proposing.

NARRATION

The telling of a story often conveys information or enhances an assertion. Relating a sequence of events involving interesting people and places sparks our listeners' interest and imagination. An effectively told story will hold or gain attention as well. The narrative should always clarify or support a major idea; otherwise we will detract our listeners from our purpose. As was the case with the use of examples, narrative is an excellent method of translating an abstract idea to our listeners' realm of understanding.

Placement of a narrative in our speech is also crucial. For instance, in competitive speaking, a contestant may want to create an indelible impression by dramatically unfolding a narrative in the introduction. In other cases, we may estimate that we can successfully hold attention until the conclusion, where narration may create a lasting impression. We must decide whether the narration would be more effective in the body of the speech or elsewhere. We must carefully analyze our purpose and determine how to make the most effective use of narrative.

STATISTICS

Stating a problem in terms of size and quantity can greatly aid listener comprehension. The impersonality of figures can be incorporated into our audience's realm of reality to provide powerful argument. For instance, in a speech to convince listeners to buy UNICEF products, a speaker stated, "One box of cards can buy 185 tablets containing PAS, a drug that helps cure TB." The figures enabled listeners to know exactly where their funds would be allocated and the importance of their use. If we wanted to impress upon our listeners the importance of cleaning up camping areas, we could say that, "The debris left after one weekend of camping, if laid side by side, would cover X number of miles, or the entire town of Y." Information delivered in such a manner is far more effective than simply stating that, "campers' litter makes an unbearable mess."

Statistics can make generally objective statements which can be helpful when speaking to an audience not already convinced to our point of view. For instance, a statement such as "This school just isn't what it used to be" is open to immediate debate. However, if we said, "In 1970, the mean IQ in this school was 108 and in 1976, the mean IQ is 100," we would actually be stating that on a given test, students in 1970 scored on the average higher than in 1976. Even though the merits of the test could be debatable, we have presented a basis for comparison. Thus, statistics can effectively pinpoint qualities found in large populations or areas.

We must be sure to use figures sparingly and to try to present them in round numbers. Once the figures become the focal point of our speech, instead of serving as support, their effectiveness is destroyed.

We have now discussed how the use of definitions, citations, examples, narration, and statistics can make our speeches more convincing and better understood. The different forms of supporting material vary in appropriateness and it is up to us to decide how to use support. Factors assisting us in these decisions depend on the audience's composition, the speech purpose, the speaker's background and experience, and the speech topic, to name a few.

Once our supporting materials are placed in the structure of the speech outline, the body of the speech is complete. It still remains for us to initially interest and motivate our audience in an introduction and to summarize and make a final, enduring impression in a conclusion. By using the elements of organization described in this chapter, we will accomplish the goal of effectively guiding an audience through our speech.

KEY CONCEPTS

Organizational patterns
  Chronological
  Relationship
  Motivational
  Topical
  Spatial
  Problem-solution
  Contrast

Supporting materials
  Definition of terms
  Examples
  Citations
  Narration
  Statistics

1. Adequate structuring of a message is crucial.
2. The speaker has the responsibility to create a clear progression from point to point in a speech to insure the audience's attention and comprehension.
3. Organizational patterns vary in their suitability for a particular speech topic and purpose.
   a. Topics that evolve around the ordering of time should use the chronological sequence.
   b. Topics that have subsections all relating to the whole should use the topical sequence.
   c. Topics that have space as the common denominator should use the *spatial* sequence.
   d. Topics that involve problem solving or attempts to provide audience action might use the motivated sequence.
   e. Topics that explore differences and similarities might use the contrast sequence.
   f. Topics that explore cause and effect would use the relationship sequence.
   g. Topics that concern problem solving might use the problem-solution sequence.
4. Supporting materials enhance the speech structure.
   a. Speakers should define terms unfamiliar to the audience.
   b. Citations and quotations can assist the speaker in gaining the respect of listeners.
   c. Examples can assist communicating complex or unfamiliar concepts.
   d. Narration may convey information or enhance an assertion.
   e. Statistics can aid listener comprehension.

Chapter 12
Presenting the Message

P R E V I E W

¶ *What is style?*
Style is the product of words chosen to convey the speaker's ideas, the structural framework in which the words are wrapped, and the manner in which the message is delivered to the listening audience

¶ *What is the principal way a speaker directs or commands meaning in a speech?*
One directs or commands meaning by selecting a particular language and style for the speech

¶ *Is there any single correct speech style?*
No! The appropriate style will be determined by the goal of the speaker

¶ *Why use visual aids?*
Visual aids can assist the speaker in clarifying the message and portraying ideas or an atmosphere that is difficult by words alone

¶ *Why practice a speech?*
We practice a public communication to refine our message, vocal quality, and body responsiveness

¶ *What five vocal qualities should we, as public speakers, be concerned with when delivering a message?*
Pitch
Rate
Volume
Diction
Timbre

¶ *Should the speaker encourage audience participation in the speaking situation?*
The total speaking system should be evaluated in order to deter-

mine the most effective and appropriate participation level the speaker wishes to achieve.

OBJECTIVES

After reading this chapter, you should be able to
1. explain how personal word meaning can create communication breakdowns.
2. define the term *style* as applied to speaking.
3. explain the advantages and disadvantages of using visual aids.
4. identify the major elements of vocal quality that influence public communication.
5. define the following terms, *pitch, rate, volume, diction,* and *timbre.*
6. differentiate between active and passive audience participation.

STARING into the television cameras, the late President Johnson proudly announced his selection of former attorney general Nicholas Katzenbach as the new undersecretary of state. "He has stood here for the cause of freedom," Mr. Johnson said. "He has pursued justice for all Americans." The President proceeded to talk about the new position. "Now the scope of his work is the world, and the qualities of mind and spirit which have made him the champion of social change and human progress at home will make him their advocate throughout the world."

The purpose of the President's address to the American public was obvious, the organization was apparent, and the content of the speech was typical for White House appointments. However, the exact words, structural framework, and manner of presentation were unique to Lyndon B. Johnson. He had a habit of setting extravagant standards for his appointees; he customarily not only announced his appointments, but congratulated himself on them and congratulated the country as well.[1] His message presentations reflected his own special style of speaking.

Every message that is transmitted to an audience has its own style. The style is the product of the words chosen to convey the speaker's ideas, the structural framework in which the words are wrapped, and the manner in which the message is delivered to the listening audience. In this chapter we will be concerned with the final stage in message development—the selection of a message

1. Newman, E., *Strictly Speaking* (New York: Warner, 1975), pp. 61–62.

style and the presentation of that message to a group of individuals. We will explore the concept of style and how it affects our messages. We will examine how visual aids may be utilized to assist the speaker in effectively reaching their intended goal. Special attention is given to factors that affect the speaker's vocal delivery of the message. Finally, we will investigate audience participation in message presentations.

Before we select the language or adopt a particular style for our message, we should ask ourselves, "What do words mean?" It is pointless to research a topic, structure the ideas, and present our message, if our audience will fail to understand what we're actually attempting to communicate. If true communication is to take place, the words we use to package our message must have common meaning for both speaker and audience. We must ask ourselves, "Who determines the meaning of words used in our messages?" In *Through the Looking Glass*, Lewis Carroll provides the following explanation of word meaning:

"I don't know what you mean by 'glory,'" Alice said. Humpty Dumpty smiled contemptuously. "Of course you don't—till I tell you. I meant 'there's a nice knock-down argument for you.'"

"But 'glory' doesn't mean a nice knock-down argument," Alice objected.

"When I use a word," Humpty Dumpty said, in a rather scornful tone, "it means just what I choose it to mean—neither more nor less."

"The question is," said Alice, "whether you can make words mean so many different things."

"The question is," said Humpty Dumpty, "which is to be master . . ."[2]

According to Humpty Dumpty, the meaning of a word depends solely on the speaker. The speaker is master and words mean just what they are chosen to mean—neither more nor less. However, Humpty Dumpty is also saying that words have private meaning, that is, we use words in a very personal, idiosyncratic fashion. For example, Kevin Jackson, a high school student taking part in a forensic competition, watched intently as his teammate brought her performance to a finish. The girl on stage had done a monologue of Black poetry. Kevin, informally evaluating her performance, leaned to the man sitting next to him and said, "Man, she sure is bad!" The man knitted his brow. "That's funny, I thought she was really good," he said. Jackson stared, his face one large

2. Carroll, L., *The Complete Works of Lewis Carroll* (New York: Random House, Inc., 1939), p. 214.

wrinkle of confusion, sputtered his words back to the man loudly, "Say, what? What are you talking about? That's what I said—she's really bad, in fact, she's the baddest on our team."

A communication breakdown occurred because the speaker used a word that had private meaning, meaning that developed from his own personal experiences—experiences not shared by his listener. Kevin Jackson came from Compton, a predominantly Black community in Southern California. For Kevin the word *bad* meant *good*. He used the term to express his positive reaction to the poetry presentation. The man he spoke to was from Westminster, California, a largely white area. This man had always used the word *bad* to express a negative evaluation. Neither individual was using the word *bad* incorrectly, but each one had a different frame of reference when attaching meaning to the particular word. We have all experienced public speakers using private terms or slang to establish greater rapport with an audience. Politicians, particularly white ones, appear incongruous and patronizing when they use ghetto slang to gain support from a Black constituency.

We should be aware of the personal meaning given by both speaker and audience to the words in a message and its potential for creating misunderstanding between speaker and audience. We also should realize that communication breakdown as a result of private word meaning can occur in any speaking situation. The words we select to transmit our message can easily confuse our audience if their personal experiences, group affiliations, and cultural background differ from our own.

In selecting the language and style for a message, an understanding of private meaning is very useful. We want to avoid the use of words that confuse or offend our audiences because of private associations. As public speakers we do not want to be placed in a position in which we must say to our audience: "I know you believe you understand what you think I said, but I'm not sure you realize that what you heard is not what I meant."

Selecting Language and Style

The principal way one directs or commands meaning in a speech is by selecting a particular language and style. Style is a term used in speech when referring to a speaker's choice of words, the ordering of sentences and paragraphs in a message for a specific purpose, and the manner in which the message is presented. An effective speaking style is built around a defined purpose and uses language that leads the audience to a position desired by the speaker.

When developing a speech for presentation, the speaker should choose words to fit the audience. This does not mean that speakers adjust or change the purpose of the message to accommodate an audience. It means that the speaker's choice of words and message structure should be tempered to the background, temperaments, and attitudes of the audience.

The concept of style may become clearer to you after we examine how the style of a speech can vary. In the following four examples we shall take one topic, the use of automobile seatbelts, one main theme, the importance of using seatbelts for safeguarding life, and develop four distinct speech styles.

Speech 1, Style 1

How many of you have seen people so mutilated by a car accident that they were scraped off the asphalt into blood-drenched pillowcases? How many of you have seen bodies so sliced up into tangled strips of flesh by broken windshields that they look like the result of a meat grinder gone berserk? Do you realize the agony a collision can cause when you are hit by a car going thirty, forty, or even fifty miles an hour? Do you realize the potential danger every time you get into a car?

No, no, you don't realize the agony or danger. You just think, "That can't ever happen to me." You sit in your cars and forget that in front of you is thick plate glass, and that, if hit by another car you, yes *you*, could break that glass by the impact of your skull crashing through it. The horror is not just in the death, or disfigured face of someone who flew, like a crazed bird, through the jagged edges of broken glass. No, the horror is in the fact that it was by choice. Yes, in a sense people don't die from auto accidents; many times they commit suicide. How? By not listening to warning after warning. How? By not using their safety belts.

If you think safety belts are a laughing matter or something unimportant, then look at photographs of twisted, grotesque bodies. Every one of them could have been spared the flight through their windshields. Look at them, hard and cold, and then tell me what's a laughing matter and what's unimportant.

If you've got any sense at all you *will* use safety belts; if not, *your* picture may be the next one I show to tomorrow's audience. It is your choice.

Speech 2, Style 2

The technocracy of our age behooves us to continually develop and employ methods for insuring our safety. Since the Industrial Revolution, progress and prevention have never moved simultaneously forward. Early steel mills, for instance, produced their product without regard to the dangers of toxic fumes, unbarracked melting pots, or the problems of excessive temperatures to which employees were subjected. The mid-nineteenth century produced one sweat shop after another; health, safety, and general protection of people, as well as the environment, went unheeded.

Today it seems much has been accomplished in ways of insuring our safety. The laws of the land provide for the inspection of all industries for safety factors. Workers themselves have opened channels to communicate their grievances through labor unions, legislators, and the media.

But let us get very specific about safety—automobile safety. The automobile of the 1970s is mandatorily equipped with safety belts. The belts are light weight, sturdy, easily installed, and easy to use. The basic waist belt is now augmented by shoulder belts for additional safety. This simple safety system has spared thousands, perhaps hundreds of thousands, of lives. Unfortunately, this accomplishment is seldom mentioned by anyone. In fact, people seem to complain more about the minor discomforts of safety belts, than acknowledging the impressive quality of their use as a safety device.

It is about time we end the complaints and praise the benefits of safety belts, for in a complicated age where physical danger is ever present, the safety belt solidly prevents physical harm in a safe and sane fashion. Moreover, it is achieved at little cost to the automobile manufacturer and with only minor discomfort to car passengers.

SPEECH 3, STYLE 3

I wish we lived in a world that had no inconveniences, but we don't. Unfortunately too many things seem to require our time; there is always the added inconvenience of doing this or that before we can just sit back and enjoy ourselves. Most of us, for instance, appreciate a good home-cooked meal, don't we? The inviting fragrance of a succulent steak, served with hot potatoes and fresh, brightly colored vegetables. Sounds good doesn't it? But few of us enjoy the work it takes, such as buying the ingredients or the general running around the kitchen to prepare the meal. Sometimes the amount of time involved in meal preparation is five times greater than the time it takes to eat the meal! And the cleanup afterwards seems worse!

Anyway, I really do wish we lived in a world that had no inconveniences, but we don't. One little item that bothers us all is the use of safety belts in our cars. Yes, ladies, I know that the safety belt wrinkles your dresses. Yes, fellas, I know you like to drive without tight belts strapping you to your seat. But friends, safety belts are a minor inconvenience that can give more pleasure than any good home-cooked meal can. Do you know what that pleasure is? You're right. Safety belts give everyone the pleasure of protecting his or her own life. Needless to say that this pleasure is more lasting than any meal.

Studies show that it takes five seconds or less to put on a safety belt. That's not too much trouble for saving a life, is it? How about it? Is your life worth five brief seconds of prevention? The fact that safety belts really do save lives is beyond question. I've got the statistics here, if you want to hear them, but you look like an audience that is intelligent and practical. Your own common sense tells you the real value of "buckling up." I don't have to waste your time quoting laundry lists of statistics to get my point across, do I?

Your own practical sense tells you, ladies, that slightly wrinkled dresses are a small price to pay for safety. Men, you know a little less freedom of movement in the driver's seat is nothing when it comes to preserving your life.

I still wish we lived in a world that had no inconveniences, but we don't. Until we find such a world, all of us will spend time cooking food and, yes, "buckling up for safety." Thank you for listening.

SPEECH 4, STYLE 4

Woody Allen has said four things about death that are worth quoting:

"Death is an acquired trait.

"It is impossible to experience one's own death objectively and still carry a tune.

"Eternal nothingness is O.K. if you're dressed for it.

"I do not believe in an afterlife although I am bringing a change of underwear."[3]

These humorous statements actually illustrate a serious point: death often is a joke to us. The reason is fear. We are generally so afraid of death that we make it a fantasy. Thus death becomes laughable. But we do this not only with death, but with other uncomfortable thoughts; injury, money, and loneliness are among the most common subjects used for comedy.

Now I'm certain you've heard that safety belts can save lives. You've seen billboards with pictures of dead or near-dead victims that say, "If only they would have used safety belts." Well, that's fantasy to most of us—death is still a joke—particularly when seen on billboards.

All I have to say to you is to keep your sense of humor, but keep your perspective, too. Safety belts may never save your life, but they will not harm you either. And they could keep you from slightly banging your head, or keep your arms from getting twisted or sprained. It's the safety from minor discomforts that you'll appreciate. That's a point for safety belts that is neither melodramatic nor irrelevant. Protect yourself a little; the belts are in your car anyway, so use them. Thus, I'll join with Woody Allen and laugh about death, just as when Nat comes to the door to answer a knock:

3. Allen, W., *Getting Even* (New York: Warner, 1972), p. 31.

NAT: Who are you?
DEATH: Death.
NAT: Who?
DEATH: Death. Listen—can I sit down? I nearly broke my neck. I'm shaking like a leaf.[4]

All four examples, though diverse in style, sought two basic goals. First, each speech attempted to use clear language to describe specific concepts or events. You'll notice that the goal of clarity did not make the four styles similar. Clarity does not dictate any particular style. Second, each speech developed a personal way of saying what had to be said, that is, develop by word choice and use of language figures (such as metaphor or simile) a particular atmosphere or ambience. This ambience is hard to pinpoint, but it is the total sense of character, or unique manner of language expression in a speech—the pattern of rhythm, use of figurative language, syntax and sentence structure, and the like.

Let's examine the first speech. It's easy to see that the speaker uses an aggressive, even abrasive style. The speech begins with rhetorical questions (those asked for dramatic or audience rapport purposes, but not meant to be answered aloud by the audience) such as "How many of you have seen . . . ?" and "Do you realize . . . ?" The abrasive quality comes in the form of a negative response. "No, no you don't realize. . . ." The language first accuses the audience, then convicts it. The speech does nothing to accommodate the possible range of audience opinions. It does not accept the audience members as equals, but continually scolds them and assumes the audience is guilty. Certainly this style is one that does little to invite audience participation or to build an atmosphere of friendly concern on the part of the speaker.

The words chosen for this speech such as *scraped, sliced, crashing,* and *jagged* are highly descriptive. These words qualify action and are used to add impact or punch to the thoughts.

The series of rhetorical questions build a relentless rhythm in pressure. "How" was used four times in succession, not to suggest ideas, but to emphasize the speaker's dogmatic stance. The student of public communication should recognize that such devices as rhetorical questions, language figures, and rhythm are basic properties of style.

It is up to the speaker to determine what kind of style is appropriate for the message. Perhaps, in the case of our first speech, the audience was so opposed to using safety belts that nothing less than harsh language could be influential. The speaker did attempt

4. Ibid., backcover.

to include the audience with the word *you* (used twelve times), but the audience was pointed at, not invited to the message.

The second speech provides a strong contrast in approaching the same message. Its style neither attacks nor is it very direct, for it begins with what sounds like a general classroom lecture. The second speech reports more than directs. The style is more scholastic in rhythm and form, being more essay than oratory. You might notice that the language is more sophisticated, for example, the words *technocracy* and *behooves* appear in the first sentence. Unlike the first speech, which used a great deal of emotional language to evoke its strong images, it is very unemotional. The speech has what might be called aesthetic distance, that is, a psychological control of emotional response. This distance allows intensity of emotion to be channelled in less obvious ways. It is not that the speaker lacks feeling, but that feelings are balanced and tempered by less emotional language.

Sometimes a style with too much aesthetic distance runs the risk of impersonality. However, in the second speech the audience is never separated from the speaker. The speech uses the pronouns, *us* and *we* to gain the audience with the speaker.

The third speech is more informal and inviting in its language and construction. The speech is open and friendly. The audience is referred to as *ladies, fellas* and *friends*. This style also uses *we* and the *we* is unquestionably personal. This style is quite sympathetic to the audience's attitudes and instead of using words to condemn their opinions, the language accepts the audience's opinions as valid. This style presents the message without abrasion or distance of the other two styles. In the third speech the rhetorical question is positive, e.g., "Do you know what that pleasure is? You're right." This speech confers worth on the audience by saying they are, intelligent, practical, and filled with common sense. It acknowledges and respects contrary opinions and invites the audience to reconsider the position of the speaker. The rhythm is casual, not pressured or measured, but close to natural speech.

The examples used in style three are commonplace; no sophisticated terms or syntax intrude on the friendly tone. The language is consistently amicable, light without being frivolous.

The fourth speech is related to the third, but has a decidedly humorous tone. The humor in this case is based on that of the well-known American humorist, Woody Allen. One unique aspect of this speech is that it eliminates rhetorical questions. In a way, the removal of rhetorical questions limits an audience's sense of participation yet, as in all stylistic matters, it is the total effect of the language and style that determines the distance between speaker and audience. The words *you* and *you're* are used when the speaker refers to the audience. Moreover, the speaker does include himself at times with the audience when he uses the pronoun *us*. Using humorous language is one way a friendly, open style can be achieved.

There are innumerable styles a speaker may choose. The four presented here reflect just some of the diversity possible and demonstrate the variety of effects and rhythms that result when a speaker varies his or her choice of language and style.

When all four speech styles are evaluated perhaps the third one may be the most enjoyable, for the message is carried with language that established a position without attacking any existing opinions. Nonetheless, the preferred style must be determined by the goal the public speaker has in mind. There is no one correct style for public speaking. There isn't any style that can be called right or wrong. The goal of the speaker is to select a style that contributes to the achievement of the public communication goal.

The next section in this chapter deals with selecting visual materials.

Selecting Visual Materials

Visual aids may include physical three-dimensional models, still photographs, film, graphs, tables, and mixed media. The use of visual aids during a speech should be limited to appropriate situations and only to enhance the message. Visual aids too often are fillers, used to draw attention away from the speaker. Drawing attention to a photograph or chart is not necessarily wrong, as long as it doesn't detract from the message. Ezra Pound, an American poet, cautioned young poets not to "retell in mediocre verse what has already been done in good prose."[5] Likewise, the public speaker should not use mediocre visual aids when the language of the speech itself could present a clearer "picture" of the message.

The problem with visual aids is that they must be seen to be effective. Often the limitation of space or poor audiovisual machinery makes it difficult for an entire audience to see a visual aid. For example, most of us have attended lectures where either an opaque or a slide projector was clumsily used as a visual aid.

"May I have the lights out?" A pause. Finally, someone takes the initiative and turns out the light.

5. Pound, E., "A Retrospect," in *Modern Poets on Modern Poetry*, edited by James Scully (London: Fontana/Collins, 1973), p. 32.

"It seems somebody left the backdoor open, could someone get that door?" Another pause, then the sound of the door closing is heard.

"Thank you. Well, these slides will show you, in graphic detail, the art of clam digging."

A student next to the projector tells his friend, "The rumble of the machine sounds like Niagara Falls."

The machine clicks, but nothing happens.

"Did anyone check this machine?" Another click, then a slide is flashed upside down on the screen. Everyone laughs.

This example points out that certain visual aids require technical rehearsal. Such a rehearsal is best when it can be done in the facility where the speech is to be given. One should always double check any machine, lighting, location of wall sockets, and the like before the presentation. The result of poor preparation can cause audience distraction and often reduce the credibility of the speaker.

The advantage of visual aids is that they can translate a thought or emotion into another medium. The old adages, "A picture is worth a thousand words" and "I won't believe it till I see it" reflect the importance people attach to seeing the subject. The choice of a particular visual aid should be made in accordance with the message being considered and how it best can present the subject. For instance, a speaker might state, "It is interesting to note the gross national products of the USSR as compared to the USA for the last decade." A chart or graph used in illustrating this point could avoid confusing the audience with a verbal list of statistics. However, the chart should be large enough for all to see, clear in its depiction of the statistics, and should not upstage the speaker, unless that is the speaker's intention.

When using a three-dimensional model or chart, the speaker has to decide whether the aid should remain stationary (in view of the audience at all times) or whether it should be seen only for a few moments. The decision rests on whether or not the visual aid actually aids the message by always being visible. Often a greater impact is made by showing an aid only when it is needed to accentuate a certain thought or to make a description more vivid.

We can use the four speech styles on safety belts as models to illustrate the practical application of visual aids. The first speech with its highly descriptive language is tailor-made for photographs as visual aids. The speaker gets the audience to see, in colorful explicitness, the disfigurements caused by not using safety belts. The speaker might have pictures set up before speaking, to establish an aura of tension or even repulsion. On the other hand, he may want to save the shock of seeing the horror until the end of the speech. Either way, the thrust and tone of language would easily incorporate visual aids.

The second speech, with its measured pace and unemotional language, would not seem to benefit from visual aids. The speech is too general and doesn't call for visualizing any scene or depicting any statistics. In this case, it would probably be best to avoid using visual aids.

The third speech could benefit from the use of slides, such as showing a meal to visually entice the pallet. In addition, one might show a humorous picture of someone cleaning up the messy kitchen. A word of caution seems appropriate, as slides can seem overdone or pretentious. Moreover, slides require perfect timing and might actually lessen the impact of the message.

Although most speakers avoid giving laundry lists of statistics, statistics can silently speak for themselves on large charts. When the speaker says, "I don't have to waste your time quoting statistics," a casual glance at the chart could help to "quote" by merely being visible. But as is the case with any speech, successful use of visual aids depends on good preparation and smooth execution. Thus, the speaker should experiment with aids or let the speech suggest the images solely on use of descriptive language.

The fourth speech is not clearly adaptable for visual aids. Woody Allen's quotes might be displayed on plaques or even on a blackboard so the audience could view them. However, the humorous impact might be lessened if the audience saw the lines before the speaker said them. One compromise would be to have the jokes on cards, but reveal them individually. The end of the speech could have a cartoon with the Allen lines as a caption. The speaker would have to weigh the time and energy needed for the aids and their potential effect. Experimentation would be necessary to discover whether or not aids for this last speech would help or hinder the message.

Speakers must recognize that visual aids should be used to aid the impact of a message or to visualize a thought where words may prove to be weak or confusing. The aids should be easily portable and large enough to be seen by all the audience. Aids that require projectors should be tested before using, and if at all possible the speech should be rehearsed with the machine for timing. Furthermore, the speaker should become familiar with the limitations of the actual facility whether it be a classroom, a private home, or an auditorium.

Delivering the Message

After one has selected the language and style to be used in the speech and considered the use of visual materials, the actual delivery of the message must be rehearsed. How does one rehearse a speech? What are the best ways?

In *Hamlet*, Act II, Scene II, Hamlet instructs some players on acting. His advice is still valuable for anyone giving a speech:

Speak the speech . . . trippingly on the tongue, but if you mouth it . . . I had as lief the town-crier spoke . . . Nor do not saw the air too much with your hand . . . You must acquire and beget a temperance that may give it smoothness. Be not too tame neither, but let your own discretion be your tutor. Suit the action to the word, the word to the action.[6]

We can paraphrase this advice in the following manner:

Give the speech with agility of articulation, but if you pronounce your words with exaggerated distinctness I might as well have someone shouting the words. Don't overgesture with your hands; learn to balance your gestures, to look natural. But don't be limp or uncommitted with your gestures either; let appropriateness be your guide. Fit the gestures to the meaning of the word, the word to meaningful gestures.

Hamlet's advice, then, is that we practice the communication to refine our vocal quality and body responsiveness. But how does one do that? A tape recorder is one way to become familiar with the aural characteristics of one's own voice. Among the characteristics you'll hear from a recording of your voice will be pitch, rate, volume, diction, and timbre.

Pitch is the actual measurement of a voice in terms of its location on a scale. People are said to have high-pitched voices or low-pitched voices, depending on the note of a scale the voice is most used on. We can measure where the position of normal pitch is by listening to the extreme range of our voice. Mark on a keyboard the lowest note you can make, and the highest note. Somewhere in the middle of your range in the keyboard is your optimum pitch, the pitch where the voice does not strain to produce its sound.

Pitch can be manipulated to add variety to our public speaking. Speak the following sentence by saying the first word in your highest possible pitch and with each word lower your pitch, so

6. Shakespeare, W., "Hamlet," in *The Riverside Shakespeare*, edited by G. Blakemore Evans (Boston: Houghton Mifflin Company, 1974), p. 1161.

that the last word is spoken in your lowest possible register of pitch:

"I was not aware that I could ever speak with such wide variation in pitch."

Repeat the exercise, don't be afraid to sound like a cartoon character in your high pitch or like a record that is slowing to a halt in your lowest pitch. Most people are genuinely surprised at the distance between the highest and lowest note of their pitch range. Generally, people strive for optimum pitch, but a variety of pitch should be used. For instance, humorous anecdotes lend themselves to a put-on voice. The potential humor of a man speaking as a woman, or a woman as a man, is partially derived from their use of a stereotyped pitch associated with a particular sex. The creative use of pitch also can be heard in using dialects or when quoting someone.

Inflection, which is a change or variation in pitch, helps us modulate our speaking. Inflection commonly raises or lowers pitch. Inflection is used to bring out subtle meaning of words or to emphasize or deemphasize, ideas. Inflection can aid our communicating a specific point of view by bringing out the importance of certain words.

Pitch, then, should not be overlooked as an important factor in helping to make a speech come alive and in adding variety to any public communication.

Rate is the actual speed used when we speak. Probably one of the single strongest tendencies for beginning speakers is to speak too fast. Sometimes a speech is delivered so fast that all the words sound as if they run together. "IamgoingtospeaktodayontheupcomingpresidentialcandidatesandtheirchancesofwinningtheNovemberelections." Of course, speakers can have too slow a rate, "I am going to speak today on the upcoming presidential candidates and their chances for winning the November elections." Needless to say, speakers must develop an effective middle ground if they want to deliver a speech that will satisfy most audiences.

Rate also can be consciously rehearsed so that a proper and effective pace can be discovered and practiced. With slight alteration, the same type of exercise used for pitch can easily aid in discovering the range of an individual's rate. Repeat outloud the following sentence, stating the first word as slowly as possible, then speeding up gradually until at the end of the sentence you are speaking as fast as possible.

"I was not aware that I could ever speak with such a wide variation of rate."

Rate can affect greatly the drama or dramatic tone of a speech. A pause is used to break or slow down the rate of speech. A pause can be used to emphasize or deemphasize a major idea, for example. It can also produce emotion and therefore is often called a dramatic pause.

The rhythmic beat of delivering a line is also related to a speech's rate. This is the lift of a speech, the characteristic pace or rhythm we produce. Rehearsing a speech, being mindful of rate variation, and effective use of pauses, will keep the delivery from becoming monotonous.

Volume refers to the level of loudness or softness of the voice. Most beginning speakers tend to speak too softly. Some speakers believe that is the single most important element of public speaking, because the speech must be heard before it can be effective. The modern public speaker, however, relies less on his own ability to project and more on the use of a microphone. Technology has reduced the importance of building a personal capacity to raise and lower volume when we speak. The voice is amplified by electric microphones. Yet, the student in the classroom does require the ability to raise and lower volume to some extent. In the classroom one aims at the back of the room to produce enough volume to be heard throughout the room. Most people can easily raise their volume when they become angry or excited. The public speaker must control the volume level and use it to its best advantage. A simple rehearsal of your speech, using maximal and minimal volume, will indicate the range you have. Then you can strive for flexibility and control.

Diction is the general term concerned with articulation and enunication—how clear the sounds are physically formed and how distinctly they are sounded out. The greatest problem beginning speakers have with diction is that most are just sloppy. "Hey dijaeat?" instead of "Did you eat?" or "I'm gonna talk bout . . ." instead of "I'm going to talk about . . ." Other common errors in diction are "sport" for "support" and "jist" for "just."

Diction can be improved by consciously noting the problems and practicing clear, correct pronunciation. A tape recorder quickly reveals how we enunciate words. Listen critically. A common error is to omit sounds. For example, the *t* sound on common words may be *swallowed* or not distinctly spoken in "throa*t*," "la*t*er," "sof*t*ly," "distinc*t*ly," and so on. Similar problems result in omitting the *d* and *p* sounds in such words as "hel*d*" and "dam*p*."

Aside from omission, we add sounds that don't belong in words. "Athlete" has two syllables, "ath'let," but it is often pronounced with three syllables, "ath'e lete." The "uh" sound is added improperly. "Chimney" is a two syllable word often pronounced "chim-in-knee" or "across" becomes "acrosst."

Perhaps the most common reason for less precise diction is plain laziness. We lose speed when we accurately pronounce words, but we gain better diction. With a little application lazy speaking could become distinct, well-articulated speech.

Timbre is the resonant or distinct tonal quality of voiced speech. When we refer to a person's voice as thin or dry (being without color), we are referring to the degree of timbre in the voice.

Timbre is improved by building a proper vocal use of breath control and muscle control. The color or rich quality of a voice is developed by achieving proper resonance. All speaking is a combination of the elements we have discussed: pitch, rate, volume, dition, and timbre.

The motivation and care one takes to prepare and deliver a speech will be reflected in the speaking event. All of us can improve by rehearsing and developing a creative approach and response to the subject of public communication.

This brief identification of pitch, rate, volume, diction, and timbre is meant only to give each term a working definition. Each element is important enough for books to have been written about them, analyzing in depth the meaning of these five components of speech. It should be remembered that these five elements are just signposts of speaking, many other categories could be used.

Audience Participation

The last element to be discussed is the role an audience takes as participants in the speaking event. The practical suggestions for improving one's delivery presented in this chapter were given to promote the communication channels of a speaker addressing an audience. The term *audience* is derived from the act of hearing and refers to a group of listeners or spectators. The important point to remember is that a good speaker invites the audience to attend, or listen, to a message. Even more, a speaker wants an audience to share in the speech. The speaker wishes to impart a message, but the audience is to take part in that message.

How does an audience participate in a public communication situation? The audience may, for example, participate passively by showing their approval or disapproval through body expression. This feedback is passive in that the audience receives the message without much resistance. They just sit there, whether scowling or smiling; their physical movements are restricted, their voices submissive. Passive participation is still a strong communication response and can be negative or positive.

Whereas some audiences are passive, others *can be* active. Active participation refers to a direct sharing in the speaker's message. An active participant is not usually submissive. He might stand up and cheer, yell, boo, or even throw things at the speaker. The active participant also may not be physically restricted.

It should be emphasized that audiences are collections of individuals, and that each person responds with a unique mixture of passive and active elements. Participation is a neutral term that only can be qualified by the situation.

How much audience participation should a speaker elicit or expect? This is a question of judgment, and the speaker should be aware that, to a degree, the person speaking controls the amount and kind of participation an audience may give, for instance:

How many of you are sick and tired of the same political speeches that promise all and produce nil? Come on! Let me see you wave your hands if you are ready for a change. Are you with me? Let me hear you say "Yeah!" Louder! I feel a new age of leadership is coming, friends, and are we ready for it? Let me hear you say it out loud, "Yeah!"

In this example the audience's participation is clearly and energetically directed. Response is being drawn out of the audience by using specific actions to unite and verify the group's positive attitude toward the message.

Once again, the general rule is that the total speaking system should be evaluated in order to determine the most effective and appropriate participation level the speaker wishes to achieve. The total speaking situation includes the types of background the audience might have, social environment, the physical speaking area, the atmosphere in both temperature and emotion, the message, the historical setting, and the personal state of the speaker.

K E Y   C O N C E P T S

Style	Rate
Ambience	Diction
Visual materials	Dramatic tone
Pitch	Passive participation
Volume	Active participation

PROPOSITIONS

1. Style is the product of the words chosen to convey the speaker's ideas, the structural framework in which the words are set, and the manner in which the message is delivered to the listening audience.
2. Communication takes place when the words used in a message have common meaning for both speaker and audience.
   a. Communication breakdown occurs because a speaker uses words that have private meaning.
   b. Communication breakdowns as a result of private word meaning can occur in any speaking situation.
   c. The words we select to verbally transmit our message can easily confuse our audience if their personal experiences, group affiliations, and cultural background differ from our own.
3. The principal way one directs or commands meaning in a speech is by selecting a particular language and style.
   a. Ambience is the total sense of character or unique manner of language expression in a speech.
   b. There is no one correct style for public speaking.
4. The goal of the public speaker is to select a style that contributes to the achievement of the public communication goal.
5. Visual aids should only be used to enhance the message.
   a. Space limitations or poor audiovisual machinery will decrease the effectiveness of visual aids.
   b. Certain visual aids require technical rehearsal.
   c. Poor visual aid preparation can cause audience distraction and often reduce the credibility of the speaker.
6. The delivery of a speech should be rehearsed before presentation to an audience.
   a. Practice refines our vocal quality and body responsiveness.
7. Pitch can be manipulated to add variety to our public speaking.
   a. Inflection helps us modulate our speaking.
8. Rate can make a speech come alive as well as add variety.
9. The proper combination of pitch and rate can keep an audience from becoming unattentive and bored.
10. A speech must be heard before it can be effective.
11. A speaker wants an audience to share in the speech.
12. The total speaking system should be evaluated in order to determine the most effective and appropriate participation level the speaker wishes to achieve.

Chapter 13
Evaluating Public Communication

P R E V I E W

¶ *What is basically involved in the evaluation of public communication?*
Evaluation is a comparison of actual results with the speaker's expected outcomes

¶ *What are the basic components of a general frame of reference that may be utilized as a basis for making evaluations?*
The basic components are: (1) the objectives of the sender, (2) the efforts incurred in the utilization of a message and a channel, and (3) the actual outcomes involving audience responsiveness or behavior

¶ *What kinds of outcomes should a communicator consider when evaluating the effectiveness or impact of public communication?*
There are five qualities or types of outcomes to be considered: (1) Dominant outcomes, (2) idiosyncratic outcomes, (3) anticipated outcomes, (4) secondary outcomes, and (5) surprise outcomes

¶ *What is the foundation of a useful framework for evaluating outcomes?*
The general framework begins with the implementation of some system that enables you to plug in the outcomes that should occur, and to see whether you are attaining or maintaining these outcomes. (See Figure 13:1)

¶ *What are some of the outcomes that pertain predominantly to the message sender in public communication?*
1. Credibility
2. Influence
3. Authority
4. Capability

¶ *What are some of the outcomes that pertain predominantly to the efforts in public communication?*
1. Manageability
2. Efficiency
3. Cost
4. Effectiveness

¶ *What are some of the outcomes that pertain predominantly to the message in public communication?*
1. Validity or value congruency
2. Ethical acceptability
3. Quality of appeal
4. Clarity
5. Attention-inducing potential

¶ *What are some of the outcomes that pertain predominantly to the channels in public communication?*
1. Channel efficiency
2. Audience coverage
3. Exposure capacity
4. Adaptability
5. Flexibility

¶ *What are some of the outcomes that pertain predominantly to the audience effect in public communication?*
1. Satisfaction
2. Involvement
3. Commitment

¶ *What are some of the outcomes that pertain predominantly to audience behavior in public communication?*
1. Behavior change
2. Attitude change
3. Opinion shift
4. Increase in information
5. Retention of information

OBJECTIVES

After reading this chapter, you should be able to
1. discuss methods for assessing or evaluating the public communicators impact on the audience.
2. identify and describe the factors that are useful in determining the kinds of outcomes that are actually occurring.

3. devise and explain a general framework or scheme that may be used to evaluate the effect of any given public communication.

DURING a so-called energy-crisis, the Department of Transportation of a large western state engineered a plan to force motorists to conserve fuel. Steps were taken to enforce car pools in order to reduce the number of cars driven daily on the roadways. As an incentive, certain fast lanes were reserved solely for the use of cars that participated in the pool; any motorist who drove in the fast lane without three or more passengers was stopped by the State Highway Patrol, given a warning, and threatened with a fine if he or she persisted in violating these regulations.

The entire conservation plan was launched by a massive multimedia communication effort. Unfortunately, the effort fell far short of its goal. The public revolted, state enforcement was frustrated, and the conservation plan, including enforced car pooling and exclusive fast lane privileges, was abandoned. As a matter of fact, the abandonment of the program was almost as costly as its construction. By most accounts, the Department of Transportation had bungled what could have been a worthwhile program.

Public communication is a costly enterprise, demanding the efforts of both the sender and the receivers of messages, and consumes time and money. Consequently, common sense and business sense would prescribe a need for discovering exactly what the payoffs are. Is the audience responding in a manner commensurate with the speaker's efforts? This chapter deals with a discussion of methods for assessing or *evaluating* the public communicator's impact on the audience.

Evaluation is a comparison of actual results with the speaker's expected outcomes. We should try to establish a general frame of reference against which to base our judgments. We may begin with the model presented below:

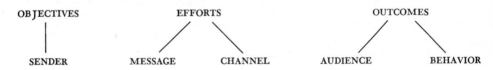

With this model, we can proceed to pinpoint the factors that are useful in identifying the kinds of outcomes that are really occurring. We will be doing that type of tagging as the chapter progresses.

To sharpen our understanding of the methods and issues that are involved, we will be discussing (1) the complexity of outcomes that can be influenced by public communication, and (2) the general framework upon which evaluation of public communication can be implemented. We can begin with an examination of how we can determine the outcomes.

Determining the Outcomes

The study or evaluation of outcomes can be somewhat complex. It involves a determination of what we may be inclined to see or not see as an outcome, and *what* we may, in turn, see or not see as its cause (input). We are again back to the old nemesis called perception. Perception of an outcome or a cause varies with each observer. Consequently, we must find ways to "standardize" the patterns of observation and definition. Most of us are inclined to think about the outcome of a message presentation in terms of whether we were able to produce the intended outcome throughout the entire audience or in some major part of the audience, for example, among opinion leaders. In other words, when listing or tagging the outcomes, we are likely to emphasize *anticipated* outcomes only. If we intended to inform our audience about some new, important issue, we normally consider the outcomes after the presentation in terms of whether the majority of our audience did, in fact, acquire knowledge and understanding of the issue. Often overlooked is the probability that other, *unexpected* outcomes may have occurred. One question that we often forget to ask is: did some audience members develop unfavorable attitudes? It is useful to *know* of these developments, especially if you are going to be involved in a series of presentations concerning the same issue. Another question might be: did people acquire something other than was intended? If so, in what area am I not being specific enough? What part of the presentation needs some machining or retooling?

Through these questions, we can begin to notice how a number of outcomes can result from a single public communication. The public communication may affect several receivers and produce a different response in each. Your credibility as a source—the audience's perception of you—may change; their interest in the problem may decrease; attitudes may become more set; or chances for future exposure may diminish.

There is one other interesting twist to the concern about outcomes. Is it not conceivable that neither sender nor receiver may see any of the kinds of outcomes that we have been discussing?

Can we say, then, that the message has *no* outcome? In the first place, there is no such thing as no outcome or no output. When you present a message, some outcome *will* take place. The response may be overt or undetectable; the outcome may not manifest itself for some time; it may be quite temporary; and so on.

Given the idea that outcomes may be many, varied, and complex, we should try to obtain precise information or feedback as to what our message is doing to the audience, or what the audience is doing to our message and to us. We must be able to identify the various types of outcomes.[1] For example, which of the following types of outcomes did your presentation create?

1. *Dominant* outcome—Did the outcome occur among a majority of the audience? If so, was it the output that I wanted?
2. *Idiosyncratic* outcome—Did the outcome occur only among a small minority of the audience? If so, why?
3. *Anticipated* outcome—Did the outcome that was detailed in your objectives occur?
4. *Secondary* outcome—Did "something else" occur that you could or could not accept? If the secondary outcome is acceptable, is there some way that you may try to enhance it; if it is unacceptable, how may you counteract it?
5. *Surprise* outcome—Did an unanticipated outcome occur? Was it idiosyncratic? Where did you go wrong with your audience analysis or presentation strategy?

A surprise outcome can be delightful, but you can't build your career on them. As a public communicator you try to minimize the possibility of surprise outcomes.

An assessment of the five outcomes—dominant, idiosyncratic, anticipated, secondary, and surprise—is important because your continued efficiency and effectiveness in presenting public communication will depend on your ability to use the consequences of a previously presented message as a basis for devising future plans and strategies. How to make such assessments will be detailed throughout the remainder of this chapter. Let us explore the general framework upon which evaluation can be conducted.

A General Framework for Evaluating Outcomes

The general framework begins with the implementation of some system that enables you to plug in the outcomes that should occur,

1. Clevenger, T., *Audience Analysis* (Indianapolis: The Bobbs-Merrill Company, Inc., 1966), p. 40.

and to see whether you are attaining or maintaining those outcomes. The attainment of the outcomes could be evaluated through any of a vast assortment of checks or tests that may be available, or that you may have to devise.

Let's build up to it. Remember that the ultimate test of the effectiveness of public communication is whether or not audience behavior is influenced. Remember also that evaluation is the process of comparing actual audience behavior in designated activities with *desired behavior,* as expressed in the communication objectives. Desired behavior should be measured in as concrete and final a form as possible. This procedure is followed in various communication contexts, among which public communication is equally important. The following list, for example, suggests some of the ultimate criteria that count in three communication areas:

Marketing communications—Increased or at least sustained sales; building of customer loyalty as evidenced, for example, in resistance to price competition.
Employee communication—Reduced absenteeism and turnover; better performance as ambassadors for the company; reduction in grievances and days lost through strikes.
Financial communications—Maintenance of high price-earnings ratio; ease of floating new issues; high rate of proxy returns in support of management.[2]

The items in each of these three communication environments represent the payoffs that must be achieved. In public communication, the payoffs must be: audience motivation, opinion shift, value modification, voting, joining an organization, petitioning, and so on. In order to detect, determine, or evaluate the kind and quality of payoff, we could design an evaluation model, such as is shown in Figure 13.1.

In figure 13.1, the objectives, efforts, and outcomes are the vital components under assessment. Objectives are mediated by the sender; efforts are mediated by the message and the channels, contexts, or media that you utilize; and outcomes are dramatized in audience states or moods, and in behavior. The arrows leading from each of the three major components point to the various conditions that you may wish to evaluate *after* your presentation. For example, the condition(s) that you may want to evaluate in

2. Lerbinger, O., *Designs for Persuasive Communication* (Englewood Cliffs, New Jersey: Prentice-Hall, Inc., 1972,), p. 234.

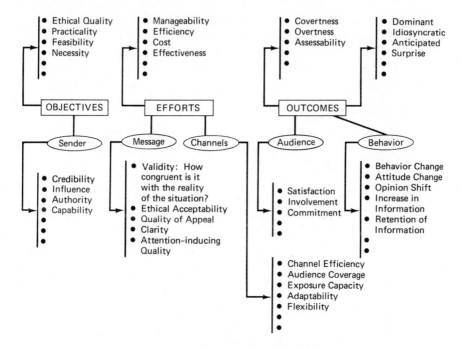

FIGURE 13.1. A scheme detailing outcomes for use in evaluating the effectiveness of public communication.

your message may concern its validity, or ethical acceptability, or its basic appeal. As far as the channel, context, or situation is concerned you may want to evaluate the amount of coverage afforded by a given context, or the flexibility of the channel or medium, and so on. The lists of outcomes that we have presented in Figure 13.1 are not comprehensive; we suggest the entire scheme as a starting point, and you may have to modify and add those dimensions that uniquely fit your communication environment.

By looking at the outcomes to which the arrows point, you should be able to determine whether certain strategies are justified and whether the greatest return is being obtained for the expenditure of money and other resources.

We will not attempt to dictate exactly what tools such as questionnaires, opinion-shift ballots, cost-analysis methods, retention tests, attitude scales, or credibility tests you should use. We believe that you should use evaluative materials that are geared to your own circumstances. We will, however, end this chapter by presenting a few evaluation checksheets or forms that have been used in various contexts.

DATE _____

1. What is your overall evaluation of this session?

Very Valuable	Quite Valuable	Moderate Value	Somewhat Limited Value	Of Very Little Value
_____	_____	_____	_____	_____

COMMENTS: _____

_____

2. What was particularly valuable to you?
COMMENTS: _____

_____

3. What was of particularly little value to you?
COMMENTS: _____

_____

4. What additional information would you like to have in relation to our session?
COMMENTS: _____

_____

5. Will you be with us at the next session?   Yes _____   No_____
COMMENTS: _____

_____

6. OTHER COMMENTS: _____

_____

FIGURE 13.2. Evaluation form used to test reaction to one presentation that is built into a series of presentations.

Evaluation Form

DATE: _____

PROGRAM: _____

(In answering Questions I and II, please draw a circle around the number which most closely reflects your rating on the scale where 1 is the lowest and 6 is the highest rating.)

    I. I rate my *degree of interest* in the _____ as it was presented:

          Low   1   2   3   4   5   6   High

    II. I rate the *value received* from the _____ as follows:

          Low   1   2   3   4   5   6   High

    III. I received from this _____ the following *benefits* which will help me in my own understanding of the issues.

    IV. The _____ weaknesses seemed to be:

    V. Suggested improvements would be:

    VI. Additional comments: (facilities, individual exhibits and presentations, time of program, etc.)

FIGURE 13.3. Form utilized to assess the strengths and weaknesses of a message detailing a new idea or issue.

Instructions for Using the Speech Evaluation Checklist:

In the "Evaluations" column, use ratings from 1 to 7 along a continuum for "needs improvement" (1) to "well done" (7) to indicate your evaluation of the successive component-factors. In the "Comments" column, you should write brief explanatory notes that reflect and amplify the reasons for your ratings.

SPEECH EVALUATION CHECKLIST

Factors	Evaluations	Comments
1. *Specific Purpose*		
Clear and to the point		
Appropriately narrowed in scope		
Appropriate for listener-agents		
Appropriate for context		
2. *Introduction*		
Attention of listener-agents secured		
Interest of listener-agents developed		
Specific purpose related to listener-agents		
3. *Body*		
Main points fulfilled specific purpose		
Main points appropriately patterned		
Main points emphasized		
Main points unified and coherent		
Developmental materials varied and helpful		
Transitions effective		
Internal summaries helpful		

Problem Resolution

Factors	Evaluations	Comments
4. *Conclusion*		
Final summary effective		
Final appeal appropriate		
5. *Facilitative Materials*		
Visual aids helpful to purpose		
Visual aids used effectively		
Humor used effectively		
6. *Language Usage*		
Language clear		
Language appropriate to listener-agents		
Language appropriate to context		
Language vivid		
7. *Delivery*		
Vocal variety utilized		
Pronunciation & articulation appropriate		
Phrasing and pausing effective		
Vocalized pauses avoided		
Good posture practiced		
Ease of movement demonstrated		
Gestures natural		
Facial expressiveness varied		

Factors	Evaluations	Comments
8. *Ethos Development*		

Knowledge demonstrated	
Trustworthiness shown	
Dynamism/Magnetism shown	

OVERALL EFFECTIVENESS

FIGURE 13.4. Evaluating public speech communication: A checklist for Assessing the Organization of a Message. Presented in Thomas Scheidel, *Speech Communication and Human Interaction*, (New York: Scott, Foresman, 1972) pp. 377, 383–384.

K E Y   C O N C E P T S

Evaluation	Anticipated outcome
Dominant outcome	Secondary outcome
Idiosyncratic outcome	Surprise outcome

P R O P O S I T I O N S

1. Evaluation is a comparison of actual results with the speaker's expected outcomes.
2. Perception of an outcome or a cause varies with each observer.
3. A number of outcomes can result from a single public communication.
   a. An outcome occurring among a majority of audience members is called a dominant outcome.
   b. An outcome occurring only among a small minority of the audience is called an idiosyncratic outcome.
   c. An outcome that was intended is called an anticipated outcome.
   d. An outcome that was unanticipated is called a surprise outcome.

Appendix:
Public Communication Exercises

The Chart

PREPARE a chart of your daily public communication activities during a normal week. A sample chart is shown below. A class discussion of the summary of the charts prepared by fellow class-mates will illustrate the important role of public communication in daily life.

Date_____ Name_____

Time	Type of Public Com- munication	Goal	Objective	Source	Receiver(s)
8:00					
8:30					
9:00					
9:30					
Through- out the day					

The Journal

The public communication journal is used to provide feedback on how well you are able to integrate the material in the text and use it. In the journal you are asked to keep a record of events, ideas, and feelings about public communication. You should write in the journal at least two or three times a week for fifteen minutes each time. You can choose to respond to reading in the text, to react and tell what you think about the ideas presented and why, rather than to summarize the material. You can describe effective and ineffective public communication efforts and try to analyze them by using the principles discussed in the class and/or presented in the text. You may react to classroom activities as well.

The journal is to be collected by the instructor at regular time intervals during the course. The instructor may respond to your comments.

The Scrapbook

You should keep a scrapbook of public communication activities, such as newspaper articles, magazines clippings, or pictures that illustrate principles discussed in class or presented in the text. You should make sure that all examples are properly annotated for their source. You also should write a short paragraph regarding each example indicating the principle illustrated by the example.

Forms of Public Communication

Discuss in groups of three to five students the relative amount of time each person spends in different types of communication activities. Ask yourself the following questions: (1) what kind of job each member has, (2) whether the work entails dealing with people, and how much, (3) whether they spend more time listening or talking in work, (4) what types of public communication are used at work, (5) what types of public communication are they exposed to away from work. In addition, ask them how successful or unsuccessful they are in public communication activities and why.

Inputs of Public Communication

This exercise can be done by a single individual or group. Each person should prepare a list of inputs related to a specific public communication activity that has occurred within the last five weeks. If the exercise is performed by a group of people, the members should compare and contrast the inputs occurring in the public communication activities.

Outputs of Public Communication

This exercise can be done by a single individual or group. Each person should prepare a list of outputs relating to public communication activities that have occurred in the last three weeks. If the exercise is performed by a group of people, the members should compare the different outputs occurring in the public communication activities.

Public Communication: Goals and Objectives

A group of three to five students should select ten speeches from the last two issues of *Vital Speeches*. First, each person should list the goal and objective for each speech. Then, the group members should compare lists. If differences exist, the group should attempt to find the basis for differences in individual judgments.

A Model of Public Communication

Prepare a diagrammatic model of public communication representing public communication as a system. List and explain each element of your model.

What Are Your Values

A group of individuals should rank-order the following list of items:

_____ Sports car
_____ Stereo
_____ Typewriter
_____ Refrigerator
_____ C.B. radio
_____ Television
_____ Microwave oven
_____ Pencil sharpener
_____ Tape recorder
_____ Swimming pool

Compare the list of each individual. Are they *different? How?* What values might be creating the differences?

Values and Advertising

Take a magazine published in the last month. Select ten different advertisements and identify the values illustrated in each advertisement.

What Are Your Beliefs

List five of the beliefs you have about education. Discuss the beliefs with other students in class. Try to discover how you developed the beliefs.

Topic: Education (or any other topic you should choose)

	Belief	Basis for Belief
1.		
2.		
3.		
4.		
5.		

Attitudes, Values and Beliefs—Discovery and Evolution

Divide into groups of three to five students. The group is to begin by responding to each of the statements listed below in terms of "what conditions would need to exist, or what evidence would you need presented, before you would have considerable confidence in the truth of the statement?

1. Most people are dishonest.
2. We don't reveal ourselves.
3. She is beautiful.
4. The world is going to hell.
5. Honor your father and mother.
6. I love you.
7. Opposites attract each other.

Each group should discuss areas of agreement and disagreement and attempt to keep adequate record of the various views taken by group members.

After this part of the exercise has been completed, you should investigate the origin of your values, beliefs, and attitudes.

Behavior and Belief, Value and/or Belief

Attitudes, values, and beliefs are often revealed in behavior. From your observations of others, select three attitudes, values, and/or beliefs and list the behaviors you have observed that reflect that value, attitude, and/or belief.

Feedback I

Each person should make two simple line drawings on a sheet of paper. Select a partner. Each person will describe to his/her partner the line drawing. The partner should not be allowed to see the design the communicator has drawn, nor the partner allowed to talk to the communicator. The communicator is not allowed to see what the partner is drawing. After completing the first drawing, the communicator gives verbal instructions to enable the partner to duplicate the second design, except that in this case feedback will be allowed. The communicator can observe the drawing of the partner, interrupt him/her with instructions, and the partner may ask questions. The two drawings should be compared and the role of feedback discussed.

Feedback II

Select a short speech from Vital Speeches. Have five people assist you with the exercise. Tell the speech to the first person while the other four are in the next room. Ask him/her to tell the story to the second person brought into the room. The second person will relate the story to the third person and so on. After the speech has passed to the fifth person, note the variations (additions, deletions, distortions, and omissions) between the original speech and the fifth person's version. Why did these variations occur?

Reaching Consensus

Divide the class into groups of four or five students. Each group should use group consensus in reaching a decision on the ranking of fifteen items involved in a moon survival situation. Each of the fifteen survival items *must* be agreed upon by each member before it becomes part of the group decision. Consensus may be difficult and conflict will probably arise.

Your group represents the crew of a space ship that was scheduled to land at a space station on the lighted surface of the moon. Because of radar error during powered descent, you have landed some 200 miles away from the station. The rugged terrain on which you have landed caused much damage to your ship and, because your survival depends on reaching the space station, the most critical items available must be selected for the 200-mile trip. Following is a list of the fifteen items left intact and undamaged after the landing. Your task is to order these items in terms of their importance in helping you reach the space station.

Select a group reporter and, on the basis of the group's consensus on the importance of the items, place the number 1 in front of the most important item, and 2 in front of the second most important, and so on through number 15, the least important.

_____ Box of safety matches
_____ 50-foot length of rope
_____ Portable heating unit
_____ Carton of dehydrated milk
_____ Stellar map
_____ Magnetic compass
_____ Signal light
_____ Solar powered FM transmitter-receiver
_____ Carton of dehydrated food
_____ Parachute silk
_____ Two .45 caliber pistols and cartridge
_____ Two 100 lb. tanks of oxygen
_____ Inflatable life raft
_____ Five gallons of water
_____ First-aid kit with injection needles

Reaching Consensus II

Divide the class into groups of four or five members. Each group should use group consensus in reaching a decision on the "Plane Crash" case study that follows. All ten items must be listed in the order in which you believe they should be done. Place the number 1 by the most important, and so on through 10.

CASE STUDY: PLANE CRASH

Imagine that you were in a plane that lost its direction in a bad storm and crashed on a desert island. The plane burst into flames shortly after it crashed, and all that is left are the bodies of the dead (including the crew), two loaded pistols, and your group. You must order the following ten actions to be taken by the group. Any group that has not completed its decision within twenty minutes is considered dead.

_____ Choose a leader
_____ Get rid of the pistols
_____ Set up rules for group behavior
_____ Explore the island
_____ Find drinking water
_____ Establish a shelter area
_____ Set a signal for outside help
_____ Decide who will handle the pistols
_____ Find food
_____ Bury the dead

After twenty minutes the groups will present the decisions to the class. The class should at this point attempt to reach a unanimous decision. Following the decision-making part of the exercise, the participants should discuss whether it was easier or more difficult to arrive at consensus in the smaller or larger group environment. Examine the inputs that produced changes in decisions at the group and class levels.

Source Inputs I

Select four public figures that you have heard speak. List the source inputs that make them effective or ineffective public communicators.

Source Inputs II

Select four students you have heard speak. List the source inputs during their public communication. List the inputs that would make each a more effective public communicator.

Source Inputs III

Select two short speeches from *Vital Speeches*. Edit each speech down to a five minute presentation. You will present both speeches to another basic speech class or general education class. Before reading the speeches, attribute each to individuals whose name you give to the audience. For one speech you use the name of a person whom the audience recognizes as knowledgeable on the subject covered by the speech—a person of authority. For the other speech use the name of someone who would be recognized but not considered as an authority on the speech topic.

After reading each speech, ask the class to evaluate the accuracy of the material presented in the speech on a five-point scale that ranges from: 1-fully authentic; 2-partially authentic; 3-don't know; 4-vaguely authentic; 5-not authentic.

Add all the scores for the first and second speech and divide that sum by the number of persons providing the average perceived authenticity rating for each speech. Discuss the resultant averages in terms of source credibility.

Source Evaluation Scale

The following scale may be used to compare the variety of judgments we make regarding different speakers. Along the left of the scale are a number of descriptive items. You are to rate the speaker on each of these items. Along the right side of the scale are two columns. You are to rate each of these columns in relation to the descriptive items on the left side of the page.

Column I Rate how you see yourself
Column II Rate how you see the *person being rated* on this scale

Use a five point scale for your ratings: o = nonexistent; 1 = low; 2 = high; −1 is contrary to; and −2 is opposite.

Descriptive Items   Perceptions

	I	II
1. Openness—speaks freely and gives frank opinions about feelings		
2. Ability to relate—is able to feel with or identify with audience		
3. Leadership—initiates ideas and exerts control only when necessary		
4. Acceptance—accepts what others say as important		
5. Stimulation—excites people by his/her words and actions		
6. Responsiveness—reacts quickly to changing situations and to what people say and do		
7. Supportiveness—gives others aid and assistance		
8. Affection—shows warmth and ability to emphathize		

Audience Analysis I

To develop skill in audience analysis and predicting audience response, prepare a worksheet like the example below on your classmates. (For attitude predicted and attitude actual, 1 = disagrees 2 = undecided or no opinion 3 = agrees.)

Name	Topic	Attitude Predicted	Attitude Actual

Audience Analysis II

Distribute to each student in class a paper that instructs him or her to listen only, to watch only, to watch and listen to the speaker, or to ignore the speaker entirely. One fourth of the class is assigned to each behavior. The instructor will ask a speaker who is unaware of the instructions to give a short five minute presentation. After he or she has given the speech, the class will discuss the speaker's feelings and behavior with the speaker. The class should then discuss the speaker's behavior. Finally, various members of the class should describe their feelings and problems created by the instruction.

Audience Analysis III

Audience Response Form A: Following is a form that can be used to evaluate the public communication.
1. The goal of the speech was to:
2. The objective of the speech was to:
3. I feel that the speaker (did) (did not) accomplish his or her goal. (circle one)
   a. The reason the speaker did not accomplish the goal was:
4. At the beginning of the speech my personal attitude toward the speaker's point of view was: (circle one)
   very favorable / favorable / neutral / unfavorable / very favorable
5. I thought your credibility was: (circle one)
        high   medium   low
6. I found your message: (check the items that apply)
   —— well-supported   —— unsupported
   —— well-organized   —— confused and disorganized
   —— logically sound   —— illogical and unsound
   —— adapted to me   —— unrelated to me
   —— stimulating   —— unstimulating
7. At the conclusion of the speech my personal attitude toward the speaker's point of view was:
   —— the same as at the beginning
   —— moved in the direction of the speaker's views
   —— moved away from the speaker's views

Audience Response Form B: List the name of each speaker. Listen to each speech carefully; then, using the 5-point scale listed below, place before each descriptive word a rating on the scale that most closely approximates your judgment of the behavior.

Too Little		Proper Level		Too Much
1	2	3	4	5

—— Aggressiveness   —— Interesting
—— Animated   —— Pleasant
—— Clear   —— Motivating
—— Courteous   —— Sensitive
—— Fluent   —— Sincere
—— Friendly   —— Trustworthy
—— Dynamic   —— Tactful

Presenting a Public Communication

Create a petition representing the least popular stand on a campus issue. The instructor will send groups of three to five out on campus with the petition. At least two group members must present speeches to the campus students in order to persuade them to sign the petition. The speakers may use any legitimate appeal to get the signatures except telling the audiences that the petition is part of a class project. Members of the group who are not giving the speeches should take notes on the speakers inputs and the audience's outputs. The group should try to get as many signatures as possible within the time period alloted, for example, one class period. The group members should discuss their experiences with the entire class at the next class meeting.

Analyzing the Public Communication

This exercise should be a major exercise if it is used in your class. You should describe and analyze a public communication situation you have personally observed or been a part of. The situation should be a relatively complex public communication system that presented problems for the speaker and audience. You should analyze the situation using the principles and concepts presented in class and this text.

The exercise should be done near the end of the term so that you are throughly familiar with the concepts and terminology of public communication. However, your instructor may assign this exercise earlier in the term so that you can begin thinking about it.

Your observations should be written down for the instructor and presented to the class in a five to ten minute oral presentation. The audience should have an opportunity to question you on your analysis.

Selected Bibliography

ALLYN, J., and L. FESTINGER. "The Effectiveness of Unanticipated Persuasive Communication." *Journal of Abnormal and Social Psychology*, 62 (1961), pp. 35–40.

ALY, B. and L. F. ALY. *A Rhetoric of Public Speaking*. New York: McGraw-Hill Book Company, 1973.

ANATOL, K. W. E. *Fundamentals of Persuasive Speaking*. Palo Alto, Calif.: Science Research Associates, 1976.

ANDERSON, M. P., E. R. NICHOLS and H. W. BOOTH. *The Speaker and His Audiences Dynamic Interpersonal Communication*. 2nd ed. New York: Harper & Row, Publishers, 1974.

APPLBAUM, R. L. and K. W. E. ANATOL. *Strategies for Persuasive Communication*. Columbus, Ohio: Charles E. Merrill Publishing Company, 1974.

ARISTOTLE. *Rhetoric*. Trans. Lane Cooper. New York: Appleton-Century-Crofts, 1932.

ASANTE, M. K. and J. K. FRYE. *Contemporary Public Communication: Applications*. New York: Harper & Row, Publishers, 1977.

BAKER, E. B. "The Immediate Effects of Perceived Speaker Disorganization on Speaker Credibility and Audience Attitude Change in Persuasive Speaking." *Western Speech*. 29 (1965), pp. 148–161.

BAKKE, E., and C. ARGYRIS. *Organization Structure and Dynamics*. New Haven, Conn.: Labor and Management Center, Yale University, 1954.

BARKER, L. L. *Listening Behavior*. Englewood Cliffs, N. J.: Prentice Hall, 1971.

BENNETT, E. "Discussion, Decision, Commitment, and Consensus in Group Decisions." *Human Relations*. 8 (1955), pp. 251–274.

BERELSON, B., P. LAZARSFELD and W. McPHEE. *Voting: Study of Opinion Formation in a Presidential Campaign*. Chicago: The University Press, 1954.

BERELSON, B. and G. Steiner. *Human Behavior: Inventory of Scientific Findings*. New York: Harcourt Brace Jovanovich, Inc., 1964.

BETTINGHAUS, E. P. *Persuasive Communication*. 2nd Ed. New York: Holt, Rinehart and Winston, 1973.

BRADLEY, B. E. *Fundamentals of Speech Communication: The Credibility of Ideas*. Dubuque, Iowa: Wm. C. Brown Company, Publishers, 1974.

BROWN, J. W., R. B. LEWIS and F. F. HORCLEROAD. A-V *Instruction: Technology, Media, and Methods.* 5th Ed. New York: McGraw-Hill Book Company, 1977.

BURGOON, M. *Approaching Speech Communication.* New York: Holt, Rinehart, and Winston, 1974.

CAMPBELL, J. A. *An Overview of Speech Preparation.* Palo Alto, Calif.: Science Research Associates, 1976.

CHESBRO, J. and C. HAMSHER. *Orientations to Public Communication.* Palo Alto, Calif.: Science Research Associates, 1976.

CLEVENGER, T. *Audience Analysis.* New York: The Bobbs-Merrill Company, Inc., 1966.

COHEN, A. R. *Attitude Change and Social Influence.* New York: Basic Books, Inc., Publishers, 1964.

COLLINS, G. and H. GUETZKOW. *A Social Psychology of Group Processes for Decision Making.* New York: John Wiley & Sons, Inc., 1964.

CRONKHITE, G., *Persuasion: Speech and Behavioral Change.* New York: The Bobbs-Merrill Co., Inc., 1969.

CRONKHITE, G. *Communication and Awareness.* Menlo Park, CA: Cummings Publishing Company, 1976.

DAHL, R. *Modern Political Analysis.* Englewood Cliff, N. J.: Prentice-Hall, Inc., 1963.

DANCE, F. E. X. and C. E. LARSON. *Speech Communication Concepts and Behavior.* New York: Holt, Rinehart and Winston, 1972.

DAVISON, W. P. "On the Effects of Communication." *Public Opinion Quarterly.* 13 (Fall 1959), p. 344.

DESOLA POOL, I., et al. *Handbook of Communication.* Skokie, Ill.: Rand McNally & Company, 1973.

DOOLITTLE, R. *Orientations to Communication and Conflict.* Palo Alto, Calif.: Science Research Associates, 1976.

DURANT, WILL. *The Life of Greece.* New York: Simon & Schuster, Inc., 1939.

DURANT, WILL. *Caesar and Christ.* New York: Simon & Schuster, Inc., 1944.

EHNINGER, P. *Influence, Belief, and Argument: An Introduction to Responsible Persuasion.* Glenview, Ill.: Scott Foresman, 1974.

FARACE, R. V., P. R. MONGE and H. M. RUSSELL. *Communicating and Organizing.* Reading, Mass.: Addison-Wesley Publishing Co., Inc., 1977.

FENELSON, *Dialogues on Eloquence.* Trans. by Wilbur S. Howell. Princeton: Princeton University Press, 1947.

FERGUSON, C. W. *Say It with Words.* New York: Alfred A. Knopf, Inc., 1959.

FESTINGER, L. "A Theory of Social Comparison Processes." *Human Relations.* 7 (1954), pp. 117–140.

FESTINGER, L. and N. MACCOBY. "On Resistance to Persuasive Communications." *Journal of Abnormal and Social Psychology.* 68 (1964), pp. 359–66.

FRENCH, J. and B. RAVEN, "The Bases of Social Power." in D. Cartwright (ed.). *Studies in Social Power.* Ann Arbor, Mich.: The University of Michigan Press, 1959.

GIBSON, J. *Speech Organization: A Programmed Approach.* San Francisco, Calif.: Rinehart, 1971.

GRUNER, C. R. "An Experimental Study of the Effectiveness of Oral Satire Modifying Attitude." *Speech Monographs.* 32 (1965), pp. 145–65.

GRUNER, C. R. "A Further Experimental Study of Satire As Persuasion." *Speech Monographs.* 33 (1966), pp. 184–85.

GRUNER, C. R., *et al. Speech Communication in Society.* 2nd ed., Boston: Allyn & Bacon, Inc., 1977.

GRUNER, C. R. "Satire As a Reinforcer of Attitude." Paper presented at SCA Chicago, December, 1972.

HARRISON, R. P. *Beyond Words: An Introduction to Nonverbal Communication.* Englewood Cliffs, N. J.: Prentice-Hall, Inc., 1974.

HART, R. P., G. W. FRIEDRICH and W. D. BROOKS. *Public Communication.* New York: Harper & Row, Publishers, 1975.

HAYNES, J. *Organizing a Speech: A Programmed Guide.* Englewood Cliffs, N. J.: Prentice-Hall, Inc., 1973.

HENLE, M. "Some Effects of Motivational Processes on Cognition." *Psychological Review.* 62 (1955), pp. 423–452.

HEUN, L. and R. HEUN. *Developing Skills for Human Interaction.* Columbus, Ohio: Charles E. Merrill Publishing Company, 1975.

HIGHET, G. *The Anatomy of Satire.* Princeton, N.J.: Princeton University Press, 1962.

HOVLAND, C. I., T. L. JONES and H. H. KELLY. *Communication and Persuasion.* New Haven: Yale University Press, 1953.

HOVLAND, C. I. and M. SHERIF. *Social Judgment: Assimilation and Contrast Effects in Communication and Attitude Change.* New Haven, Conn.: Yale University Press, 1961.

JAMIESON, K. *A Critical Anthology of Public Discourse.* Palo Alto, Calif.: Science Research Associates, 1978.

JANIS, I. and S. FESHBACH. "Effects of Fear-Arousing Communications." *Journal of Abnormal and Social Psychology.* 48 (1953), 78–92.

JONES, E., and H. GERARD. *Foundations of Social Psychology.* New York: Wiley & Sons, Inc., 1967.

JONES, J. A. and G. R. SERLOUSKY. "An Investigation of Listener Perception of Degrees of Speech Disorganization and the Effects on Attitude Change and Source Credibility." Paper presented at the ICA convention, Atlanta, Georgia, 1972.

KARLINS, M. and H. ABELSON. *Persuasion: How Attitudes and Opinions Are Changed.* New York: Springer Publishing Co., Inc., 1970.

KATZ, D. "The Functional Approach to the Study of Attitudes." *Public Opinion Quarterly.* 24 (Summer 1960), pp. 163–204.

KELMAN, H. C. "Processes of Opinion Change." *Public Opinion Quarterly.* 25 (Spring 1961), pp. 57–78.

Selected Bibliography

KELLEY, H., and E. VOLKHART. "The Resistance to Change of Group-Anchored Attitudes." *American Sociological Review.* 17 (1952), pp. 453–465.

KELMAN, H. C. and C. I. HOVLAND. "Reinstatement of the Communicator in Delayed Measurement of Opinion Change." *Journal of Abnormal Social Psychology.* 48 (1953), 327–35.

KENNEDY, GEORGE. *The Art of Persuasion in Greece.* Princeton, N.J.: Princeton University Press, 1963.

KIESLER, C., and J. SAKUMURA. "A Test of a Model for Commitment." *Journal of Personality and Social Psychology.* 3 (1966), pp. 349–353.

KNAPP, M. L. *Nonverbal Communication in Human Interaction.* New York: Holt, Rinehart and Winston, 1972.

KRUGER, A. N. *Effective Speaking: A Complete Course.* New York: Litton Educational Publishing, Inc., 1970.

LASSWELL, H., and A. KAPLAN. *Power and Society: A Framework for Political Inquiry.* New Haven, Conn.: Yale University Press, 1950.

LAZARSFELD, P., B. BERELSON and H. GAUDET. *The People's Choice.* New York: Columbia University Press, 1948.

LERBINGER, O. *Designs for Persuasive Communication.* Englewood Cliffs, N. J.: Prentice-Hall, Inc., 1972.

LETH, P. C. and S. A. LETH. *Public Communication.* Menlo Park, Calif.: Cummings Publishing Co., 1977.

LEVENTHAL, H. and J. C. WATTS. "Sources of Resistance to Fear-Arousing Communications on Smoking and Lung Cancer." *Journal of Personality.* 34 (1966), pp. 155–175.

LOOMIS, J. "Communication, the Development of Trust and Cooperative Behavior." *Human Relations.* 12 (1959), pp. 305–315.

MARTIN, H. H. and C. W. COLBURN. *Communication and Consensus: An Introduction to Rhetorical Discourse.* New York: Harcourt Brace Jovanovich, Inc., 1972.

McCROSKY, J. C. *An Introduction to Rhetorical Communication.* 2nd ed. Englewood Cliffs, N. J.: Prentice-Hall, Inc., 1972.

McCROSKY, J. C., C. E. LARSON, and M. L. KNAPP. *An Introduction to Interpersonal Communication.* Englewood Cliffs, N. J.: Prentice-Hall, Inc., 1972.

McCROSKY, J. C. and R. S. MEHRLEY. "Effects of Disorganization and Nonfluency on Attitude Change and Source Credibility." *Speech Monographs.* 36 (1969), pp. 13–21.

McCROSKEY, J., and L. WHEELESS. *Introduction to Human Communication.* Boston: Allyn & Bacon, Inc., 1976.

McGUIRE, W., "An Information-Processing Model of Advertising Effectiveness." Paper presented at the symposium on Behavioral and Management Science in Marketing, Center for Continuing Education, The University of Chicago, July 1969.

McEDWARDS, M. G. *Introduction to Style.* Belmont, Calif.: Dickenson Pub. Co., Inc., 1968.

MEASELL, J. *An Overview of Speaking Situations*. Palo Alto, Calif.: Science Research Associates, 1978.

MERTON, R. *Social Theory and Social Structure*. Glencoe, Ill.: The Free Press, 1949.

MILLER, G., and M. BURGOON. *New Techniques of Persuasion*. New York: Harper & Row Publishers, 1973.

MILLER, G. R. and M. STEINBERG. *Between People*. Chicago: Science Research Associates Inc., 1975.

MILLS, J. and E. ARONSON. "Opinion Change as a Function of the Communicator's Attractiveness and Desire to Influence." *Journal of Personality and Social Psychology*. 1 (1965), pp. 173–177.

MINNICK, W. C. *The Art of Persuasion*. Boston: Houghton Mifflin Company, 1957.

MONROE, A. H. and D. EHNINGER. *Principles and Types of Speech Communication*. 6th ed. Glenview, Ill.: Scott, Foresman and Company, 1974.

MORTENSON, C. D. *Communication: The Study of Human Interaction*. New York: McGraw-Hill Book Company, 1972.

MYERS, G. E. and M. T. MYERS. *Communicating When We Speak*. New York: McGraw-Hill Book Company, 1975.

NEWMAN, R. P. and D. R. NEWMAN. *Evidence*. Boston: Houghton Mifflin Company, 1969.

OSBORN, M. *Orientations to Rhetorical Style*. Palo Alto, Calif.: Science Research Associates, 1976.

PALAMOUNTAIN, J. *The Politics of Distribution*. Cambridge, Mass.: Harvard University Press, 1955.

PEARCE, W. B. and B. J. BROMMEL. "Vocalic Communication in Persuasion." *Quarterly Journal of Speech*. 58 (1972), pp. 298–306.

PEARCE, W. B. and F. CONKLIN. "Nonverbal Vocalic Communication and Perceptions of a Speaker." *Speech Monographs*. 38 (1971), pp. 235–37.

PHILLIPS, G. M. and N. J. METZGER. *Intimate Communication*. Boston: Allyn & Bacon, Inc., 1976.

PIERCE, J. R. *Communication*. San Francisco, Calif.: W. H. Freeman and Company, Publishers, 1972.

PLATO, *Gorgias*. Trans. by W. R. Lamb. Cambridge, Mass.: Harvard University Press, 1925.

PLATO, *Phaedrus*. Trans. by H. N. Fowler. Cambridge, Mass.: Harvard University Press, 1914.

QUINTILIAN, *The Institutio Oratoria of Quintilian*. Trans. by H. E. Butler. Cambridge, Mass.: Harvard University Press, 1953.

Rhetorica ad Herennium. Trans. by Harry Caplan. Cambridge, Mass.: Harvard University Press, 1954.

ROBERTSON, T. C. *Consumer Behavior*. Glenview, Ill.: Scott, Foresman and Company, 1970.

ROBB, M. *Fundamentals of Evidence and Argument*. Palo Alto, Calif.: Science Research Associates, 1976.

Selected Bibliography

Rosnaw, R. and E. Robinson. eds. *Experiments in Persuasion*. New York: Academic Press, Inc., 1967.

Ross, R. S. *Speech Communication: Fundamentals and Practice*. 3rd ed. Englewood Cliffs, N. J.: Prentice-Hall, Inc., 1974.

Roth, R., Violent demonstrations bring sorrow to the capital, Philadelphia Sunday Bulletin, May 9, 1971. In: H. Simons. *Persuasion Understanding, Practice and Analysis*. Reading, Mass.: Addison-Wesley Publishing Co., Inc., 1975.

Saint Augustine. *On Christian Doctrine*. Trans. by D. W. Robertson, Jr. Indianapolis: The Bobbs-Merrill Co., Inc., 1958.

Samovar, L. and J. Mills. *Oral Communication: Message and Response*. Dubuque, Iowa: W. C. Brown Company, Publishers, 1972.

Schelling, T. "An Essay on Bargaining." *American Economic Review*. (June, 1956.), pp. 281–306.

Sharp, H. and T. McClung. "Effects of Organization on the Speaker's Ethos." *Speech Monographs*. 33 (1966), pp. 83–91.

Sherif, M. "Superordinate Goals in the Reduction of Intergroup Conflict." *American Journal of Sociology*. 63 (January, 1958), pp. 349–350.

Shils, E., and M. Janowitz. "Cohesion and Disintegration in the Wehrmacht in World War II." *Public Opinion Quarterly*. 12 (1948).

Simons, H., N. N. Berkowietz, and R. J. Mayer. "Similarity, Credibility, and Attitude Change: A Review and Theory." *Psychological Bulletin*. 73 (1970), pp. 1–15.

Scott, W. and T. Mitchell. *Organizational Theory: A Structural and Behavioral Analysis*. Homewood, Ill.: Richard D. Irwin, Inc., 1972.

Smith, C. R. *Orientations to Speech Criticism*, Palo Alto, Calif.: Science Research Associates, 1976.

Smith, C. R. and D. M. Hunsaker. *The Bases of Argument: Ideas in Conflict*. New York: The Bobbs-Merrill Co., Inc., 1972.

Steele, E., and W. C. Redding. "The American Value System." *Western Speech*. 26 (Spring 1962), pp. 83–91.

Sturdivant, F., and D. Granbois. "Channel Interaction: An Industrial-Behavioral View." paper delivered to the December, 1967, American Marketing Association Professional Dialogue Session on Channels of Distribution, Washington, D. C.

Thompson, J., and W. McEwen. "Organizationl Goals and Environment." in Amitai Etzioni (ed.). *Complex Organizations*. New York: Holt, Rinehart and Winston, 1962.

Triandis, H. C. *Attitude and Attitude Change*. New York: John Wiley & Sons, Inc., 1971.

Tubbs, S. L. and S. Moss. *Human Communication*. 2nd ed., New York: Random House, Inc., 1977.

Verderber, R. *The Challenge of Effective Speaking*. 2nd ed. Belmont, Calif.: Wadsworth Publishing Co., Inc., 1973.

VOHS, J. L. "An Emperical Approach to the Concept of Attention." *Speech Monographs.* 31 (1964), pp. 355–360.

VOHS, J. L. and G. P. MOHRMANN. *Audiences, Messages, Speakers.* New York: Harcourt Brace Jovanovich, Inc., 1975.

WALTER, O. *Speaking to Inform and to Persuade.* New York: Macmillan Publishing Co., Inc., 1966.

WATTS, W. "Relative Persistance of Opinion Change Induced by Active Compared to Passive Participation." *Journal of Personality and Social Psychology.* 5 (1967), pp. 4–15.

WEAVER, C. H. *Human Listening Processes and Behavior.* New York: The Bobbs-Merrill Co., Inc., 1972.

WILSON, J. F. and C. C. ARNOLD. *Public Speaking as a Liberal Art.* 3rd. ed. Boston: Allyn & Bacon, Inc., 1974.

ZIEGELMUELLER, G. W. and C. A. DOUSE. *Argumentation: Inquiry and Advocacy.* Englewood Cliffs, N. J.: Prentice-Hall, Inc., 1975.

Index